INTERACT

(WITH)

INFORMATION TECHNOLOGY

New Edition

2

Roland Birbal
Michele Taylor

DYNAMIC LEARNING

HODDER
EDUCATION
AN HACHETTE UK COMPANY

Orders: please contact Bookpoint Ltd, 130 Park Drive, Milton Park, Abingdon, Oxon OX14 4SE. Telephone: +44 (0)1235 827827. Fax: +44 (0)1235 400401. Email education@bookpoint.co.uk Lines are open from 9 a.m. to 5 p.m., Monday to Saturday, with a 24-hour message answering service. You can also order through our website: www.hoddereducation.com

© Roland Birbal and Michele Taylor 2020

This edition published in 2020

Published from 2015 by
Hodder Education,
An Hachette UK Company
Carmelite House
50 Victoria Embankment
London EC4Y 0DZ

www.hoddereducation.co.uk

Impression number   10 9 8 7 6 5 4 3 2 1
Year   2024 2023 2022 2021 2020

Cover photo © *GraphicCompressor* – stock.adobe.com

Illustrations by Stéphan Theron, Val Myburgh and Wimpie Botma

Typeset in Glypha LT Std 45 Light 11/14 pt

Printed in India

A catalogue record for this title is available from the British Library.

ISBN: 978 1 5104 7397 3

Contents

Being IT safe – taking care of IT things (2)

Objectives

At the end of the chapter, you will be able to:

❏ identify the common ports and cables used in a computer system and its peripherals

❏ explain the proper hardware-handling methods when connecting and disconnecting peripheral devices

❏ identify ways to properly care for and maintain your computer equipment and accessories.

If you look at your laptop or computer, you will notice a number of different types of ports. A port is a physical dock that allows you to connect an external or peripheral device to your computer.

A peripheral device is an external device that works with the computer to perform a specific function when it is connected. Many of these devices cannot function without the use of the computer. Some examples of peripheral devices are:

* keyboards
* mice
* printers
* projectors
* flash drives
* speakers
* microphones.

In Chapter 1, we will look at the types of ports located on your computer, the cables that connect the devices to these ports and how to take care of them.

Figure 1.1 Cables connected to ports on a laptop

Types of computer ports and cables

The following main ports and cables allow devices to connect to computers:

* Computer power cords
* Universal serial bus (USB) ports and cables
* Video ports and cables
* Audio ports and cables
* Ethernet ports and cables.

Computer power cords

Figure 1.2 A computer power cord

The computer power cord supplies electrical power to your computer from an alternating current (AC) wall power socket. Always make sure that you turn off your computer before you connect or disconnect your power cord. Pulling out your computer power cord without shutting down your computer can corrupt the data on your computer hard drive or damage the computer's hardware.

Laptops need an adaptor that can convert the electrical power from the wall socket to the correct wattage that they need to work. Laptop adaptors come in many shapes and sizes, with each specific to the brand and model of laptop.

Figure 1.3 Laptop adaptors showing different power connectors

Figure 1.4 The USB logo

Universal serial bus (USB) ports and cables

Most peripherals will connect to your computer using an external universal serial bus (USB) port. This port is rectangular in shape and inscribed with a small logo. USB ports come in three sizes:

* The standard size
* The mini size
* The micro size.

Three types of USB ports are available in the standard size:

* USB type A port
* USB type B port
* USB Type-C ® port (USB Type-C ® and USB-C ® are registered trademarks of the USB Implementers Forum).

The USB type A ports

The USB 2.0 port, which is usually black, and the USB 3.0 port, which is usually blue, are both USB type A ports. The main difference between the two is the speed at which the transfer of data takes place. The USB 3.0 transfers data at a faster speed than the USB 2.0. A variety of devices can be connected to these ports, such as external hard drives, printers, mice, scanners, flash drives and many more. The USB cable plugs directly into the USB port.

Figure 1.6 USB type A 2.0 (black) and USB 3.0 (blue) ports

Figure 1.7 USB type A and type B cables

Once you have finished using a USB device, you must disconnect it safely from the computer. This ensures that the action being performed by the computer is stopped before the USB device is disconnected. For example, in the case of a flash drive, stopping the drive ensures that data is not being written to the flash drive. If the flash drive is not stopped before it is disconnected, the data on it can become corrupted.

USB type B ports

A USB type B port is usually used for the cable that sends data from the computer to the printer.

Figure 1.8 USB type B port (printer port)

Did you know?

The PS2 ports and cables are rarely used today, although they are still found on much older computers and some gaming systems. These cables and ports are both colour-coded, with purple for the keyboard and green for the mouse.

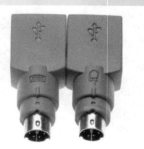

Figure 1.5 PS2 ports and cables

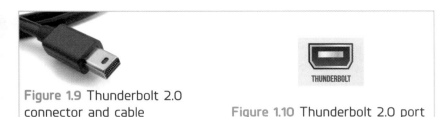

Figure 1.9 Thunderbolt 2.0 connector and cable

Figure 1.10 Thunderbolt 2.0 port

Figure 1.11 Thunderbolt 3.0 connector and cable

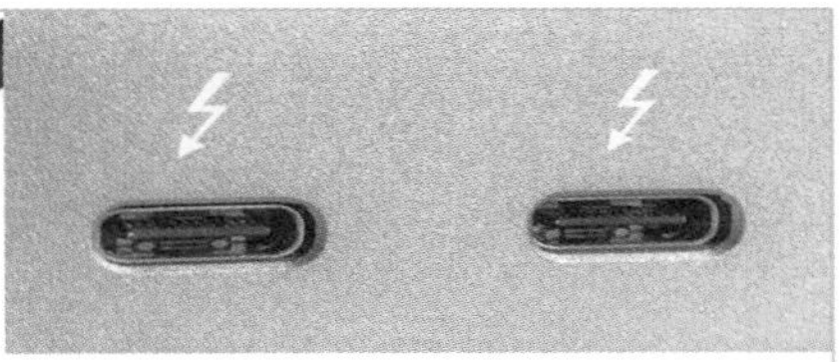

Figure 1.12 Thunderbolt 3.0 port

USB Type-C® ports

The USB Type-C ® port is usually used for the cable known as the Thunderbolt cable. The two types of ports and cables are the Thunderbolt 2.0 and the Thunderbolt 3.0, which is the later version and transmits data at a faster rate. They usually have a lightning bolt symbol on the cable and near the port.

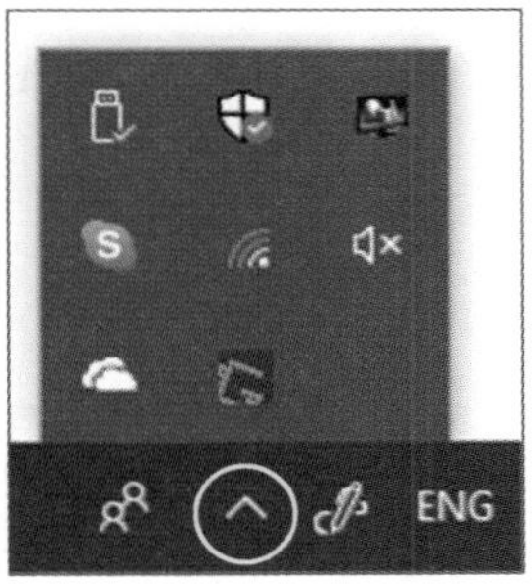

Follow these steps to disconnect your USB device safely, as shown in Figures 1.13 and 1.14.

Step 1: Click the **Show/hide** icon on the taskbar to display the icons that are not shown.

Step 2: Click on the **Flash drive** icon or the device icon that you want to disconnect.

Step 3: Click **Eject**.

Figure 1.13 The Show/hide icon on the taskbar

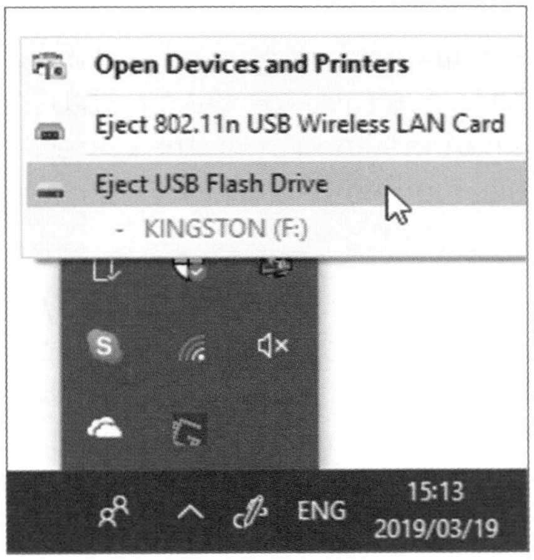

Figure 1.14 Ejecting a USB device

You can also eject the USB device from the Explorer folder, as shown in Figure 1.15. Follow these steps:

Step 1: Right click on the device in your Explorer folder.

Step 2: A pop-up menu will appear.

Step 3: Select **Eject** from the menu.

Figure 1.15 A pop-up menu from the Explorer folder showing 'Eject'

Figure 1.16 Video port

Figure 1.17 Video cable and connector

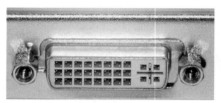

Figure 1.18 DVI port

Figure 1.19 DVI cable and connector

Video ports and cables

The different types of video ports include the following:

* Video graphics array (VGA) ports
* Digital video interface (DVI) ports
* High-definition multimedia interface (HDMI) ports
* Display ports.

Video graphics array (VGA) ports

The video graphics array (VGA) port allows you to attach a monitor or screen to your computer's video card. This port is found mainly on older computers, monitors and television sets. Many laptops, projectors and monitors also still have VGA ports.

This port has 15 holes and requires a 15-pin cable connector. The shape of the port indicates how the pins fit into it. The cable connector can only fit in one direction. Forcing the cable into the port will only bend the pins and damage both the port and the cable. Therefore, you will need to make sure that the connector and the port are lined up in the correct position before you insert the cable. Figures 1.16 and 1.17 show a video port and a cable with a connector.

Digital video interface (DVI) port

The digital video interface (DVI) port also connects your computer to a monitor. The DVI is a high speed digital interface between the computer and monitor. Some laptops and computers still carry this type of port. Take note of the curve of the port and the cable connector, as well as the position of the pins, as this indicates the direction in which the cable should be inserted into the port. Figures 1.18 and 1.19 show a DVI port and a cable with a connector.

High-definition multimedia interface (HDMI) ports

Most new computers, monitors, televisions and projectors have HDMI ports. These ports come in three sizes:

* The standard HDMI port
* The mini-HDMI port
* The micro-HDMI port.

The mini-HDMI and micro-HDMI ports are usually found on small and highly portable devices such as digital cameras and camcorders and mini projectors known as pico or pocket projectors.

Figure 1.20 Standard HDMI, mini-HDMI and micro-HDMI ports

Figure 1.21 Standard HDMI, mini-HDMI and micro-HDMI connectors on cables

Display ports

A display port is the latest development in types of video ports. It gives a much better picture quality, in other words a higher-resolution picture, than the HDMI port. Figure 1.22 shows a display port cable and connector, and Figure 1.23 shows display ports.

Figure 1.22 A display port cable and connector

Display port   Display port   HDMI port   Display port

Figure 1.23 Display ports

Emerging technology

USB 4.0 port technology
According to estimates, the USB 4.0 port technology will be released in the year 2020. This new technology is likely to provide a data transfer rate of approximately 10,000 Mbps (megabits per second), which means that the USB 4.0 will be 16 times faster than the USB 3.0, which offers a data transfer rate of 625 Mbps.

Audio ports and cables

Audio ports allow you to connect your speakers, headphones and microphone to the computer. The cable is known as a 3.5 mm jack audio cable. You will usually see the pink and green or blue audio ports, or you may see the symbol of a headphone or microphone near the port, which indicates the type of port that it is.

* The pink port connects the microphone to the computer.
* The green port connects the computer speakers and headphones to the computer.
* The blue port, usually called the **in-line port**, is used to playback and record sounds from devices such as an MP3 player, electric guitar, turntables and DVD players.

If a computer has grey, black and orange ports, then these are used for surround sound speakers. Figure 1.24 shows the different types of audio ports, and Figure 1.25 shows audio cables.

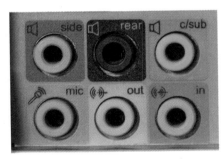

a Audio ports – different colours

b Audio ports – symbols

Figure 1.24 Different types of audio ports

Figure 1.25 Audio cables (3.5 mm)

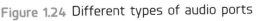

Ethernet ports

Figure 1.26 Ethernet (RJ-45) ports on a modem

Figure 1.27 RJ-45 cables with connectors (jacks)

Ethernet (RJ-45) ports and cables

An ethernet port is a networking port that connects your computer directly to the internet or to other computers. It looks like an oversized telephone port. Ethernet ports can be found on your computer, laptop, printer, television and internet modem.

Exercise 1

1 Explain what a port is.

2 Explain the difference between a DVI port and a display port.

3 Explain the difference between a USB port and an HDMI port.

4 Thunderbolt ports can be found on what type of device?

5 Why is ejecting a flash drive safely important?

Did you know?

The 'RJ' in RJ-45 stands for 'Registered Jack'. An RJ-45 is an ethernet jack, while an RJ-11 is a telephone jack. Although these jacks and ports look alike, the RJ-11 telephone jack is smaller than the RJ-45 ethernet jack. See Figure 1.28 and Figure 1.29.

Figure 1.28 RJ-45 ethernet jack and port

Figure 1.29 RJ-11 telephone jack

Caring for and maintaining your computer equipment

Care and maintenance of devices are important. As many of these devices are expensive, you may need them to last a long time in order to get the full benefit of the device. Always power down and disconnect your devices before cleaning them to prevent damage.

In *Interact with IT* Book 1 Chapter 3, we discussed how to care for computers devices. Here are a few key points to remember:

* Always use the correct 'on-screen' procedure to shut down your computer, rather than directly using the on/off switch.
* Avoid exposing your computer to too much dust by covering it with a dust cover when you have finished using it. An excess of dust may affect the circuitry.
* Avoid using USB drives, CDs and DVDs that were used to store information in computers from outside the lab. These storage devices may contain viruses that will affect your computer. A virus is a piece of **software** that may cause your computer to malfunction.
* Do not pile objects onto the computer keyboard, as their weight may damage the keys.
* Do not move a computer system when it is switched on and operational.
* Do not eat or drink in the computer laboratory. Liquids can cause short circuits or electric shocks, and the crumbs from food can cause inner computer parts to malfunction.
* Do not install any software without your teacher's permission.
* Avoid excessive printing, as paper and printing cartridges are expensive. Be sure that what you print is something you really need to see or store as a printed version.

Some devices, such as memory cards, disks and ink cartridges, can be easily damaged and should be stored in a cool dry place.

Keyboard, mouse and ports

Dust and dirt can affect your mouse and keyboard. These devices may eventually stop working if dust and dirt are allowed to accumulate in them. Dust and dirt clog ports, reduce airflow into and out of the system, and can eventually cause your system to overheat.

You can clean these devices by wiping them down with a lint-free damp cloth. Do not spray water directly onto the device or the port. You can also use a can of compressed air to blow out any dust particles from hard-to-reach places. Do not use any chemicals or cleaning agents on your devices.

Figure 1.30 Using compressed air to clean a keyboard

Monitor or screen

Dust particles, fingerprints, smudges and stains can make your computer monitor dirty. Use a soft, dry lint-free cloth, such as a micro-fibre cloth. You can also dampen the micro-fibre cloth with a little water. However, make sure that you wring as much water as possible out of the cloth, so that it does not run down into the sides or corners of the screen.

Do not use any abrasive chemicals such as alcohol, ammonia-based cleaners, sprays and other glass cleaners on your screen. Your screen is coated with anti-reflective coating and these chemicals will strip the coating, which can make your screen cloudy or cause more serious damage. Do not use paper towels or household rags, they are also abrasive and can scratch the surface of the screen.

Do not spray water directly onto the screen, as it may run down into the corners and seep under the housing. This can damage the sensitive materials and parts inside in the monitor or screen.

Printers, scanners, projectors exteriors and hand–held peripherals

Clean these devices, which include printers, scanners, projectors exteriors and hand-held peripherals, using a soft, dry lint-free micro-fibre cloth. You can also dampen the micro-fibre cloth with a little water. However, make sure that you ring as much water as possible out of the cloth to avoid damaging the devices.

Cords and cables

Figure 1.31 Roll cables neatly and tie them with cable ties so that they do not become twisted and tangled.

Use cable ties to organise cords and cables, as jumbled cords can be easily damaged if they are twisted or tugged. Cords that are jumbled or disorganised also look unsightly and can be a tripping hazard if not organised neatly and packed away. Do not overload outlets or power strips by plugging in too many devices, as they may become a fire hazard.

Computer batteries

Do not overcharge your laptop batteries by keeping them plugged in all the time. This affects the ability of the battery to recharge, which reduces its lifespan (length of time it can function). As a result, the battery eventually will not be able to hold its charge, and you may even need to use the power adaptor for your computer or laptop to work. Rather wait until your laptop or computer runs down to 20% of its full charge before you plug it in again to fully charge it again.

Blocked vents

Blocked vents obstruct the airflow into and out of your computer system. This can cause the system to overheat and damage the parts of it. Your system needs to remain cool in order to function correctly. Therefore, remove all clutter from around your computer so that the airflow is not obstructed. Try to work on a solid surface, as resting your laptop on your bed or lap while working can obstruct the airflow into and out of the computer, and cause it to overheat.

Shutting down your computer

Shut down your computer correctly every night. This will save on electricity, and allow important Microsoft updates to be installed on your Windows computer, which only happens in shutdown mode.

Avoid holding down the power button to shut down the computer. This is called **cold booting** and should only be done in emergencies, such as when your computer is frozen. Cold booting can also damage your hardware and software. Make sure that you shut down your computer correctly by using the shutdown button of your operating system.

Protecting the environment from digital technology

Follow these guidelines to protect the environment from digital technology:

* Do not print information unless it is absolutely necessary. Cutting down on paper usage reduces the number of trees that need to be harvested.
* Reduce the need for electricity by switching off your devices when they are not in use. This will reduce the need for fuel (usually oil, gas or coal) to generate electricity.
* Dispose of computers and other electronic devices safely by taking them to disposal sites designated specifically for electronics. These sites have the facilities to safely extract any heavy metals from the devices and dispose of it as hazardous waste. Then the parts are sorted for recycling.

Figure 1.32 Used office printers ready to be disassembled inside a recycling plant.

Summary 1

1 A port is a physical dock that allows you to connect an external or peripheral device to your computer.

2 The computer power cord or adaptor supplies electrical power to your computer from an AC wall power socket.

3 A USB port is a rectangular-shaped port that can connect most peripherals to your computer.

4 Video ports allow you to attach a monitor or screen to your computer's video card.

5 Video graphics array (VGA), digital video interface (DVI), high-definition multimedia interface (HDMI) and display ports are all video ports.

6 The HDMI ports and cables come in three sizes: standard, mini and micro.

7 Audio ports connect your speakers, headphones and microphones to the computer.

8 The ethernet (RJ-45) cable and port, also called the networking port, connects your computer to the internet or another computer.

9 Cleaning and maintaining your computer equipment can keep your system functioning correctly for a long time.

Questions 1

Matching questions

Match each name to its correct image.

1 Display   a   b

2 Power cord

3 VGA   c   d

4 USB

True or false questions

1 There can be as many as six audio ports on a computer.

2 The ethernet port is also known as a telephone port.

3 The Thunderbolt port is a USB port.

4 You should not spray water directly onto a computer screen while cleaning it.

5 You should not use compressed air to clean your computer ports.

6 You should shut down your computer using the shutdown button in your computer's operating system.

Short-answer questions

1 List three common types of computer cable.

2 Explain why it is necessary to use cable ties to keep your cables and cords organised.

3 Explain how to shut down a computer correctly.

4 Explain why it is important to safely disconnect a USB flash drive from a computer.

5 You are told that your computer has two USB 2.0 ports and a USB 3.0 port. Explain the difference between the two ports.

6 What do the following acronyms stand for?

a HDMI   b DVI

c VGA   d USB

Project

1. Create a poster to illustrate how to care for and maintain a peripheral device of your choice.

2. Create a picture chart to show at least six (6) examples of cables and matching ports.

Crossword

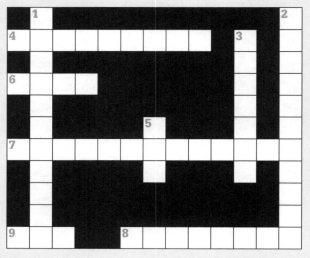

Across

4. This supplies electrical power to your computer

6. This video port comes in three sizes: standard, mini and micro

7. This is used to clean debris out of a keyboard

8. The name given to the port that connects a computer to the network or internet

9. A video port found on older computer systems that attaches the monitor or screen to the computer's video card

Down

1. The name given to shutting down the computer while holding down the power button

2. A type of USB port that has a lightning bolt symbol

3. This video port is the latest development in video ports

5. A type of port that most peripherals use to connect to your computer

STEM project

Jody is a civil engineer and takes her company-issued laptop computer to worksites on a daily basis. Her laptop sometimes falls, gets wet or is exposed to dust and different chemicals. After only six months, she notices that some ports on the laptop and keys on the keyboard no longer work. Her company's IT Department is issuing her a new laptop, but it also plans to send along 'worksite-friendly' guidelines to Jody and other field employees with precautions that they must follow in the future to care for their laptops. You and your classmates have been asked to help the IT Department write these guidelines and advise on the most suitable and user-friendly presentation format for this particular type of work situation.

1. Which possible aspects of caring for her laptop computer could Jody have been careless about? List all aspects that you and your classmates can think of.

2. Decide on the content and format of the guidelines. What process did you and your classmates follow to decide on the content and format? Write a brief outline of this process.

3. Put the guidelines together and present to a form or grade doing CSEC IT.

4. What feedback did you get? From the feedback, are there any improvements you can make?

Hints

1. Revise all that you have learnt about the proper care of a computer.

2. What durable, portable material can be used to put the guidelines on?

3. A checklist at the end of your guidelines can be useful.

Why do we need input devices?

A computer needs various input, output and storage devices so that it can accept data, process that data and produce useful output. All the input, output and storage devices connected to and dependent on a computer for operation are called peripherals. Input devices are pieces of equipment that are used to enter data into the computer.

Figure 2.1 Two peripherals in this photograph are input devices: the keyboard and the mouse.

Data collection

Data capture is the first stage of entering data into a computer. It is at this point that the various input devices are used to input data that the computer will process and/or store.

There are two main ways to input data:

* **Manual data input:** Data is entered directly into the computer by hand, one transaction at a time. Examples of devices used for manual data input are keyboards, mice, touch screens, light pens, graphics tablets and voice input devices.
* **Automatic data input or data capture:** Data is entered directly into the computer from source documents. **Source documents** are documents on which data is first recorded before it is entered into the computer. Data entered from these documents is transferred directly from the document into the computer's memory. As the data is captured at the source, for example from **barcodes** on supermarket items or from national lottery slips using optical mark readers (OMRs), it is entered directly into the computer.

The diagram in Figure 2.2 shows these two data capture methods.

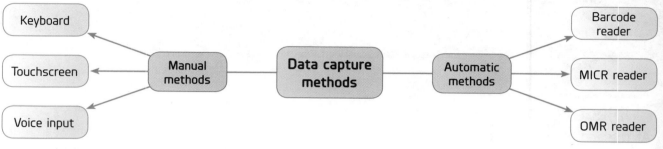

Figure 2.2 Data capture methods

Typical input devices

The peripherals shown in Table 2.1 are examples of typical input devices. We will look at some of these input devices in this chapter.

Table 2.1 Input devices

Keyboard	Barcode scanner
Mouse	RFID
Joystick	Magnetic reader
Digitising tablet	Smart card
Touch-sensitive screen	Voice data entry system
Light pen	Sound capture device
Digital stills camera	Video capture device
Magnetic ink character recognition (MICR) reader	Motion-sensing device
Optical character recognition (OCR) reader	Biometric system
	Remote-control device
Flatbed scanner and drum scanner	Motion-sensing device
Optical mark recognition (OMR) reader	

We will look at the following types of input device in this chapter:

* Keyboards
* Pointing devices
* Scanning devices
* Audio and video input devices.

Keyboards

The most common input device is the keyboard. Keyboards play an important role with the input of data in the form of letters, numbers and symbols into the computer. The two main types of keyboard are:

* alphanumeric keyboards
* special-function keyboards.

Figure 2.3 An ergonomic keyboard

Alphanumeric keyboards

An **alphanumeric keyboard** contains letters, numbers and symbols in particular layouts. This keyboard, which is modelled on the typewriter keyboard, is known as a QWERTY keyboard (based on the sequence of letters at the top left). As each key is pressed, a unique digital code is sent to the computer. For example, the code 01100001 is produced when the 'a' key is pressed and the code 1100010 is produced when the letter 'b' is pressed.

Keyboards can be attached to a computer in the following ways:

* With a cord connected to a USB port
* Wirelessly through radio frequency or **WiFi** signals
* On-screen, where the keyboard appears on the computer screen
* Built-in, where the keyboard is part of the computer, (for example, a laptop).

Did you know?

The traditional keyboard known as the QWERTY keyboard, which is still widely used today, was patented in 1867 and was designed to slow down the speed of typists so that the typewriter keys would not jam. Do research to find out about another keyboard design that allows for faster typing and less errors, but is not being manufactured.

Users who spend long hours on the keyboard may prefer to use an ergonomic keyboard, which is a standard keyboard designed for greater comfort and usability. Similarly, a person who plays computer games may prefer to use a gaming keyboard. These keyboards include programmable keys so that gamers can customise the keyboard to the game being played.

Special-function keyboards

Special-function keyboards are designed for a particular purpose. Examples include the following:

* **The Braille keyboard** has its keys marked with raised dots to help users who are blind. Users can type and enter text or instructions for the computer by feeling the Braille symbols on the keys.
* **The eye-controlled keyboard**, which was designed mainly for people with physical disabilities, lets a user enter information by focusing their eyes on individual keys on the keyboard displayed on the screen. Letters, numbers, symbols and function keys are all accessible.
* **The concept keyboard** contains a flatbed of contact switches covered by a flexible membrane. Whole words, pictures or symbols are superimposed over each contact switch, to which the computer is then programmed to respond appropriately. These keyboards are used in education as an early-learning aid, in restaurants so the operator can visually add up the cost of standard menu items, and in places where a normal keyboard would be at risk.

Figure 2.4 A Braille keyboard

Pointing devices

Pointing devices are used by graphical operating systems such as Windows to show the motion of a pointer or cursor, and to enable the user to control and select objects on the display.

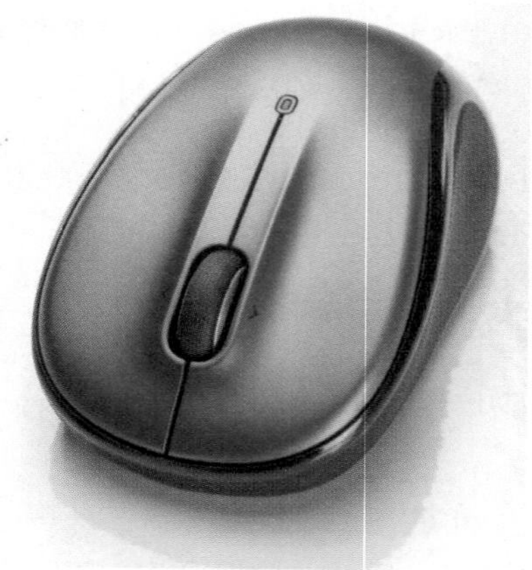

The mouse

The **mouse** is a pointing device that a user operates by moving over a flat surface. This movement is mirrored by a pointer on the monitor screen. On the top of the mouse are two buttons that allow you to make selections on your screen, move objects around the screen, and paint or draw. These buttons have the following uses:

* **Clicking:** This involves pressing and releasing the left mouse button quickly. This is often used to select a pull-down menu in a **program** or an item on the screen.
* **Double clicking:** This involves pressing and releasing the left mouse button twice. This is often used to open a document, a graphic or a program.
* **Dragging and dropping:** This involves placing the pointer over an item on the screen and clicking and holding down the left mouse button. While holding down the left button, you can move (drag) the object (file or icon) to another location on the screen. When you release the button, the object remains in its new location. This is often used when copying a document to USB storage or hard disk.
* **Right clicking:** This involves pressing the right mouse button, which displays a list of commands on the screen, depending on which program you are using at the time. By moving the pointer, you can select one of these individual commands, which will perform a specific action.

In addition to a regular mouse, you can also choose from other options, with some based on your personal preference and others designed for comfort. We look at some of these options below.

The optical mouse

The **optical mouse** can slide over most surfaces as it does not have a ball. It emits a small beam of red light that bounces off the surface into a sensor. The sensor sends coordinates to the computer, which in turn moves the cursor or pointer on the monitor screen, according to these coordinates. A mouse can be wired (attached to the computer by a USB cable) or wireless (connected by radio-frequency (RF) technology).

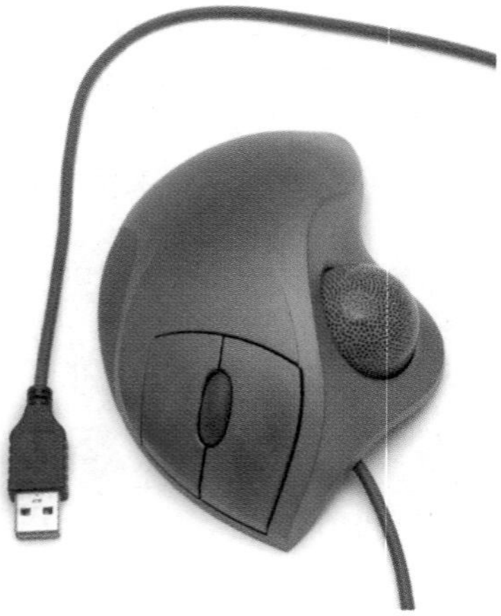

The trackball mouse

The trackball mouse has a large ball on top rather than underneath, which you roll with the palm of your hand or fingers. This type of mouse is not as precise as a regular mouse for some actions, but people who suffer from repetitive strain injuries may find them more comfortable to use. Figure 2.6 shows a thumb-operated trackball mouse..

Figure 2.5 A mouse allows you to select, move and control objects on your computer screen.

Figure 2.6 A trackball mouse

Figure 2.7 A pointing stick mouse

The pointing stick mouse

The pointing stick mouse is found on laptop computers and looks like a pencil eraser. It protrudes from the keyboard between the B, G and H keys (see Figure 2.7). Pushing on the pointing stick with your finger moves the pointer around the screen. Once again, buttons placed close by allow you to select features on the screen.

The touchpad mouse

The touchpad mouse contains a touch-sensitive pad and is usually found on laptops. The pad is a pressure- and motion-sensitive flat surface of about 5 cm × 5 cm, over which you move your fingers to control the cursor or pointer on the screen. Buttons placed close to this surface allow you to select features on the screen.

The eye-controlled mouse

The eye-controlled mouse allows users with disabilities to use computers through eye movements. The user wears glasses or special equipment to carry out a command. The user looks at an icon and blinks once to select the command.

Joysticks

A **joystick** is a device that lets you control the movement of an object on the screen by operating a small lever. This device is used mainly for computer games such as flight simulators.

Figure 2.8 A joystick

Digitising tablets (graphics tablet)

To digitise data means to convert it from an analogue form (like a picture) to a digital form. A **digitising tablet** is a board that can detect the position of a pointing device, such as a stylus or a puck, on its surface. A **stylus** is a pen-like pointing device for a graphics/digitising tablet. A **puck** is a mouse-like device that is moved over the surface of the tablet. It has cross-hairs to position it accurately and a number of buttons for different actions. You can easily enter drawings and sketches onto the computer using the digitising tablet.

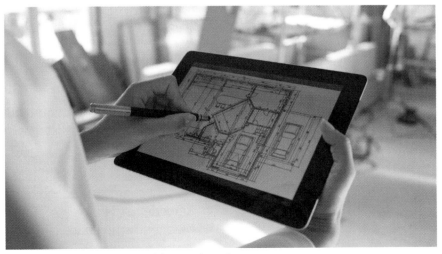

Figure 2.9 A digitising tablet and stylus pen

Touch-sensitive screens

Touch-sensitive screens let you interact with the computer by touching the screen. The pointing device in this instance is your finger. There are three types of touchscreen:

* **Pressure sensitive:** The screen consists of two layers with a gap in between. When you touch the screen, the two layers come into contact and the electrical flow that follows lets the sensors determine the touch point.
* **Capacitive surface:** 'Capacitive' means the ability to collect and hold an electrical charge. The screen consists of a glass panel covered with an electrode layer. When you touch the screen, some of the electrical charge moves from the screen to your finger, and the sensors use this drop in electrical charge to determine the touch point.
* **Light beam:** The surface of the screen is covered with a grid of invisible infrared light beams. When you touch the screen, you disturb the light beams and the sensors use this disturbance to determine the touch point.

For example, capacitive surface or light beam touchscreens are the types mainly used in bank ATM machines. These touchscreens allow you to perform actions on your bank account by following instructions and options on-screen, using your finger to choose the option you wish.

Light pens

A light pen is shaped like a pen and is connected to a VDU or monitor. It allows you to point and make selections more accurately on a screen. The tip of the light pen contains a light-sensitive element that, when placed against the screen, detects the light from the screen and enables the computer to identify the location of the pen. Making selections with a light pen on a touch-sensitive screen is far more accurate than using your finger. Light pens also allow the user to draw directly onto the screen. However, they are not as accurate as a digitising tablet and drawing can become uncomfortable.

Scanning devices

The different types of scanning devices include the following:

* Scanners
* Magnetic ink character recognition (MICR) readers
* Optical mark readers (OMRs)
* Optical character recognition (OCR) readers
* Barcode readers
* Magnetic strip codes.

Scanners

Scanners use laser beams and reflected light to translate drawings, photos and even text into digital form. These images can then be processed by a computer, displayed on a monitor, stored on a storage device or communicated to another computer. There are many types of scanners, for example:

* **Flat-bed scanner:** The picture is placed on a flat scanning surface and the image is captured, similarly to how a photocopying machine works. Household versions of **flatbed scanners** are inexpensive, costing less than 100 United States (US) dollars.

* **Hand-held scanner:** This scanner performs the same tasks as that of a flatbed scanner. It is used to scan physical documents into their digital forms that can be stored, edited, transferred and emailed digitally. The quality of the image provided by this scanner is poor, but it is useful for quick data capture. They can be used in various settings including retail, warehouse and distribution centres.

* **Drum scanner:** These are normally used in the publishing industry (magazines, books) to capture images with high detail. These scanners tend to be expensive, costing perhaps thousands of US dollars.

* **Sheet-fed scanner:** The sheet that contains the image is fed through rollers and the picture is scanned as the paper passes through.

Figure 2.10 A flatbed scanner

Figure 2.11 **A MICR reader**

Magnetic ink character recognition (MICR) readers

Magnetic ink character recognition (MICR) readers are mainly used in the banking industry to read data on cheques. Bank cheques have the following information encoded on them:

* The cheque number
* The bank branch number
* The customer's account number.

After the customer has written a cheque, the bank also encodes the amount of money onto the cheque using an encoding machine. This machine prints the amount onto the cheque in a special magnetic ink that contains iron oxide. The cheques can then be read by an MICR reader. As the document passes into the MICR reader, the shapes of the characters are recognised electronically. When the cheque is cashed, the bank transfers the money from the customer's account to the account of the person or business who has cashed the cheque.

Optical mark recognition (OMR) readers

An optical mark recognition (OMR) reader detects the position of dark patches on a sheet of paper. The documents to be read have empty boxes pre-printed on them. The user makes pencil or ink marks in the appropriate boxes. The intensity of the reflected light from these marks on the form is detected by the OMR reader. This is sometimes called mark sensing. The computer records the positions of the marks and analyses them to determine the meaning of the data. OMR readers are used mainly in assessing multiple-choice examinations or questionnaires given out by market researchers. Another huge application of OMR is in electronic lotteries, where participants can quickly and easily mark their selection of numbers on a machine readable ticket.

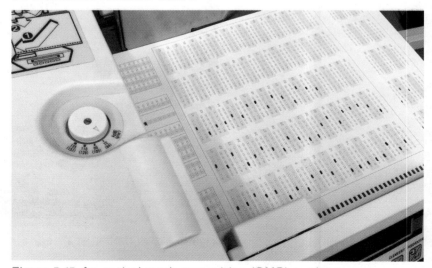

Figure 2.12 **An optical mark recognition (OMR) reader**

Optical character recognition (OCR) readers

Optical character recognition (OCR) technology is software that scans documents containing texts and converts them into documents that can be easily edited, stored or searched. This text can be typed or handwritten or taken from a scanned document, image, graphic or even a photo.

Figure 2.13 Post offices use OCR readers to sort letters.

An OCR reader has an optical scanner for reading text. A photoelectric device shines a light on the characters, which allows the reader to detect their shapes by sensing the patterns of reflected light. The reader looks at each pattern, for example, a letter such as 'R', individually. Sophisticated software allows the reader to compare each pattern with a set of stored patterns until the closest match is found. This match is translated into electronic text in the computer, so it can be manipulated by the user.

Figure 2.14 A barcode

Barcode readers

A **barcode** is a set of vertical lines of differing thickness with a string of numbers printed at the bottom (see Figure 2.14). When used in a supermarket information system, barcodes provide a lot of information. When the cashier at the checkout counter passes an item over the scanner in the counter, a laser beam scans the item's barcode and the beam is reflected back from the barcode into the scanner. The information provided by the differing line thicknesses in the barcode is then sent to a computer for processing.

The store's computer can tell from the information in the barcode that one unit of this particular item has just been sold. This information helps the store manager decide when to order more stock of the item. Using the item number detected in the barcode, the computer also searches its memory to find the matching item number. The computer can then send information to the cashier's display screen, such as the price and name of the item.

When the customer receives his or her receipt, the computer will have printed the name and price of the item on the receipt, as well as added up the total price of all the items bought. The barcode reading system, therefore, is a fast and error-free data entry method into the store's computer. This system also provides a quick method of recording the sale of items. Barcodes are also used in other information systems such as libraries and warehouses.

Figure 2.15 Libraries use barcode scanning to keep a record of all books borrowed and returned.

Figure 2.16 The magnetic strip on the back of a typical bank card

Magnetic strip codes

A magnetic strip is a short length of magnetic-coated plastic tape printed on the surface of, or sealed into, a ticket or card. It contains information to identify the ticket or card and its user. The card is read by swiping it, which involves moving the magnetic strip through a reader so that the strip can be read.

These strips are used on bank cards to identify the card holder's bank account, so that the card holder can perform banking transactions. Cards with encoded magnetic strips can quickly identify and allow access to card holders entering buildings. These cards can also be used for security purposes. Examples of other uses include phone cards and debit cards for cell phones. The magnetic strip on these cards contains information about the amount of money left 'on' the card.

Audio and video input devices

The different types of audio and video input devices include the following:

* Voice data entry or **voice recognition systems**
* Sound capture devices
* MIDI instruments
* Biometric systems
* Digital cameras
* Smart cards
* Digital video cameras
* Motion-sensing devices.

Voice data entry or voice recognition systems

Figure 2.17 Smartphone using Personal assistant voice app

Voice recognition systems require the use of a microphone. This system accepts the spoken word as input data or commands. Human speech is complex, because it carries tones, inflections and emphasis of various parts of words and phrases. The computer is programmed to recognise certain patterns of speech. Using a microphone, human speech is coded into a sequence of electronic signals. These signals are compared to a set of stored patterns. If they match, the command or data being entered is accepted by the computer and processed.

Simple commands can be used to control machines or even 'type' letters in a word processor. Voice recognition has become important in many areas of our lives. It has made life easier for people with movement difficulties, such as those who are paralysed, and who, with suitable equipment, can now operate a wheelchair, lighting and even open doors using voice commands.

Figure 2.18 A sound studio has the equipment and software to produce audio recordings.

Sound capture devices

All modern computers have a built-in microphone to capture sound. This means that you can record your voice, for example, to make comments that are embedded in a word-processing document. Your computer must have a sound card to record voice or music. The sound card digitises the sound information into a form that the computer can understand.

MIDI instruments

Electronic musical instruments can have a MIDI port (musical instrument digital interface) for input into the computer. The sounds are digitised and stored as a file, and can be displayed on the screen, edited and played back, using appropriate software. A sound studio has the equipment and software needed to record, digitise, store and edit different types of audio, for example, voice and instruments.

Biometric systems

'Biometrics' refers to the automatic identification of a person based on their individual body characteristics. The features that can be measured include face, fingerprints, hand geometry (the pattern of lines on your hand), iris, retina, vein and voice.

Figure 2.19 A fingerprint reader on a laptop

Figure 2.20 Biometrics requires the person to be physically present in order to be identified.

Fingerprint readers are now built into some computer keyboards (see Figure 2.19). Retinal-identification devices use a ray of light to identify the distinctive network of blood vessels at the back of the eyeball. Using biometrics to confirm a person's identity is becoming widely used, as they are considerably more accurate than current methods such as passwords or PINs (personal identification numbers), which are used with ATM cards.

Biometric technologies require that the person to be identified is physically present at the point of identification. They can potentially prevent unauthorised use of ATMs, cell phones, smart cards, desktop PCs, workstations and computer networks.

Digital cameras

Unlike the old-style film cameras, which used photographic film to store a picture, digital cameras capture an image and store it in memory as long strings of numbers. A digital camera does not use film. When you press the button to take a photograph with a digital camera, an aperture (opening) opens at the front of the camera and light streams in through the lens. The incoming light hits the image sensor chip, which breaks it up into millions of pixels. The larger the number of pixels that a camera has, the clearer the image and the more detail it can capture. The sensor measures the colour and brightness of each pixel and stores it as a number. Your digital photograph is stored as a long string of numbers describing the exact details of each pixel it contains.

Figure 2.21 A digital camera

A digital camera has the following advantages:

* It gives us instant photographs.
* It allows us to edit our pictures.
* It makes it easier for us to print or share photographs using smartphones, email and websites.

In addition, the memory in a digital camera can be erased so that more images can be captured.

Smart cards

A smart card (also called a chip card) is one of the main ways people make most payments today. This card is similar to the debit card used in ATMs except for one major difference. The smart card has a small microchip attached to it, which makes it very secure and gives it an advantage over the magnetic strip cards. While the magnetic strip on the back of normal cards can be altered or forged, it is difficult to tamper with the computer chips attached to smart cards.

The microchips also hold more memory than magnetic strips. For example, one smart card could hold information for credit card use, debit card use and prepaid services, such as cell phone time bought from a phone company. When a customer goes to a refitted ATM and inserts the smart card, money from the customer's account can effectively be downloaded to the card itself.

Businesses need to have a retail terminal to handle smart card transactions. A business places the customer's smart card into the retail terminal, where electronic money (e-money) is transferred from the cardholder's card to the retailer's smart card, which is housed in the retail terminal. The retailer can take their smart card out of the machine at any time and go to the bank or an ATM to credit their account.

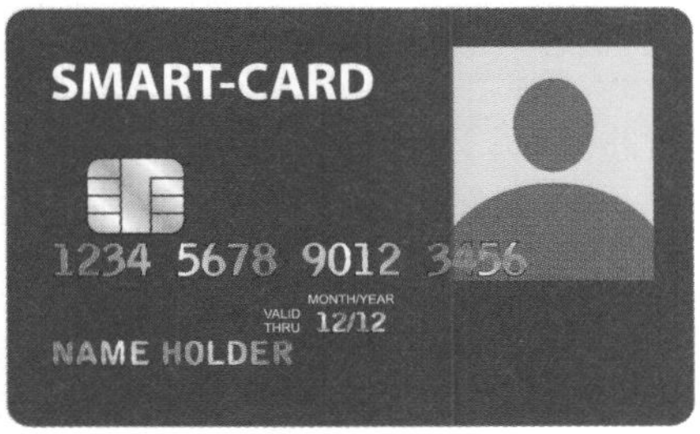

Future uses are already being considered for the cards, based on technological advances. Eventually, smart-card chips could store data about a person, such as voice prints (recordings of the holder's voice), fingerprints and retina scans. An individual person may therefore eventually need only one card for all their everyday living.

Figure 2.22 **A smart card**

Digital video cameras

Modern electronic video cameras or camcorders use a light-sensitive microchip called a charge-coupled device (CCD) to convert what the lens 'sees' into digital (numerical) format. Similar to a digital camera, each frame is stored as a long string of numbers, instead of as a photograph. A video camera takes many pictures per second to give an impression of movement. So, a movie recorded with a digital video camera is a series of frames, each stored in the form of numbers.

Most video cameras today record the digital information on a hard drive or on flash memory. The advantage of storing movies or recordings in digital format is that you can edit them on your computer, upload them onto websites, and view them on different types of devices from smartphones and tablets to computers and television sets.

Motion-sensing devices

Motion sensing devices such as game controllers communicate with a game console or personal computer using wired or wireless technology. The console or computer translates a player's natural gestures, facial movements and full-body motion into input. While these devices were originally developed for gaming, they are now being used in the US military for flight simulation and weapon usage exercises. The medical field also uses motion input for training. For example, doctors can practise new technologies in a simulated environment.

Figure 2.23 **Motion sensing (gaming example)**

Summary 2

1. Input devices are used to enter data into the computer for processing.

2. Data capture is the first stage of inputting data into the computer. The two main data input methods are manual and automatic.

3. Source documents are documents on which data is first recorded.

4. A keyboard is one of the most important input devices. The QWERTY keyboard can be used to type in data for use by a wide range of applications. Examples of other types of keyboard include the Braille keyboard, eye-controlled keyboard and the concept keyboard.

5. A typical mouse is a hand-held pointing device that moves a pointed arrow on a computer screen. It is often used to select a pull-down menu, open a document or program, or copy a document to a flash drive or hard disk by dragging and dropping the icon.

6. Trackballs, pointing sticks and touch pads are found mainly on laptop computers and perform the same function as a mouse.

7. A light pen is a hand-held device that has a light-sensitive photoelectric cell at its tip connected by a wire to the computer.

8. A digitising tablet enables you to enter drawings and sketches into a computer. It consists of a tablet that is connected to the computer and which is also connected by a wire to a stylus or puck (wireless is also available). You use the stylus or puck to 'sketch' an image on the tablet. This image then instantly appears on the computer screen.

9. Scanners use laser beams and reflected light to translate drawings, photos and even text into digital form.

10. A barcode is made up of columns of thick and thin lines at the bottom of which a string of numbers is printed. These numbers hold information about a product or item.

11. Magnetic strip codes on a card are used to identify the card and its user. They are commonly found on bank cards and cards that allow access to secure buildings.

12. Magnetic ink character recognition (MICR) readers are used mainly in the banking industry to read data on cheques.

13. Optical mark recognition (OMR) readers process marked data by detecting and measuring the positions of dark patches on a sheet of paper. OMR is mainly used for assessing the answers given to questions in multiple-choice examinations or questionnaires and electronic lotteries to select numbers.

14. Optical character recognition (OCR) involves the reading of text from paper and translating that text into electronic text in the computer, which can then be edited, stored or searched.

15. A smart card, also called a chip card, is similar to the debit card used in ATMs except that a smart card has a small microchip attached to it that allows it to store more information.

16. Voice recognition is the ability of a computer to accept spoken words as input for processing.

17. Biometrics refers to the automatic identification of a person based on their individual body characteristics. The features that can be measured include face, fingerprints, hand geometry, iris, retina, vein and voice.

18. Some electronic musical instruments have a MIDI port (musical instrument digital interface) for inputting sound into a computer, which can be stored and manipulated.

19. Digital cameras and digital video cameras capture images and store them on flash memory.

20. Motion-sensing devices, such as game controllers, translate a player's natural gestures, facial movements and full-body motion into input.

Questions 2

Copy and fill in the blanks questions

1 All the input, output and storage devices connected to and dependent on a computer for operation are called _____.

2 _____ devices are pieces of equipment that are used to put data into the computer.

3 The first stage of getting data into a computer is known as _____.

4 Entering data directly into the computer one transaction at a time by hand is known as _____ data input.

5 The process of entering data directly into the computer from source documents is known as _____.

6 Documents on which data is first recorded before it is entered into the computer are known as _____ documents.

7 The _____ keyboard contains a flatbed of contact switches covered by a flexible membrane.

8 A/An _____ keyboard is designed for comfort and usability.

9 A _____ is a set of vertical lines of differing thickness with a string of numbers printed at the bottom.

10 _____ devices are used by graphical operating systems to enable the control and selection of objects on the display.

True or false questions

1 Input devices are pieces of equipment that are used to put data into the computer.

2 Data can only be entered manually into a computer.

3 Source documents are documents that are output by the computer.

4 A joystick can be used mainly for computer games such as flight simulators.

5 Drawings and sketches can be easily entered onto the computer using the digitising tablet.

6 An OCR reader can only read typed documents.

7 A stylus is a pen-like pointing device for a graphics or digitising tablet.

8 OMR readers are used mainly in assessing multiple-choice examinations or questionnaires given out by market researchers.

9 A sound card is used to digitise sound information into a form that the computer can understand.

10 Passwords and personal identification numbers are more reliable than biometric systems for maintaining security.

Multiple-choice questions

1 Which of the following is NOT an alphanumeric keyboard?

    a QWERTY

    b Gaming

    c Concept

    d Ergonomic

2 Which of the following is NOT an example of a pointing device?

    a Touchscreen

    b Trackball

    c Touchpad

    d Pointing stick

3 Which of the following is used in banks to read cheques?

    a OMR

    b OCR

    c MICR

    d Barcodes

4 Which of the following can be used in a library to hold information about books?

   a OMR

   b OCR

   c MICR

   d Barcodes

5 Natural gestures and facial movements are used in:

   a voice input.

   b touch input.

   c motion input.

   d OCR.

6 One device that reads data directly from the source is a:

   a keyboard.

   b barcode reader.

   c touch screen.

   d light pen.

7 A document on which data is first recorded before it is entered into the computer is known as a:

   a primary document.

   b secondary document.

   c source document.

   d main document.

8 All of the following are special-function keyboards except for the:

   a QWERTY keyboard.

   b Braille keyboard.

   c eye-controlled keyboard.

   d concept keyboard.

9 Which of the following is an input device that is used mainly for computer games such as flight simulators?

   a Joystick

   b Keyboard

   c Mouse

   d Stylus

10 Which of the following input devices is used to translate drawings, photos and even text into digital form?

   a MICR

   b OCR

   c Scanner

   d OMR

Short-answer questions

1 **a** Why do computers need input devices?

   b Give three examples of manual input devices.

2 Explain the following terms:

   a Peripherals

   b Data capture

   c Source document

3 **a** Give two examples of applications in which data is captured directly from the source.

   b Explain what happens to the data after it is captured at the source.

4 State which type of keyboard may be used by the following individuals:

   a A person who is blind

   b A person who is not be able to use their hands or feet

   c A cashier at a restaurant

   d A person playing computer games

5 For each of the following devices, give an application for where it can be used.

Device	Application
Plotter	
Biometric system	
Audio input device	
Smart card	
Game controller	

6 a Use the information in the table to match the number of the device with the letter for the task that the device performs.

   b For each device give an example of where it can be used.

	Input device		Function
1	Scanner	a	A board that can detect the position of a pointing device, such as a stylus, on its surface
2	Digitising tablet	b	A device that can read codes with name and price information
3	OMR reader	c	A device used mainly in the banking industry to read data on cheques
4	MICR reader	d	A device that can translate drawings, photos and even text into digital form
5	OCR technology	e	A device that detects the position of dark patches on a sheet of paper
6	Barcode reader	f	Software that scans documents containing texts and converts them into documents that can be easily edited, stored or searched.

7 a Explain what a pointing device is in terms of computers.

   b Give an example of a pointing device.

c Which type of operating system allows for the use of pointing devices?

d Name three input devices that can be used to point on the computer screen, and explain why different pointing devices are needed.

8 a Give three examples of different types of mouse and the purpose of each one.

   b Explain the differences in the way that each mouse operates.

9 Use an example to explain how each of the following devices is used:

   a Joystick

   b Digitising tablet

   c Touch-sensitive screen

   d Light pen

10 Explain the differences between the following:

   a A plotter and a printer

   b OMR and OCR

   c A flatbed scanner and a drum scanner

Research questions

1 Do research on the internet and then answer these questions.

   a Define 'motion input'.

   b Name three disciplines in which motion input can be used.

   c Explain the purpose for which motion sensing is used in one of the disciplines that you named in (b).

2 You are the manager for a new supermarket in your neighbourhood that services several people with disabilities. You have decided to hire a disabled person who is differently abled to assist with clerical work. Using your choice of disability that the person may have, give an example of the office job that you can hire this individual to perform, and the device or devices that you may need to obtain to allow the individual to perform the job correctly.

Crossword

Down

1   A type of sensing device that can translate a player's natural gestures and facial movement into input

2   A tablet that enables you to enter drawings and sketches into a computer

3   A device used mainly for assessing the answers given to questions in multiple-choice examinations

6   A set of thick and thin lines in columns, with a string of numbers printed along the bottom

Across

1   A device used mainly in the banking industry to read data on cheques

4   The automatic identification of a person based on their individual body characteristics

5   The documents on which data is first recorded

7   A device that uses laser beams and reflected light to translate drawings, photos and text into digital form

STEM project

Virtual Mags, a small tyre sales and services company, is moving from a paper-based accounting system to a computer-based system. The company has been in operation for the past ten years and has accumulated a large amount of paper and many receipts. The data entry clerk employed to help with the computerising is worried, as she is only knowledgeable about two types of devices that can be used to enter data: a keyboard and a mouse. Her concern is that if she only uses these two methods, completing this task will be nearly impossible. What help can be given to the data entry clerk? Your teacher will divide you into two groups. Each group will present the options for data entry to the other group for review.

1   Clearly state the problem in this situation.

2   Produce a complete list of all methods of data entry and the available devices that can be used. How did you approach getting the information for this list?

3   Prepare your advice for the data entry clerk on the best option that will allow her to finish the task on time. Give reasons for your advice. How will you present your advice to the clerk?

4   How did the other group respond to the advice you gave the data entry clerk? Based on their response, describe how you can improve your advice.

Hints

1   Where do you plan to get your information on available input devices, for example, from computer shops, businesses, online research, and so on?

2   What may be limiting factors in these scenarios?

3 Output devices

What are output devices?

Output devices are pieces of equipment that are used to get information or any other response out of a computer. If the output can be read by people, it is said to be **human readable**, for example, output to a computer screen or printed on paper. If the output cannot be read by people, but only by machines, it is said to be **machine readable**, for example, barcodes, output stored on storage devices, and so on.

Figure 3.1 Human-readable output devices

Types of output devices

Output can be further classified into softcopy and hardcopy output:

✳ **Softcopy** output or temporary output refers to information displayed on a screen or transmitted in audio or voice form through speakers. This kind of output disappears when the computer is switched off.

✳ **Hardcopy** output or permanent output refers to output printed onto paper.

We will also look at a few output devices that can be classified as both input and output devices.

Softcopy output devices

We will look at the following softcopy output devices:

* Display screens
* Video graphics card
* Sound output devices.

Display screens

Display screens, also called monitors or visual display units (VDU), are the main devices for displaying softcopy output. Screens are made in a range of sizes and can be either colour or monochrome (black and white). However, monochrome screens are found on older computers and are mostly non-existent today. The two types of display screens are:

* cathode ray tube (CRT) display screens
* flat-panel displays.

Cathode ray tube (CRT) display screens

A cathode ray tube (CRT) display screen was very common until the early 2000s, when they were replaced by newer 'flat panel' display technologies such as liquid crystal display (LCD), plasma display and organic light-emitting diode (OLED) display. Although they are no longer used in the production of television sets, cathode ray tubes are still used to make display screens for industrial applications.

Figure 3.2 A cathode ray tube (CRT) monitor

A cathode ray tube (CRT) computer screen has the same technology as that of a CRT television screen. The images shown on the screen are made up of individual dots called pixels. A **pixel** (short for picture element) is the smallest unit on the screen that can be turned on and off or coloured in different shades. The number of pixels determines the resolution of the screen.

The **resolution** is the clarity or sharpness of an image when displayed on the screen. Screens with more pixels have a higher resolution, which means that they can show more detail in an image. If the screen resolution is low, the images are displayed with jagged edges. A screen with high resolution displays images with very sharp, clearly defined lines and curves. Some software packages, for example computer-aided design (CAD) packages need high-resolution screens so that designs can be viewed and worked on in great detail. Most types of gaming software also require high-resolution screens.

Did you know?

Did you know that the CRT was invented in 1897 by the German scientist Karl Braun? This technology was first used in the cathode ray oscilloscope, which was a scientific instrument used to display data about electric currents. Later, it became the basis of the technology used in television sets. The Scottish inventor, John Logie Baird, carried out the first successful transmission of moving television images in 1925.

Flat panel display screens

Portable computers such as notebooks and laptops, television sets and most desktop computers use flat panel display screens. These screens consist of two plates of glass with a substance between them that creates the image on the screen. The different types of flat screens are:

* liquid crystal display (LCD) screens
* electroluminescent display (EL) screens
* gas-plasma display screens.

A typical 48 cm (19 inches) flat-screen monitor has a resolution of 1680 x 1050 pixels. The 95 cm (37.5 inches) Acer XR382CQK flat screen monitor, which costs about US$1 000, has a resolution of 3840 x 1600 pixels.

Figure 3.3 A flat screen monitor

Video graphics card

A video graphics card, also called a video display adapter, is a circuit board installed in most computing devices. This graphics card displays graphical data with high clarity, colour, definition and overall appearance. As the quality of graphics card increases, so the image produced becomes clearer, smoother and more defined. Most gamers and people who do a lot of video editing use high-end graphics cards or may install an additional graphics card in their computer system.

Figure 3.4 A video graphics card

Sound output devices

Sound output is another form of softcopy output. Some sound output devices are:

* speakers
* voice-response systems.

Speakers

A simple speaker can make a range of sounds available to the computer user. Computer-generated sound, music output, computer-synthesised voice and the normal speaking voice are now standard forms of output that can be produced using a speaker. Audio (sound) cards need to be installed in microcomputers to obtain good sound quality for music or games. The audio card is a circuit board in the computer that processes sound, in a similar way to the video graphics card described earlier.

Figure 3.5 Modern speakers provide computer users with good sound quality for music and games.

Voice response systems

A voice response system (VRS) is an interface that responds to voice commands. The system selects from a set of digitised prerecorded words, phrases, music, alarms or other sounds stored on hard disk. The system combines these prerecorded words into responses based on selections made by the user. For example, many phone banking systems use voice response systems. As a caller selects options on their telephone keypad, this information is sent to the bank computer, which then outputs voice information to the caller.

People with visual or other physical impairments who may be unable to use a mouse or keyboard can use a voice response system to give the computer instructions to carry out various tasks. At present, VRS systems are available to operate standard household activities, such as turning lights and fans on and off, or closing and opening a garage door.

Hardcopy output devices

Some hardcopy output devices that we will look at in this section are:

* printers
* plotters
* 3D printers
* speech generating devices (SGDs)
* multimedia projectors.

Printers

Printers are used to present and store all kinds of information on paper, such as letters, legal documents, scientific data, graphs, photographs and advertising material. There are no limits to the amount and type of information that can be printed onto paper, as you can see from the paper-based material around you, in your classroom or in your home. There are many different kinds of printers, which vary in their speed and print quality, depending on the print output required.

Printers can be divided into two broad categories:

* Impact printers
* Non-impact printers.

Impact printers

Impact printers produce their output when the print head, which contains a number of metal hammers, strike an inked ribbon placed between the print head and the paper. These hammers may contain complete characters or they may contain 'dots' that are used to build up a character.

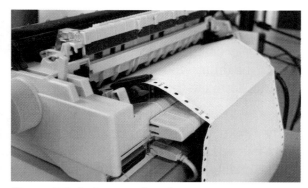

Figure 3.6 A dot matrix printer

A dot matrix printer

One of the most common types of impact printer is the **dot matrix printer**. A dot matrix printer contains a print head with pins (18 or 24) arranged in a rectangular matrix of rows and columns. These print one character at a time, depending on how the pins within the head are aligned. When a character or image is to be printed, the pins needed to form the character move forward and strike an inked ribbon, which then strikes the paper. Ink is transferred from the ribbon to the paper. Dot matrix printers are slow, with printing speeds ranging from 50 to 500 characters per second (cps).

Dot matrix printers do not produce good-quality printing. A 24-pin print head, which prints the best quality for this type of printer, can print 144 dots per inch (dpi). Although these printers are becoming obsolete, companies still use them because of their reliability, low operating cost and ability to print multiple copies of documents such as invoices.

Line printers

A **line printer** is an impact printer that appears to print a line at a time. Some of these printers print up to 3 000 lines per minute. The two main types are chain printers and band printers, which contain characters on a rotating band. Although line printers have been mostly replaced by high-speed laser printers, some businesses still use them as they are cheap to operate and can print on multi-part forms.

Non-impact printers

Non-impact printers are faster, quieter and produce better quality print than impact printers. Characters and images are formed without the printing mechanism making any direct physical contact with the paper. The main types of non-impact printers are:

* laser printers
* inkjet printers
* thermal printers.

Laser printers

Most large companies, as well as institutions such as schools, now have **laser printers** due to their ever-reducing cost. The printers have a very high-quality output (letter quality or LQ), with resolutions varying from 300 dots per inch (dpi) to 1 200 dots per inch (dpi) and printing at high speeds. Laser printers are also called page printers, and some of these printers can produce more than 70 pages per minute. Although colour laser printers and black and white laser printers are available, the colour printers are much more expensive.

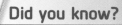

Did you know?

Did you know that the fastest black and white laser printers can produce around 100 fully printed pages per minute? The fastest colour laser printers are only slightly slower, and can produce about 70 pages per minute.

Figure 3.7 A laser printer

Laser printers use similar principles to photocopying for printing. A laser beam creates an image of a page on a light-sensitive drum that is treated with a magnetically charged powder called toner. The paper is then pressed against the drum, while heat and pressure are applied. The image is then transferred to the paper.

Inkject printers

Inkjet printers produce their output by spraying small, electrically charged droplets of ink from four nozzles through holes in a matrix, at high speed onto paper. The quality of printing, which varies from 320 dpi to 720 dpi, is very high.

Inkjet printers can print text or graphics in colour or black and white. The main difference between inkjet printers and laser printers is that inkjet printing sometimes smudges.

Inkjet printers are cheap compared to laser printers. Inkjet printers can print between 22 and 50 pages per minute depending on the size of the printer.

Figure 3.8 An inkjet printer

Thermal printers

Thermal printers, like dot matrix printers, have a print head that is made up of pins arranged in a matrix. These pins are heated electrically and burn the characters onto heat-sensitive paper. Thermal printers can print at a rate of up to 60 pages per minute. They are specialty devices used in cash registers, barcode systems, label makers and calculators. They are not used for general-purpose word-processing or report documents.

Plotters

A **plotter** is a peripheral printing device used to draw high-quality and high-resolution graphics, charts, graphs, maps and vectors or coordinate graphics onto large sheets of paper (see Figure 3.10).

Figure 3.9 A thermal printer

Although plotters are slow, they can draw continuous lines and often in a variety of colours. They are useful for producing architectural drawings, building plans (blueprints), maps and CAD (computer aided design) drawings, where accuracy is required. The paper is sometimes laid on a flatbed (flatbed plotter) or on a rotating drum (drum plotter). There are three main types of plotter:

* **Pen plotters** use a mechanical arm or rail that holds a pen that can be moved across the page.
* **Inkjet plotters** work in the same way as inkjet printers by spraying ink onto the paper.
* **Electrostatic plotters** work in the same way as laser printers.

Figure 3.10 A plotter

3D printers

A **3D printer** is a device that creates a physical object from a digital model by layering materials such as metal alloys, polymers, plastics or even food ingredients. The creation of a 3D printed object is achieved using **additive processes**. In an additive process, an object is created by laying down successive layers of material until the object is created. Each of these layers can be seen as a thinly sliced horizontal cross-section of the eventual object. 3D printers are used in many fields, such as aerospace engineering, dentistry, archaeology, biotechnology and information systems. For example, a 3D printer might be used in the field of archaeology to physically reconstruct ancient artefacts that have been damaged over time.

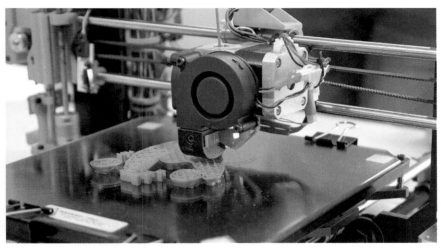

Figure 3.11 A 3D printer

Speech-generating devices (SGD)

A **speech-generating device (SGD)** is an electronic output device that is used to help individuals with severe speech impairments or other issues who have difficulty in communicating. Although SGDs vary in their design, most consist of several pages of words or symbols on a touch screen from which the user may choose. As the user makes their choices, suggestions are made for the next symbol or word based on what they might want to say. Most speech-generating devices can produce electronic voice output either through speech synthesis or digital recordings of someone speaking.

> **Did you know?**
>
> The famous theoretical physicist Stephen Hawking used a speech-generating device to communicate.

Multimedia projectors

A multimedia projector is a visual output device used to create and deliver dynamic multimedia presentations (presentations in which sound, photos, video, text and other moving graphics may be combined to create interesting effects). The liquid crystal display (LCD) projector is now a common device in most schools and organisations.

The LCD projector has its own built-in lenses and light source, and can connect directly to a computer, television set, video or DVD player, and video camcorder. Images from these devices are projected through the LCD projector onto a screen or wall. Versions of the LCD projector now include an arm extension on which a digital video camera is attached. This video camera allows real-time videos and pictures to be instantly projected through the LCD projector onto a screen. For example, the camera can be directed at a page in a book or at someone performing a demonstration, and this video camera image is then projected through the LCD projector onto a screen or wall.

Figure 3.12 A multimedia projector

Multimedia projectors are used frequently in classrooms, offices and gatherings at which multimedia presentations are made. For example, a teacher can integrate elements of sound, text, video and graphic into a lesson. In a marketing meeting, a presenter could alternate seamlessly between spreadsheets, animated ad content and live feeds from social media sites.

Input and output devices

Some devices, which include touch-sensitive screens and headsets, can perform both input and output functions.

Touch-sensitive screens

A touch-sensitive screen is a visual display screen that lets the user interact with the computer by touching the screen. The screen is covered with a plastic layer behind which are invisible beams of infrared light. Depending on the application for which the screen is being used, the plastic layer may contain symbols, buttons, words, numbers or menus. Many laptops and smartphones have touch-sensitive screens to carry out various actions. Additionally, the automatic teller machines (ATMs) in most banks have touchscreens, with buttons (keys) showing the different transactions, which the user needs to press to carry out. Touchscreen devices are also found in restaurants (the cash register) and some tourist information centres.

Figure 3.13 A touch-sensitive screen

Headsets

Headsets are devices that combine a pair of earphones and a microphone (see Figure 3.14). They work in the same way as the headsets used by disc jockeys when they play music. The headset can be connected to a computer using a USB connector. Once connected, it inputs sound through the microphone and outputs sound through the earphones. Headsets are popular with musicians who use computers to produce music.

Figure 3.14 Headsets combine earphones with a microphone.

Summary 3

1. Output devices are pieces of equipment that are used to get information or any other response from a computer.

2. Output can be human readable or machine readable.

3. Softcopy output is temporary and disappears when the computer is switched off.

4. Hardcopy output is permanent output that is usually printed onto paper.

5. Monitors or VDUs are softcopy output devices, and types include CRT, LCD and plasma.

6. A pixel (short for picture element) is the smallest unit on the screen that can be turned on or off or coloured in different shades.

7. Resolution is the clarity or sharpness of an image when displayed on the screen.

8. Printers are hardcopy output devices and can be classified as character, line and page printers.

9. Printers can be divided into two broad categories: impact printers and non-impact printers. Impact printers include dot-matrix and line printers. Non-impact printers include inkjet, laser and thermal printers.

10. Sound is softcopy output. Examples of sound output that use a speaker include computer-synthesised voice, computer-generated sound, music output and the speaking voice.

11. A plotter is a specialised output device designed to produce high-quality graphics in a variety of colours. A plotter is used, for example, in CAD, to draw accurate graphics, charts, graphs, maps and vectors or co-ordinate graphics on large sheets of paper.

12. Touch-sensitive screens and headsets are examples of devices that perform both input and output functions.

Questions 3

Copy and fill in the blanks questions

1. _____ devices are used to get information or any other response out of a computer.

2. Output that cannot be read by humans it is said to be _____ readable.

3. _____ output or temporary output refers to information displayed on a screen.

4. _____ output or permanent output refers to output printed onto paper.

5. A _____ is the smallest unit on the screen that can be turned on and off or coloured in different shades.

6. _____ is the clarity or sharpness of an image when displayed on the screen.

7. A _____ is a peripheral used to draw high-quality, high resolution graphics, charts, graphs, maps and vectors or coordinate graphics on large sheets of paper.

8. A _____ is a device that creates a physical object from a digital model by layering materials such as metal alloys, polymers, plastics, or even food ingredients.

9. A _____ screen is a visual display screen that lets the user interact with the computer by touching the screen.

10. A device that combines a pair of earphones and a microphone is known as a _____.

True or false questions

1. Output stored on a storage device is an example of machine-readable output.

2. A barcode is an example of human-readable output.

3. Information displayed on a screen or in audio or voice form through speakers is referred to as hardcopy output.

4 The more pixels there are on a screen, the higher the resolution.

5 VRS systems can operate standard household activities, such as turning lights and fans on and off, or closing and opening a garage door.

6 One of the most common types of impact printer is the dot matrix printer.

7 A laser printer is an example of a line printer.

8 Laser printers can be used by businesses to print multi-part forms.

9 Non-impact printers are faster, quieter and produce better quality print than impact printers.

10 Laser printers use similar principles to photocopying for printing.

Multiple-choice questions

1 Which of the following is an example of human readable output?

  a Barcodes

  b Output on a computer screen

  c Output stored on a storage device

  d Magnetic ink characters

2 Which of the following software applications may require a screen with high resolution?

  a Word processor

  b Gaming software

  c Spreadsheet

  d Database

3 Which of the following printers would allow a user to print a multi-part form?

  a A laser printer

  b A thermal printer

  c A dot matrix printer

  d An inkjet printer

4 Which of the following printers is an impact printer?

  a A laser printer

  b A thermal printer

  c A dot matrix printer

  d An inkjet printer

5 Which of these printers has the fastest printing speed?

  a A laser printer

  b A thermal printer

  c A dot matrix printer

  d An inkjet printer

6 Plotters are useful for producing:

  a charts.

  b maps.

  c building plans.

  d all of the above.

7 Which of the following performs both input and output functions?

  a A headset

  b A multimedia projector

  c A speech-generating device

  d A 3D printer

8 All of the following are examples of impact printers, except for the:

  a dot matrix printer.

  b inkjet printer.

  c chain printer.

  d band printer.

9 Which of the following might an architectural firm purchase to print architectural drawings of building plans?

   a A laser printer

   b An inkjet printer

   c A line printer

   d A plotter

10 All of the following are characteristics of a laser printer, except:

   a fast printing speed.

   b operates quietly.

   c high-quality printing.

   d printing multi-part forms.

Short-answer questions

1 Use examples to explain the difference between the following:

   a Machine readable and human readable

   b Softcopy and hardcopy

2 Three terms associated with the quality of an image are 'pixel', 'resolution' and 'graphics card'.

   a Define the term 'pixel'.

   b Explain the term 'resolution'.

   c Give two examples of applications that might require high resolution.

   d Explain the function of a graphics card.

3 A voice-response system (VRS) is an interface that responds to voice commands.

   a Explain how a VRS works.

   b Give one example of an application of a VRS in the home.

   c Give an example of how a disabled person may use a VRS system.

   d Explain the difference between a VRS and a speech-generating device (SGD).

4 Column A in the table below lists various devices, while Column B lists different tasks. Match each device with the task that best suits it. Write only the number and the letter each time in your notebook, (for example, 6f).

	Column A: Device		Column B: Task
1	3D printer	a	Used for playing computer games
2	Touch-sensitive screens	b	Operate standard household activities, such as turning lights and fans on and off
3	Joystick	c	Creates a physical object from a digital model by layering materials such as metal alloys, polymers, plastics, or even food ingredients.
4	Speech-generating device	d	Used as an interface to carry out transactions in an automatic teller machine (ATM)
5	Voice response system	e	Used to help individuals with severe speech impairments or other issues that result in a difficulty in communicating

5 Column A in the table below lists various devices, while Column B lists individuals who may use the device. Match each device with the most appropriate individual who may use the device. Write only the number and the letter each time in your notebook, (for example, 6f).

	Column A: Device		Column B: Individual who may use the device
1	Touchscreen	a	Teacher
2	Joystick	b	Architect
3	MICR	c	Cashier at a restaurant
4	Plotter	d	Banker
5	Multimedia projector	e	Gamer

6 **a** Explain the differences between impact and non-impact printers.

    b Give an example of an impact printer and a non-impact printer.

7 Copy and complete the table below. For each printer, state its approximate printing speed and give an example of an application where it can be used.

Name of printer	Speed	Application
Dot matrix		
Line printer		
Laser printer		
Inkjet printer		

8 **a** Explain how a thermal printer works.

    b Give two examples of where a thermal printer may be used.

9 A plotter is an output device.

    a Define the term 'plotter'.

    b List three types of plotters.

    c Give two examples of applications that use plotters.

10 **a** What is a multimedia projector?

    b Explain how a multimedia projector may be used for a business presentation.

Research questions

1 You are about to open a large hardware store. You visited a hardware store to observe the operations and discuss the day-to-day operations of the business with the manager. You observed that when a customer makes a purchase, a three-layered receipt is generated: one sheet for the customer, one sheet for the cashier and one sheet for the stores department. Discussions with the manager of the store showed that he has to prepare high-quality documents to send to different companies and government offices. The manager said that they use different types of printers for the different tasks, but was unable to give further details.

    a Conduct research to determine which two types of printers would satisfy the requirements of the business.

    b Explain your choice of printers in question (a).

    c Create a table to show the type of printers required for each activity outlined above, and list three brand names for each of the two types of printer required.

    d For each printer, state the approximate cost, printing speed, manufacturer and model.

2 A home for people with disabilities has approached you to recommend the type of output devices that differently-abled people can use to help them to lead more productive lives. You are required to conduct research, and then to copy and complete this table for at least two disabilities.

Name of device	Supplier/Brand	Type of disability	How is it used	Approximate cost

Crossword

Down

1 Output that is temporary and disappears when the computer is switched off

2 A printer that produces output when the print head, which contains a number of metal hammers, strikes an inked ribbon placed between the print head and the paper

3 A type of printer used in cash registers, barcode systems, label makers and calculators

5 A specialised output device designed to produce high-quality graphics in a variety of colours

Across

1 An electronic output device that is used to help individuals with severe speech impairments

2 A type of printer that produces output by spraying small, electrically charged droplets of ink from four nozzles through holes in a matrix, at high speed onto paper

4 Output that is permanent and usually printed

6 The smallest unit on the screen that can be turned on or off or coloured in different shades

7 A type of printer that uses similar principles to photocopying for printing

STEM project

The Ministry of Social and Citizens Care (MSCC) in your country is offering to purchase IT support equipment to the value of US$2 500 for community centres, to help them with the delivery of services to their respective local communities. However, the equipment must be purchased from local suppliers. All community centres have computers and speakers, but no other IT equipment. Your community centre manager is preparing a proposal to access the funding and has asked your class to prepare the section on the IT equipment needed. Your teacher can play the role of the community centre manager.

1 What format do you plan to use for preparing the section on IT equipment? Give two reasons for selecting this format?

2 Which key steps will you take to access the information needed to prepare your section of the proposal on the IT equipment needed?

3 Prepare your presentation and present it to the community centre manager.

4 After delivering your presentation and receiving feedback, describe the improvements that you can make to your section of the proposal.

Hints

1 What information should a proposal for funding contain?

2 What are the main activities at your community centre? Which IT equipment would be most useful to support these activities?

3 List all the relevant IT devices and write short descriptions of each one. Visit nearby computer shops to get information on prices and availability.

4 Primary and secondary storage

All computers need to store and retrieve data for processing. Storage refers to the media and devices used to keep data and instructions available for immediate or later use. Storage can be grouped into two categories:

* Primary storage
* Secondary storage.

Primary storage

As you learned in *Interact with IT* Book 1, processing takes place in the central processing unit (CPU) of a computer. The CPU consists of two units, which are the control unit (CU) and the arithmetic and logic unit (ALU). The CPU takes raw data and, following a set of instructions (programs), converts it into information.

As the main part of the CPU, the control unit (CU) directs and coordinates all the activities within it. The arithmetic and logic unit (ALU) performs all the arithmetic and logic functions in a computer.

Primary storage, which is directly accessible to the CPU, holds data and instructions that the computer is processing at the time.

Figure 4.1 Primary and secondary storage devices

Primary storage is also called **main memory** or **immediate access store (IMAS)**. This type of storage consists of a group of memory chips positioned on the motherboard (main circuit board) of the computer. These chips are located here because the processing unit can only act on data and instructions that are held in primary storage. Primary storage consists of two types of memory chips:

* **Random-access memory (RAM)**
* **Read-only memory (ROM)** chips.

A memory chip is an integrated circuit (IC) made of millions of transistors and capacitors.

Random-access memory (RAM)

Random-access memory (RAM) is only filled after a computer is turned on and given something to do. RAM is available to the processor immediately and holds data and instructions (programs) temporarily, while processing takes place. It also holds the data that result from processing, which is waiting to be output or stored in a secondary storage device. Therefore, RAM is also called working memory.

Programs and data stored in secondary storage must first be loaded into RAM before they can be processed. For example, before a letter can be typed, or data entered for a **spreadsheet**, the CPU must first load the application programs, such as a word-processing or spreadsheet program, into memory. These application programs, as well as whatever the user inputs using any of the applications, are held in RAM until the application is closed or the power is turned off. As RAM is **volatile**, if these inputs are not stored on a secondary storage device, they will be lost. The term 'volatile' means that if the power is turned off or the computer is rebooted (started up again), all the information that is held in RAM will be lost. RAM chips have limited storage capacity. In 2019, a personal computer RAM storage capacity can vary from 4 GB to 32 GB. RAM is also expensive and is a major factor in the final price of a computer.

Read-only memory (ROM)

Read-only memory (ROM) chips hold the data and instructions necessary for starting up the computer when it is switched on. ROM is commonly used to store system-level programs such as the BIOS (Basic Input Output System) program. ROM chips may also hold translators for high-level languages and operating systems.

These instructions are fixed at the time of manufacture and are sometimes described as being 'hard-wired'. This ensures that the instructions stored in ROM are always there, regardless of whether or not the power is on. Therefore, ROM is non-volatile. This is necessary because, when the computer is first turned on, the system memory is empty and needs the instructions stored in ROM for the PC to **boot** up.

Figure 4.2 Chips can contain ROM and RAM memory.

Variations of ROM chips, namely, **programmable ROM (PROM)** and **erasable programmable ROM (EPROM)**, which allow some flexibility in storing data and instructions, are also available. PROM chips can be programmed using special equipment and they can also be written to, but only once. EPROM is ROM that can be deleted and reprogrammed.

Secondary storage

Secondary storage is also called auxiliary or backup storage. This type of storage is used to store data and instructions when they are not being processed. Secondary storage is more permanent than main memory, as data and instructions are 'remembered' when the power is turned off. Secondary storage is also much cheaper than primary storage and is unlimited (you can buy as much as you can afford).

The most commonly used secondary storage devices are magnetic disks, optical disks, flash memory, USB drives and, less frequently, magnetic tapes.

Magnetic disks

Magnetic disks are one of the most widely used secondary storage mediums for computers. Magnetic disks provide **direct access** to the stored data. This means that you can go directly to a specific piece of data without having to access any other data either before or after the data you want. The capacity and access speeds of magnetic disks vary with each device or medium. Types of magnetic disks include diskettes (which are now almost obsolete) and hard disks.

Hard disks

Hard disks, as the name suggests, are thin, rigid (unbending) disks made of highly polished metal. The surface of each side of a disk (also called a platter) is covered with a substance that can be magnetised. This allows data to be stored on both sides of the disk as magnetised or unmagnetised spots.

The disks constantly rotate at a high speed and may have one read or write head per disk (a moveable head) or, on more expensive disks, every track in each disk may have its own read or write head (fixed head). As each track on a fixed head disk drive has a read or write head, less time is taken to access data and instructions, as the seek time is removed.

Almost all PCs have a hard drive housed inside the system unit and attached to the motherboard by a special cable. These hard drives are not removable and vary in storage capacity from 500 GB to 8 TB or more. The hard drive usually stores **application software**, such as word-processor, database, spreadsheet, and so on, and the operating system.

Two additional types of hard drives that can be used with a PC are:

* external hard drives
* removable hard disk packs.

External hard drives

External hard drives can be used if there is no space in the system unit to house another hard drive. They may have their own power source and they connect to the system unit through a USB port. External hard drives are easy to remove and connect to another computer, which make them portable. External hard drives are available in various sizes that range from 1 TB to 8 TB. A typical example of an external hard drive is the Seagate 8TB Innov8.

Removable hard disk pack

A removable hard disk pack may contain between 6 and 20 hard disks lined up one above the other in a sealed unit. The storage capacity is usually very large and can range from 1 TB to 10 TB or more.

Figure 4.3 A hard disk drive with hard disk displayed

Figure 4.4 External hard drives are easy to connect to other computers such as laptops.

Fixed disk drives

Fixed disk drives are similar to those found in PCs. They have a large storage capacity and are more reliable than removable hard disks. A mainframe computer may have between 20 and 100 fixed disks housed in a single cabinet. Data is transmitted to the CPU using a single data path.

A RAID storage system

The term 'RAID' stands for redundant array of independent disks. A RAID storage system consists of a cabinet that contains a large number of disk drives (up to 100). Besides holding more data than a fixed disk, this storage system stores multiple copies of data on different drives. If one drive fails, the others can take over, which allows the data to be recovered. Data is transmitted to the CPU using multiple data paths.

Figure 4.5 A RAID storage system

Figure 4.6 Optical disks

Optical disks

Optical disks are read by laser lights. The disc is made mainly of a type of plastic (polycarbonate). The data is stored on a layer inside the plastic. A metal coating (usually aluminium) reflects the laser light back to a sensor.

The main types of optical disks are:

* CDs
* DVDs.

CDs

The three types of CDs are CD-ROM, CD-R and CD-RW.

CD-ROM (compact disk)

CD-ROM stands for compact disk-read only memory. This means that you can only read (access) what is on the disk, but you cannot add or change anything. The data is encoded and read optically with a low-intensity laser light. The data is represented as a series of pits and lands.

* A pit is a little depression formed by the laser burning into the data layer.
* A land is the part between the pits or the smooth surface.

Reading a CD is done by shining a laser light at the disk and detecting changing reflecting patterns. The laser beam reflecting off the smooth surface (a land) is interpreted as a 1 **bit**. There is no reflection when the laser beam enters a pit, which is interpreted as a 0 bit.

The speed at which the data is accessed depends on how fast the disk spins. The faster the disk spins, the faster the data can be transferred to the computer's memory. The speed of a CD-ROM drive is shown by a number followed by an 'X'. Typical CD-ROM drive speeds are 48X, 50X, and so on. The higher the number, the faster the disk spins, which results in faster data access.

Due to their large storage capacity (up to 800 MB), CD-ROMs are used to store software packages for sale or distribution. They are particularly useful for storing multimedia (text, graphics, sound and videos), as well as application software packages such as encyclopaedias, word processors, training programs, and games and graphics packages.

CD-R

The term 'CD-R' stands for compact disk recordable. This disk allows you to write data onto it only once using a CD recorder (burner). The disk then becomes a CD-ROM, as its contents cannot be changed. A CD-R is ideal for storing large volumes of data that do not change frequently.

CD-RW

The term 'CD-RW' stands for compact disk rewriteable. CD-RWs are now a common choice for use as backup storage. The data layer of these disks uses a phase-changing metal alloy film. By using a higher intensity laser light, this film can be melted to level out the marks made by the laser, which deletes the previously stored data. New data can then be recorded using a lower intensity laser light to burn the new data. In theory, you can erase and write on these disks as many as 1 000 times. Therefore, a CD-RW is an ideal backup storage device for storing large volumes of data that changes frequently.

DVDs

The term 'DVD' stands for digital versatile disk. The main types are DVD-ROM (read only), DVD-R (recordable) and DVD-RW (rewriteable). They look similar to a CD-R disk, but can hold much more information. A typical DVD can hold between 4.7 GB and 17 GB of information. DVDs are used mainly for storing videos of films, as the quality of sound and video output is far superior to video tapes.

Blu–ray disks (BDs)

A **Blu-ray disk (BD)** is a high-capacity optical disk developed for recording, rewriting and playing back high-definition video. A BD can store large amounts of data and was designed to replace the DVD.

Blu-ray technology enables viewers to see more depth, a wider range of colour shades, and more detail in the image than on a DVD. This is because BDs support higher resolutions and more advanced video and audio formats compared to DVDs.

The BD gets its name from the blue-violet laser beam that is used to read BDs. Compared to a DVD's red laser, a blue laser allows more information to be stored at a greater density. For example, while a DVD can store 15 GB per layer, a Blu-ray disk can store 25 GB per layer, and dual-layer disks can hold up to 50 GB.

BDs also provide much higher resolution than DVDs. While a DVD with standard definition can provide a resolution of 720 x 480 pixels, a high-definition BD has a resolution of 1 920 x 1 080 pixels.

Note!

Optical disks are becoming obsolete (outdated) because of USB drives. The result is that most desktop and laptop computers are being built without optical disk drives.

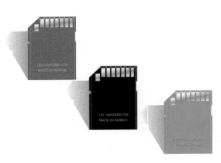

Figure 4.7 Flash memory cards

Flash memory

Flash memory is a way to store data electronically on removable and easily portable devices, such as memory cards and USB flash drives.

Memory cards

Several different brands of removable memory cards, also called storage cards, are now available. These are solid-state devices (no moving parts) that read and write data electrically, instead of magnetically.

Devices such as digital cameras, digital camcorders and cell phones may use CompactFlash, SmartMedia or other types of flash memory card. Laptop computers use PCMCIA cards, which is another type of flash memory, as solid-state hard disks.

USB flash drives

Solid-state memory devices called 'flash drives' have become a main storage medium for personal computer users. These devices, which are known by different names, such as flash drives, flash pens, thumb drives, key drives, and mini-USB drives, are small (about the size of your thumb or a large car key) and plug into a USB port on the computer. No drivers are needed for Windows XP and Windows 7, 8 or 10. You just plug it in and the computer reports a new hard drive.

These small flash drives can have storage capacities ranging from 16 GB, 32 GB and 64 GB to 128 GB, 256 GB and more. For example, the Samsung T3 SSD has a capacity of 1 TB. Some flash drives include password protection and the ability to run software directly from the USB drive.

Figure 4.8 Flash drives plug into a USB port on a computer.

Magnetic tapes

Figure 4.9 Magnetic tape cartridges

A magnetic tape is a ribbon of plastic material coated with a metal oxide film on which data is recorded as magnetised or unmagnetised spots. The magnetic orientations (locations) of the magnetised and unmagnetised spots are represented by the binary digits 0 and 1. On mainframe computers, magnetic tapes are stored on reels or in cartridges. In microcomputers, magnetic tapes are only stored in cartridges similar to those that were used to store music but of a much higher quality. As with the tape in a tape-recorder, data can be written to or read from the tape as it passes across the magnetic heads.

Magnetic tapes are not suitable for data files that are revised or updated often because they store data sequentially. This means that data is accessed in the order in which it was stored. Therefore, accessing data is very slow as you cannot go directly to an item of data on the tape. You need to start at the beginning of the tape and search for the data as the tape goes past the heads.

Magnetic tapes are erasable, reusable and durable, and are made to store large quantities of data cheaply. Although magnetic tapes are used less and less for the day-to-day backups, many businesses still use tapes for archiving and off-site storage.

Cloud storage

Cloud computing or cloud storage, also referred to as 'the cloud', is a service for maintaining, managing and backing up data remotely on the internet. This service allows users to store data on different servers online and access them from any location using the internet. The rapid growth of cloud storage has resulted in hundreds of companies offering a variety of cloud storage services. Services, such as Google Drive™, Amazon S3 and Sky Drive, allow users to save their files in one of many massive data centres.

As the cloud's popularity grows, more and more businesses are using the service as a backup program for their software and documents. This service also allows anyone to access their documents from anywhere worldwide. Users are no longer tied down to just one electronic device in one set area. Instead, for example, you can revise a version of a document on your laptop at home and then access it at work for a presentation the next day. In addition, multiple users can collaborate on projects by having access to the same file.

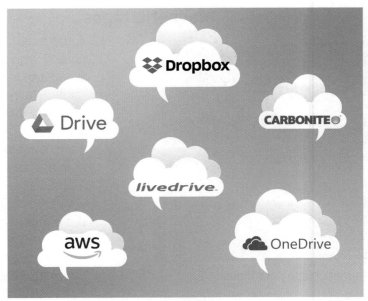

Google Drive is a trademark of Google LLC.

Figure 4.10 Cloud storage services

Advantages of cloud storage

Cloud storage has the following advantages:

* **Ease of use:** All cloud storage services have desktop folders for Mac® and PC. This allows users to drag and drop files between the cloud storage and their local storage.
* **Accessibility:** Users can access and share stored files from anywhere using an internet connection. Cloud data storage allows the data to be shared with a number of remote locations, such as an office in another part of the country or one in a completely different country, or employees working from home.
* **Disaster recovery:** Cloud data storage can be used as an offsite backup, as it is not affected by events and disasters such as theft, floods and fires.
* **Cost savings:** The relatively low cost of cloud storage often allows businesses and organisations to reduce their annual operating costs.

Disadvantages of cloud storage

Cloud storage has the following disadvantages:

* **Usability:** Cloud storage is much slower than local backups.
* **Accessibility:** You need an internet connection to access the cloud storage. If you have no internet connection, you have no access to your data.
* **Data security:** There are concerns about the safety and privacy of important data stored remotely.
* **Software:** If you want to be able to use your files locally on many devices, then you will need to download the service software on all your devices.

Summary 4

1. Storage refers to the media and devices used to keep data and instructions for immediate or later use.

2. Primary memory, which is positioned on the main circuit board, consists of RAM and ROM chips.

3. Random-access memory (RAM) is immediately available to the processor and holds data and instructions temporarily, while processing takes place. It also holds processed data that is waiting to be output or stored in a secondary storage device. Data can be read from and written to RAM. RAM is volatile, limited and expensive.

4. Read-only memory (ROM) chips hold the data and instructions necessary for starting up the computer when it is switched on. Data can only be read from ROM chips. ROM is non-volatile.

5. PROM and EPROM are variations of the ROM chip that allow data to be added – once in the case of PROM and many times for EPROM.

6. Secondary storage devices store data and instructions permanently, so that they can be used when required.

7. The type of storage chosen for a particular application is based on its storage capacity, access speed, size, portability and cost.

8. Magnetic tapes, magnetic disks (hard disks), optical disks (CD-Rom, CD-R, CD-RW and DVDs), USB drives and flash memory are secondary storage devices.

9. Magnetic tapes are erasable, reusable and cheap. Although they have large storage capacities, they only allow sequential access. Magnetic tapes are used mostly for backup purposes.

10. Sequential access refers to the accessing of data in the order in which it was stored.

11. Magnetic disks provide direct access to the stored data.

12. Direct access means that you can go directly to a specific piece of data without having to access any other data.

13. Optical disks refer to CD-ROMs, CD-Rs, CD-RWs and DVDs, which provide direct access to the stored data.

14. Cloud storage is a model in which data is stored, maintained, managed and backed up on remote servers accessed from the internet, or 'cloud'. Some advantages of cloud storage include ease of use, accessibility, disaster recovery and cost savings. Some disadvantages include being slower, requiring an internet connection, and concerns with data security and the need to load the service software onto all machines.

Questions 4

Copy and fill in the blanks questions

1. _____ memory is another name for primary storage, which is also called main memory or immediate access store (IMAS).

2. The _____ unit can only act on data and instructions that are held in primary storage.

3. A memory chip is an integrated circuit (IC) made up of millions of _____ and capacitors.

4. _____ is immediately available to the processor and holds data and instructions (programs) temporarily, while processing takes place.

5. _____ chips hold the data and instructions necessary for starting up the computer when it is switched on.

6. Instructions that are fixed at the time of manufacture on a ROM chip are sometimes described as being _____.

7 _____ storage, which is also called auxiliary or backup storage, is used to store data and instructions when they are not being processed.

8 _____ disks are one of the most widely used forms of secondary storage for computers.

9 _____ access means that you can go directly to a specific piece of data without having to access any other data either before or after the data you want.

10 _____ devices read and write data electronically, instead of magnetically.

11 _____ storage is a service for maintaining, managing and backing up data remotely on the internet.

12 _____ access refers to the accessing of data in the order in which it was stored.

True or false questions

1 All computers need to store and retrieve data for processing.

2 A magnetic disk is an example of primary storage.

3 Main memory is made of RAM and ROM chips.

4 RAM memory is volatile.

5 RAM memory is only filled after a computer has been turned on and is given something to do.

6 RAM chips are cheap and have unlimited storage capacity.

7 ROM chips hold the data and instructions necessary to start up the computer.

8 ROM chips are non-volatile.

9 A CD-ROM holds more information than a DVD.

10 Cloud storage allows users to store data online, so that they can access them from any location via the internet.

Multiple-choice questions

1 Primary storage is also referred to as:

   a backup storage.

   b secondary storage.

   c auxiliary storage.

   d immediate access store.

2 Primary storage holds:

   a the programs needed to start up the computer.

   b the software applications not being processed.

   c data and instructions temporarily, while processing takes place.

   d none of the above.

3 RAM is volatile, which means:

   a that the data and instructions held in RAM are permanent.

   b that if the computer is rebooted, all the data and instructions held in RAM are lost.

   c that RAM holds data that can be quickly accessed by the control unit.

   d all of the above.

Short-answer questions

1 Use examples to explain the differences between primary storage and secondary storage.

2 Explain why a computer needs both RAM and ROM memory.

3 Use examples to explain the difference between direct access and sequential access.

4 Magnetic tapes are still being used by many companies to store data and information.

   a Explain how data and information are stored on a magnetic tape.

   b Give two reasons why a company may choose to use magnetic tapes instead of magnetic disks.

5 Cloud storage has become a popular method of storage.

   a Explain the term 'cloud storage'.

   b List two advantages of cloud storage.

   c List two disadvantages of cloud storage.

   d Name two companies that provide cloud storage services.

Research questions

1 a List three companies located anywhere in the world that use magnetic tapes to store their backup data.

   b Give examples of the type of data and information that these companies store.

   c Give reasons why these companies continue to use magnetic tapes instead of other storage methods.

2 Different devices can be used for secondary storage. Copy the table below into your notebook. Name three products in each category that are currently being sold and fill in the other data.

Storage media	Name of the device (brand name)	Storage capacity	Average cost per MB	Application (where it can be used)
Magnetic tape				
Magnetic disk				
Flash memory				

3 List five major companies that are currently providing cloud storage services. For each company, give the approximate cost of providing the service.

Crossword

Down

1 A type of storage device that stores data and instructions permanently to be used when required

2 Memory that consists of RAM and ROM

3 A chip that is non-volatile

5 A type of access where you can go directly to a specific piece of data without having to access any other data

7 refers to the media and devices used to keep data and instructions for immediate or later use

Across

4 A type of online storage

6 A type of disk that is read by laser lights

8 A type of access where data is accessed in the order in which it was stored

9 The smallest unit of storage

10 This holds processed data waiting to be output or stored in a secondary storage device

STEM project

A large multinational company has sold a franchise to a small Caribbean entrepreneur as part of a market trial of café outlets selling cold and hot non-milk beverages. The parent company stores its training modules, accounting templates and weekly market updates in cloud storage. You have been hired by the entrepreneur to advise on the best information storage methods for his start-up franchise, taking into account the area's irregular internet service, as well as his desire to eventually expand his number of outlets.

1 Write a precise statement of what you have to do for the Caribbean entrepreneur.

2 Write brief notes on each step you plan to take in order to prepare your advisory document. You should have at least three steps.

3 Prepare an advisory document for the entrepreneur. Ask a classmate to review your document.

4 Based on your classmate's evaluation, briefly describe how you can improve your document.

Hints

1 What is a franchise? How does it work?

2 Revise the types of storage devices.

3 Compare the advantages and disadvantages of the entrepreneur using cloud storage.

5 Data storage and representation

Data representation and storage

A bistable device is one that can be set to one of two states at any one point in time. An example of a bistable device could be a light bulb. A light bulb can be either in the 'on' or 'off' state. A circuit can either pass a current or not pass a current through the bulb.

The two states of a bistable device can be represented by the digits 0 and 1. In the case of the light bulb, we can use 0 to represent the bulb being 'on' and 1 to represent it being 'off'. A computer consists of a number of two-state (bistable) devices called switches, which process and store data. Computers use the binary number system, which consists of two digits 0 and 1, to represent the two states of a switch. These two binary digits are also known as bits (short for binary digits). A single bit can represent one of two values, 0 and 1. Switches can be grouped together to store larger numbers. A group of two bits can be used to represent one of four (2^2) values:

- 00
- 01
- 10
- 11

These four values can represent four different symbols or characters. For example, the numbers 0, 1, 2, 3 could be assigned to the four bit patterns:

00	0	10	2
01	1	11	3

With three bits, we can have eight (2^3) bit patterns. This means we can now represent eight different characters, for example 0 to 7:

000	0	100	4
001	1	101	5
010	2	110	6
011	3	111	7

With four bits, we can represent 16 (2^4) characters, with eight bits we can represent 256 (2^8) characters, and so on. Therefore, with 'n' bits, we will be able to represent 2^n characters.

Figure 5.1 The binary number system consists of two digits 0 and 1.

The amount of data and instructions that can be stored in the memory of a computer or secondary storage medium is measured in bytes. A **byte** is made up of a combination of eight bits and has the storage power to represent one character. A **character** can be a letter, a number, a symbol, a punctuation mark or a blank space. A **word** is the number of bits a computer's CPU can process in one operation. Word length is the number of bits in a word. Your CPU's word length may be 64 bits or 32 bits, (in other words, 8 bytes or 4 bytes). The CPU can process a word of data several billion times per second.

Larger units of storage

Larger units of storage include kilobytes (KBs), megabytes (MBs), gigabytes (GBs) and terabytes (TBs).

* **1 kilobyte (KB)**
  1 024 bytes
* **1 megabyte (MB)**
  1 000 kilobytes or
  1 048 576 bytes
  (about 1 million bytes)
* **1 gigabyte (GB)**
  1 000 megabytes or
  1 073 741 824 bytes
  (about 1 billion bytes)
* **1 terabyte (TB)**
  1 000 gigabytes or
  1 009 511 627 776 bytes
  (about 1 trillion bytes).

Number systems

The number system that you may be most familiar with is the decimal (base 10) number system (also called a denary system). This system is used in everyday mathematical operations. However, as computers can only perform binary operations, you need to know how to do calculations using the binary number system. The next section deals with converting numbers from binary (base 2) to base 10 and vice versa.

Converting a binary number (base 2) to a decimal (base 10)

Before we convert a binary number to decimal, we need to revise some basic concepts of the decimal number system. This system consists of ten digits (0, 1, 2, 3, 4, 5, 6, 7, 8, 9) and, for this reason, is also referred to as the base 10 number system. The base of any number may be indicated as a subscript on the extreme right of the number, for example, 455_{10} means '455 to the base 10'. These digits and their combinations are used to represent numbers in the decimal number system.

Each digit in the decimal number system has a value that depends on its position or place in the number. The place values start at 10^0 for the digit of smallest value on the right. You know from your mathematics lessons that $10^0 = 1$, since any number raised to the power of 0 is 1. So 10^0 is the 'ones place' or 'ones column'. Similarly, 10^1 is the 'tens place'. The value of each place increases by a factor of 10 for each consecutive digit moving from right to left, until the digit of greatest value is reached: the digit on the far left. Again, you will remember this from your mathematics lessons.

Figure 5.2 The decimal system consists of numbers 0 to 9.

Let us look at the number 325. This number is made up of the sum (addition) of each digit multiplied by its place value. Table 5.1 on the next page shows the value of each digit in the number.

Table 5.1 The value of each digit in a number

Hundreds (H)	Tens (T)	Ones (O)
3 represents 3 H	2 represents 2 T	5 represents 5 O
$3 \times 100 = 300$	$2 \times 10 = 20$	$5 \times 1 = 5$
Adding the totals together gives 325.		

Table 5.2 shows another way to set out the information in Table 5.1.

Table 5.2 Decimal number and place value

H (10^2)	T (10^1)	O (10^0)	
100	10	1	P
100	10	1	This row shows the value of each digit in that position: the 'place value'.
3	2	5	Each digit in this row is multiplied by its place value, above.
300	20	5	Sum the totals: The result is 325.

Binary numbers are very similar to decimals, because each digit in a binary number also has a place value that depends on its position in the number. However, for binary numbers, the place value starts at 2^0 for the least significant bit (LSB) and increases by a factor of 2 for each bit that follows, again moving from right to left, as in the decimal example given in Table 5.2.

To convert a binary number to a decimal, we multiply each bit by its place value, starting from the least significant bit (LSB) on the right to the most significant bit (MSB) on the left, and then sum the totals. Example 1 shows how to do this conversion.

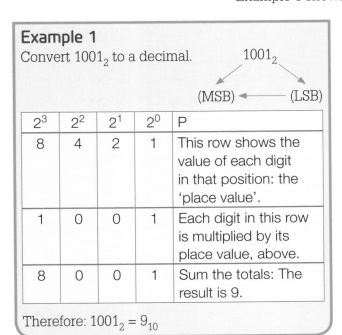

Example 1
Convert 1001_2 to a decimal.

1001_2

(MSB) ← (LSB)

2^3	2^2	2^1	2^0	P
8	4	2	1	This row shows the value of each digit in that position: the 'place value'.
1	0	0	1	Each digit in this row is multiplied by its place value, above.
8	0	0	1	Sum the totals: The result is 9.

Therefore: $1001_2 = 9_{10}$

Example 2
Convert 111001_2 to a decimal.

2^5	2^4	2^3	2^2	2^1	2^0	P
32	16	8	4	2	1	This row shows the value of each digit in that position: the 'place value'.
1	1	1	0	0	1	Each digit in this row is multiplied by its place value, above.
32	16	8	0	0	1	Sum the totals: The result is 57.

Therefore: $111001_2 = 57_{10}$

Converting a decimal number (base 10) to a binary number (base 2)

The process for converting a base 10 (decimal number) to binary (base 2) is simple. It involves dividing the decimal number by 2 and recording the remainder until the quotient is zero, and then writing out the remainders starting from the last remainder to the first. Example 3 and Example 4 show you how to do this.

Example 3

Convert the number 9_{10} to binary.

÷	9	Nine divided by 2 gives 4 remainder 1.
2	4 R 1	Four divided by 2 gives 2 remainder 0.
2	2 R 0	Two divided by 2 gives 1 remainder 0.
2	1 R 0	One divided by 2 gives 0 remainder 1.
	0 R 1	Write the remainders starting from the last remainder moving up to the first. This gives 1001_2.

Therefore: $9_{10} = 1001_2$

The process is the same for larger numbers.

Example 4

What is the binary equivalent of 225_{10}?

÷	225	225 divided by 2 gives 112 remainder 1.
2	112 R1	112 divided by 2 gives 56 remainder 0.
2	56 R 0	56 divided by 2 gives 28 remainder 0.
2	28 R 0	28 divided by 2 gives 14 remainder 0.
2	14 R 0	14 divided by 2 gives 7 remainder 0.
2	7 R 0	7 divided by 2 gives 3 remainder 1.
2	3 R 1	3 divided by 2 gives 1 remainder 1.
2	1 R 1	One divided by 2 gives 0 remainder 1.
	0 R 1	Write the remainders starting from the last remainder moving up to the first. This gives 11100001_2.

Therefore: $225_{10} = 11100001_2$

Adding binary numbers

Memorise these five calculations and remember the points that follow, as this basic information shows you how to add in binary.

1	**2**	**3**	**4**	**5**
0_2	0_2	1_2	1_2	1_2
$+\ 0_2$	$+\ 1_2$	$+\ 0_2$	$+\ 1_2$	$+\ 1_2$
0_2	1_2	1_2	10_2	1_2
				11_2

To understand how these calculations work, think of them as follows:

1: $0_2 + 0_2 = 0_2$ is the same as: $(2^0 \times 0) + (2^0 \times 0)$
$$= (1 \times 0) + (1 \times 0) = 0 \times 0$$
$$= 0$$

0_{10} in base 2 is 0_2, hence the answer shown.

Similarly:

5: $1_2 + 1_2 + 1_2$ is the same as: $(2^0 \times 1) + (2^0 \times 1) + (2^0 \times 1)$
$$= 1 + 1 + 1$$
$$= 3$$

3_{10} in binary is the same as: $(2^1 \times 1) + (2^0 \times 1) = 11_2$

When you add binary numbers, always remember that $1 + 1 \neq 2$, because the digit 2 is not used in binary; similarly $1 + 1 + 1 \neq 3$.

Now let us look at how to add in binary, using a few examples.

Example 5

Add the binary numbers 01 and 10 together.

First, place the binary numbers one above the other and make sure that the bits with the same weighting are in the same columns. This gives:

01

10

Step 1: Starting from the column on the right, add the digits: $1 + 0 = 1$. Write the 1 in the same column.

```
  01
+ 10
───
   1
```

Step 2: Add the digits in the second column: $0 + 1 = 1$. Write the 1 in the same column.

```
  01
+ 10
───
  11
```

Therefore: $01_2 + 10_2 = 11_2$

Example 6

Add 011_2 and 010_2 together.

$$
\begin{array}{r}
\text{(MSB)} \quad \text{(LSB)} \\
0\ 1\ 1 \\
+\ 0\ 1\ 0
\end{array}
$$

Step 1: Starting from the far-right column (LSB), add the digits: $1 + 0 = 1$. Write the 1 in the same column.

$$
\begin{array}{r}
0\ 1\ 1 \\
\underline{0\ 1\ 0} \\
1
\end{array}
$$

Step 2: Add the digits in the second column: $1 + 1 = 10$. Write the 0 in the same column and carry the 1 to the next column.

$$
\begin{array}{r}
\text{(carry)}\ \ 1 \qquad\quad \\
0\ 1\ 1 \\
\underline{0\ 1\ 0} \\
0\ 1
\end{array}
$$

Step 3: Add the digits in the third column: 1 (the carried bit) $+\ 0 + 0 = 1$

We now have:

$$
\begin{array}{r}
0\ 1\ 1 \\
+\ \underline{0\ 1\ 0} \\
1\ 0\ 1
\end{array}
$$

Therefore: $011_2 + 010_2 = 101_2$

Example 7

Add 1011_2 and 0011_2 together.

First, place the binary numbers one above the other, making sure that the bits with the same weighting are in the same columns.

```
(MSB)     (LSB)
    1 0 1 1
  + 0 0 1 1
```

Step 1: Add the digits in the far-right (LSB) column: $1 + 1 = 10$. Write the 0 in the column and carry the 1 to the next column.

```
            1
    1  0  1  1
  + 0  0  1  1
  _____
               0
```

Step 2: Add the digits in the second column, including the carried bit: $1 + 1 + 1 = 11$. Write the 1 in the column and carry 1 to the next column.

```
        1  1
    1  0  1  1
  + 0  0  1  1
  _____
            1  0
```

Step 3: Add the digits in the third column, including the carried bit: $1 + 0 + 0 = 1$. Write the 1 in the column.

```
        1  1
    1  0  1  1
  + 0  0  1  1
  _____
         1  1  0
```

Step 4: Add the digits in the fourth column: $1 + 0 = 1$. Write the 1 in the column.

```
        1  1
    1  0  1  1
  + 0  0  1  1
  _____
      1  1  1  0
```

Therefore: $1011_2 + 0011_2 = 1110_2$

Subtracting binary numbers

There are several ways to subtract binary numbers. In this section, we will subtract binary numbers using the borrowing method.

Example 8

Subtract $11_2 - 10_2$.

Since this subtraction does not require borrowing, you can subtract starting from the right (LSB) and moving to the left (MSB).

$$
\begin{array}{cc}
1 & 1_2 \\
1 & 0_2 \\
\hline
0 & 1_2
\end{array}
$$

Example 9

Now let us look at an example that requires borrowing.
Subtract $10_2 - 01_2$.

Start from the right column (LSB). Since 0 is less than 1 we have to borrow from the next column.

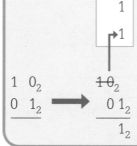

Borrowing 1 from the second column gives two 1s in the first column. So subtracting 1 would give 1_2.

Example 10

Subtract $100_2 - 011_2$.

Start from the right column. Since 0 is less than 1, we have to borrow from the closest adjacent column that has a 1. This means we will have to borrow 1 from the third column.

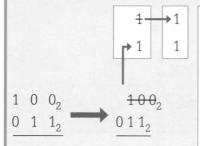

Taking a 1 from the third column gives two 1s in the second column. Taking 1 from the second column gives two 1s in the first column. Therefore, two 1s in the first column take away 1 gives 1. 1 take away 1 in the second column gives 0 and 0 take away 0 in the third column gives 0. Our answer is 001_2.

Summary 5

1 A bistable device is one that can be set to one of two states at any one point in time.

2 A bit is the smallest unit of storage.

3 A byte is made up of a combination of eight bits, and has the storage power to represent one written character.

4 A word is the number of bits a computer can process in one operation. A word length is the number of bits in a word.

5 A decimal number (base 10) can be converted to a binary number (base 2) by dividing the decimal number by 2 and recording the remainder until the quotient is zero, and then writing out the remainders starting from the last remainder to the first.

6 A binary number can be converted to a decimal by multiplying each digit by its place value starting from the least significant bit (LSB) on the right to the most significant bit (MSB) on the left, and adding the results. The place value is a factor of 2 starting from 2^0 for the LSB and increasing by a factor of 2 for each consecutive bit.

7 Binary addition can be done easily by remembering the following rules:
$$0_2 + 0_2 = 0_2$$
$$0_2 + 1_2 = 1_2$$
$$1_2 + 0_2 = 1_2$$
$$1_2 + 1_2 = 10_2$$
$$1_2 + 1_2 + 1_2 = 11_2$$

Questions 5

Copy and fill in the blanks questions

1 A _____ is the smallest unit of storage in a computer.

2 The amount of data and instructions that can be stored in the memory of a computer or secondary storage medium is measured in _____.

3 A _____ can be a letter, a number, a symbol, a punctuation mark or a blank space.

True or false questions

1 A single bit can represent one of two values, 0 and 1.

2 A byte is made up of a combination of four bits.

3 The base 10 number system is used to represent data and instructions in digital computers.

4 $01_2 + 11_2 = 100_2$

5 9_{10} converted to binary is equal to 1001_2.

Multiple-choice questions

1 A byte consists of:

   a 4 bits.

   b 6 bits.

   c 8 bits.

   d 10 bits.

2 A group of 2 bits can represent:

   a 2 values.

   b 3 values.

   c 4 values.

   d 8 values.

3 One megabyte is equivalent to:

   a 1 000 bytes.

   b 1 000 kilobytes.

   c 1 000 gigabytes.

   d 1 000 terabytes.

4 The binary number 1011_2 converted to base 10 equals:

   a 9.

   b 10.

   c 11.

   d 12.

5 When the decimal number 15 is converted to binary, the answer is:

   a 1101.

   b 0111.

   c 1110.

   d 1111.

6 $011_2 + 010_2$ is equal to:

   a 101_2.

   b 110_2.

   c 011_2.

   d 111_2.

7 Subtract 10_2 from 11_2. The result is:

   a 00_2.

   b 01_2.

   c 10_2.

   d 11_2.

Short-answer questions

1 a How many bit patterns can be represented by 3 bits?

   b Write out the bit patterns that can be represented by 3 bits.

2 Convert the following binary numbers to decimal (base 10) numbers:

   a 1100

   b 1001

   c 1111

3 Convert the following decimal numbers to binary:

   a 25

   b 205

   c 255

4 Add the following binary numbers together:

   a $1011_2 + 0011_2$

   b $1101_2 + 0111_2$

   c $1011_2 + 01011_2$

5 Perform the following binary subtractions:

   a $100_2 - 011_2$

   b $101_2 - 011_2$

   c $110_2 - 101_2$

Research questions

Do research on the internet and then answer these questions. Write the answers in your notebook.

1 What type of code is used to represent all the characters on a typical keyboard?

2 How are the characters represented?

3 How does a computer add two binary numbers?

Crossword

Down

1 A device that can be set to one of two states at any one point in time

2 The amount of bits a computer can process in one operation

Across

1 A combination of eight bits that has the storage power to represent one character

3 The general term for a letter, a number, a symbol, a punctuation mark or a blank space

4 The smallest unit of storage

5 A type of number that can be converted to binary by dividing the number by 2 and recording the remainder until the quotient is zero, and then writing out the remainders starting from the last remainder to the first

STEM project

You have applied for the post of programmer's calculator for a high-tech computer firm. In the interview, you are asked to complete the table below to assess your readiness. You must deliver a presentation to the interview panel showing the completed table and explaining your workings. You have 15 minutes to complete the table, and prepare and deliver your presentation. You have a choice of the following equipment and materials for your presentation: a whiteboard, whiteboard markers, a computer, a printer, a slide projector, transparencies and permanent markers.

3 Prepare your presentation. Which equipment and material did you select and why did you select them?

4 Once you and a classmate have completed the table and prepared your presentation, swap and review each other's work.

5 Did you both complete the table correctly? What feedback did you get on your presentation? From this feedback, describe the improvements that you can make to your presentation.

Binary	Decimal	Hex	Octal	BCD	Sign and magnitude	Two's complement
(–)001001						
		BAC		1010 1000 1110 1011		

1 Copy and complete the table. Make a note of all your workings to use in your presentation.

2 What is the most logical process to explain your workings? Write a brief outline of this process.

Hints

1 Review the conversion methods in the chapter before attempting this project.

2 Select the best equipment and materials to do an effective presentation.

6 Operating system (1)

Objectives

At the end of the chapter, you will be able to:

❏ state the two major types of software (application and system)

❏ classify application software into their different categories

❏ outline the functions of the operating system (file management, security control, provides user interface, device management, program management, multitasking and memory management)

❏ explain the functions of the different types of system software.

In the *Interact with IT* Book 1, you learned that software is the general name given to all the programs that computers use to perform different tasks. Software can be classified into two major categories:

* **Application software**
* **System software**.

Application software

Application software consists of programs developed to carry out specific tasks or solve particular problems. For example, if someone wants to create a brochure or a newsletter, they will use a desktop publishing package. If they want to keep the accounts for a club or business, they will use a spreadsheet program. Desktop publishing packages and spreadsheet packages are examples of application software.

Application software can also be grouped as follows:

* General-purpose software
* Integrated software
* Customised (specialised) software
* Custom-written (tailor-made) software packages.

Figure 6.1 Examples of application software: A spreadsheet package (left) and a desktop publishing package (right)

General-purpose software

General purpose software is not written for any specific business or organisation, but can be used or adapted to suit their specific needs. For example, a teacher can use a spreadsheet package to prepare students' end-of-term grade reports, and a word-processing package to write letters to the parents. These same packages could also be used in a business to perform different tasks, such as accounting or memo-writing. General-purpose software packages, also called 'off-the-shelf' software, are usually well tested and relatively cheap.

Integrated software

An **integrated software** package is a set of related programs combined in a single package. This type of software package allows data to be transferred easily between the programs and has a similar look across the programs. Examples include Microsoft Office, Microsoft Works, Adobe® Cerative Suite® and the iWork® package used by Apple® Macintosh® computers.

A basic integrated package may contain word-processor, spreadsheet, database, communications, graphics and presentation programs. A major advantage of these packages is the ease with which data can be transferred from one component to another.

For example, if you are working on a word-processing document, you can quickly incorporate a graph created in the package's spreadsheet component using a simple cut or copy-and-paste operation, or by using the object linking and embedding option (OLE).

The OLE option allows the transfer and sharing of information between applications. With embedded or linked objects, a document can contain information that was created in different applications. For example, a Microsoft Word document may contain a chart or table from Microsoft Excel. This information can be edited from inside the Word document that contains the object.

If an object, such as a chart, table or so on, is linked, the object in the Word file is updated every time the Excel file is updated. However, when you embed an Excel object, information in the Word file doesn't change if you modify the source Excel file. Embedded objects become part of the Word file and, after they are inserted, they are no longer part of the source file.

Figure 6.2 Integrated software allows the user, for example, to insert a graph from Excel into a Word file.

Some additional advantages of integrated software include the following:

* It takes up less disk space than individual applications.
* It allows you to move much faster from one application to the next.
* It is usually easier to learn as the **user interface** for choosing commands is the same.
* It tends to be more powerful and versatile than individual applications.
* It is less likely to crash and contains fewer errors, since it has been widely tried and tested.
* The producers' after-sales service is often good, for example, online help facilities, and users can also get support from user groups and magazines.
* It is usually cheaper than purchasing the packages individually.

Some disadvantages of integrated software include the following:

* Not all the features of single applications are included.
* Some integrated packages do not contain all the applications that may be required to complete a task.

Specialised software

Specialised software is software that is written for a specific task rather than for a broad application area. These programs provide facilities specifically for the purpose for which they were designed. For example, a payroll program will usually only be able to deal with all aspects of a company's payroll, that is, for one very specific purpose.

Other examples of specialised software are expert systems (software that operates like an expert in a particular field, for example, medical expert systems such as DIABOT), accounting programs such as Sage 300 and QuickBooks, and theatre or airline booking systems.

Customised software

Software can be customised to better meet the needs of an individual or organisation. For example, macros or plug-ins can be added to general purpose software to make the software more useful and increase its range of functions.

Macros are short programs written to automate several steps in software, such as databases, spreadsheets and word processors. Plug-ins are blocks of code that add features to the overall package. The core code of the program allows for these macros or plug-ins to be added. Macros and plug-ins can be written by experienced end-users of the program or by programmers.

Another method of customising software is to integrate several pieces of proprietary (copyrighted) and/or open-source software to fit the requirements of the user or organisation. For example, many universities and learning institutions use the CANVAS learning management system to provide digital tools and learning resources for teachers to use in one location. To better suit the needs of the university, an experienced user or in-house programmer can use an application programme interface (API) to integrate software such as Office 365, Google Drive™, student information system (SIS) and other features into the base program.

Custom-written (tailor-made) software

Custom-written software is created to meet the specific needs of a company. Every company is unique and may have unique needs. For this reason, a solution tailored to achieve a company's goals, based on their specialised requirements, offers many advantages when compared with general purpose pre-packaged applications.

Custom-written software may be written by programmers within the company, or it may be contracted out to a **software house** (a company that specialises in writing software). This may be necessary because there are no commercial applications or 'off the shelf' packages available.

The main advantage of custom-written software is that the solutions it offers give the greatest possible depth, breadth and flexibility for meeting the needs of the organisation, as is tailored to the organisation's specifications. Also, the software developer delivers and installs the software and trains the end-users in the use of the new product.

System software

System software is software that manages and supports the resources and operations of a computer system. It enables the running of application software and the management of the system resources. Four major categories of system resources include the:

* operating system
* utility programs
* device drivers
* language translators.

System software acts as a buffer between the hardware and application software. Figure 6.3 shows a conceptual arrangement of hardware, system software, application software and the user.

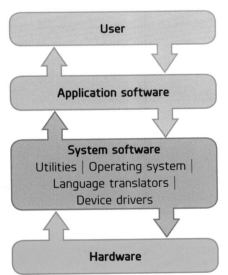

Figure 6.3 Conceptual arrangement of hardware, system software, application software and the user

Operating system

An operating system (OS) is a set of programs that governs the operation of a computer. The OS manages all software and peripheral hardware, and accesses the central processing unit (CPU) for memory or storage purposes. It also makes it possible for a system to run applications at the same time. A computer cannot function without operating system software. All PCs, laptops, tablets, smartphones and servers require an OS.

In some hand-held computers such as **smartphones** and tablets, the operating system is embedded in a ROM chip that can be rewritten when the system is updated. However, for most PCs and larger computers, the operating system is switched on as soon as you turn on, or 'boot', the computer. The term 'booting' refers to the process of loading operating system software into a computer's main memory from disk. The instructions to load the operation system are held in the BIOS, which is also known as the Basic Input Output System. The BIOS is a firmware or set of instructions that resides in a ROM chip on the motherboard. It contains the bootstrap, which is the program that takes the computer through steps that lead up to the loading of the operating system (OS). The operating system remains in main memory until you turn the computer off.

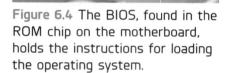

Figure 6.4 The BIOS, found in the ROM chip on the motherboard, holds the instructions for loading the operating system.

Types of operating system

The most common operating systems are Microsoft's Windows, Apple® OS X®, Linux distributions such as Ubuntu or Red Hat, and mobile operating systems for smartphones such as Android and iOS. Some older operating systems that were used in PC computers include: MSDOS, Windows 3.X, Windows 95, Windows 98, Windows ME (Millennium Edition), Windows 2000, Windows XP, Windows Vista and Windows NT. Windows 7 was the successor to Windows Vista and included enhancements such as multi-touch support, Internet Explorer 8, improved performance and start-up time and improved security.

Windows 10, which was released in 2015, is Microsoft's newest operating system for Windows. This system features fast start up and resume, built-in security, and the return of the Start Menu in an expanded form. This version of Windows also features Microsoft Edge, Microsoft's new browser. Devices such as tablets, PCs, smartphones and Xbox consoles can also use Windows 10.

Some operating systems that are still in use today include: Windows 7, Windows 10, Apple® operating systems, (for example OS9 and OS X®), OS/2, Linux and Unix. There are Unix operating systems for PCs, mini-computers and mainframe computers.

Figure 6.5 The operating system makes it possible for different applications to run at the same time.

Functions of the operating system

The functions of an operating system depend on the size and complexity of the computer system. It may also depend on whether the system is a single user system such as a PC or a multi-access system such as a mainframe or network.

* A **multi-access system** is one that allows a number of users with online terminals or PCs to interact with the same computer at the same time.
* An **online system** is one where the terminals or PCs and the computer are linked interactively.

Although the operating systems of mainframes and networks are much more complex and perform a wider range of functions than those of PCs, the functions of most operating systems can be grouped into the following categories:

* Manage computer resources
* Manage files and memory
* Maintain security
* Manage tasks and processes
* Provide a user interface.

Manage computer resources

Managing all the resources of the computer system is a large part of the operating system's function. The operating system allows application software or user programs such as word-processing, spreadsheet and database packages to communicate with the computer's hardware. For example, if you are working in a document in Microsoft Excel and you want to print the document, you simply access the print command. Excel directs the operating system to select a printer (if there is more than one) to print the document. The operating system then notifies the computer to begin sending data and instructions to the appropriate program to print the document. Figure 6.6 shows how the operating system acts as an interface between application programs and the hardware.

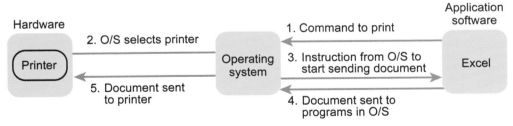

Figure 6.6 The operating system is at the centre of operations, interfacing between the software and hardware.

Manage files and memory

The operating system manages all the files on a computer. It keeps track of the program and data locations stored in the computer's memory. For example, when you open a file saved to your hard drive, you are first instructing the computer to find that file, and then open it. The operating system also allows you to find files stored in other secondary storage devices. Other file management functions include copying, erasing, renaming and backing up files. For mainframe computers, the operating system has to share storage between many programs that may be running at the same time.

Maintain security

Modern personal computers, networks and larger computers require each user to input a user name or ID and password to access the computer system. The operating system keeps a register of all names, so that only people with valid user names or IDs and passwords can access the system. This prevents access by hackers and unauthorised persons. The operating system also keeps a **log** of which users logged in, how long each user stayed on the system, and what they did. Administrators can check the log for security breaches and abuse of resources.

Manage tasks and processes

The task management function of the operating system involves allocating adequate resources and time of the CPU to each process. Based on the type of operating system, process management can be accomplished using one of the following modes of processing:

* Multitasking
* Multiprogramming
* Multiprocessing.

Multitasking

Multitasking is the ability of the computer to appear to run more than one program at the same time, although at any specific instant, the CPU deals with only one instruction for one active program. The operating system manages which instruction to send to the CPU.

Multiprogramming

Multiprogramming refers to the computer's ability to run two or more programs at the same time using a single processor.

Multipocessing

Multiprocessing refers to a computer system's ability to support more than one process (program) at the same time using multiple processors. This generally increases processing times.

Provide a user interface

Many operating system functions never appear on the computer's display screen. What you do see, though, is the user interface. The user interface is the user-controllable part of the operating system, which allows you to communicate, or interact, with it. We will examine user interfaces in more detail later in this chapter.

Note!

Here is an example to illustrate 'multitasking'. Many students like to listen to music on their computer while typing a document or playing a computer game at the same time. These tasks appear to be happening at the same time. As computers are so fast, the operating system can switch the program executed in the CPU so quickly that the user cannot tell that, in reality, the music-playing and typing functions are performed at individual moments in time. The CPU actually processes one instruction at a time, but can execute instructions from any active process.

Utility programs

Utility programs are system software programs that provide useful services, such as performing common tasks and 'housekeeping' routines. Examples of these tasks and routines include backup, disk repair and virus protection.

Device drivers

A device driver is a software application that enables a computer to interact with hardware devices that are attached to it.

Language translators

Language translators (assemblers, compilers and interpreters) are programs that translate programs written in a particular programming language into another programming language.

User interfaces

There are four types of user interfaces for both operating system and application software:

* Command-driven
* Menu-driven
* Graphical
* Touch.

Command-driven interface

The command-driven interface was an earlier interface used in computing, where you have to type in the command at the prompt on the display screen. For many years, PCs only used the MS-DOS operating system or Linux and Unix with a command line interface. Modern PCs using Windows, macOS® or Linux also have a command line or terminal interface to allow you to type commands in.

This interface has been kept in operating systems, because particularly for an experienced user, it can be a fast and efficient way to do certain functions. Beginners will find this complicated to use as you have to learn the commands and the options that go with them. An example in the Windows command prompt would be at the C:\> prompt, where C:\ generally refers to the hard disk, you can type the following command:

C:\>delete *.*

This command tells the operating system to erase all the files on the hard disk. Figure 6.7 shows an example of a command user interface.

Figure 6.7 A computer screen in MS-DOS mode

Menu-driven interface

A menu-driven interface is very different to a command-driven interface. It lists menu choices that a user can select to move from one place to another within a website or software program. A menu-driven interface does not require a user to memorise commands, which makes navigation easier for the user. Therefore, users need little training when using menu-driven interfaces. A disadvantage of a menu-driven interface is that it can be difficult for a user to find a command if they do not know where the command is located in the menu. This is particularly true for more complex systems that include multiple menus.

In addition, menu-driven interfaces are less flexible and users can only execute actions that are listed. Cashpoint machines (ATMs) contain a menu-driven interface. Some other applications that use a menu-driven interface are game consoles, websites, apps, word processors and other office software. Figure 6.8 shows the Windows 10 Disk Management menu-driven interface.

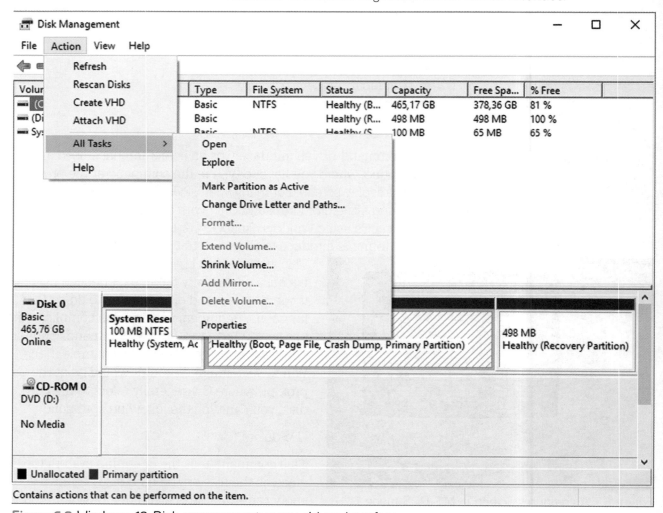

Figure 6.8 Windows 10 Disk management menu-driven interface

Graphical user interface

The graphical user interface (GUI), (pronounced as 'goo-ee'), also called WIMP (windows, icons, menus and pointing devices), is the easiest interface to use when interacting with a computer. This user interface allows you to use graphics (images), menus and keystrokes to choose commands, start programs, see lists of files and other options. Some of these images take the form of icons. **Icons** are small pictorial figures that represent programs, folders, files, tasks, procedures, and so on.

Another feature of the GUI is the use of windows. A **window** is a rectangular boxed area on a computer screen. (This is different to Windows, for example, Windows 7 or Windows 10 with a capital 'W', which is the Microsoft operating system.) The screen can show different windows at the same time, within which individual application programs may be running. Each window may show a different program, such as a word-processing document in one window and a spreadsheet in another window, or two windows may show two different documents being run by the same program. A window can also show other things, such as a directory of files on your hard drive. The windows appear over a common visual background known as the **desktop**. Figure 6.9 shows a Windows 10 graphical user interface desktop, without any windows open.

We will look at the Windows desktop as an example of a GUI later in this book.

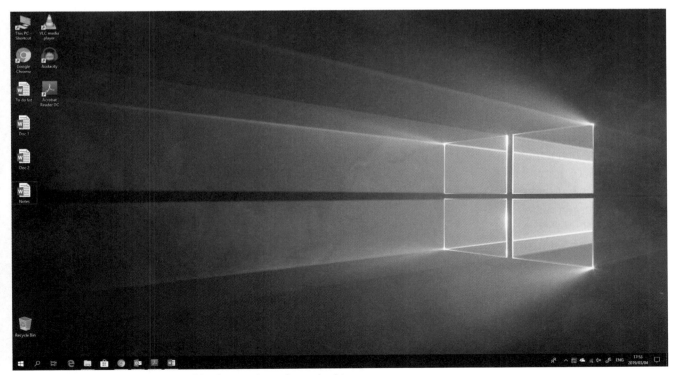

Figure 6.9 A Windows 10 graphical user interface desktop

Touch user interface

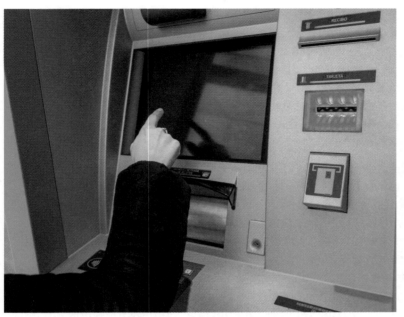

Figure 6.10 Automatic teller machine touch user interface

Touchscreen devices are found almost everywhere, from smartphones, retail stores and restaurants to cars, residential homes and commercial workplaces. They allow users to control a device or machine through a touch-based user interface. A touch user interface (TUI) is a computer-pointing technology based on touch. It is a graphical user interface using a touchpad or touchscreen display as a combined input and output device (see Figure 6.10). A TUI reduces the amount of time it takes for the user to access where they want to go in the digital world. Often it takes the form of a simplified version of a GUI, perhaps with larger finger-sized buttons.

Actions may also be simplified to reduce the amount of text you need to enter, so for example a user can touch a printed advertisement and connect directly to the online experience provided by the advertiser. This can include initiating a voice-over internet protocol (VoIP), instant messaging (IM), or electronic mail (email) by simply touching the page. Further, electronic commerce (**e-commerce**) transactions can be initiated and completed with the TUI.

The advantage of a TUI is that it doesn't need a keyboard, because you simply touch the screen. This means it is ideal for smaller devices such as smartphones and tablets. It also means that for applications such as a point of sale terminal, you reduce the number of steps that a user has to choose from (because you only give them buttons to do what you want them to), which makes it simpler to use. In addition, for a user with visual impairments, these simplified interfaces can be adapted to work with tactile or Braille input.

Specific system requirements for software compatibility

System requirements for software compatibility refers to all the computer hardware and other software needed on a computer for a particular software to run efficiently. These requirements may include the operating system, processing power, memory, secondary storage, display adapters and browsers. The system requirements for running Microsoft Office 2016 are shown in the box to the left.

Example
The system requirements for running Microsoft Office 2016 are as follows:

* **Processor:** 1 gigahertz (GHz) or faster x86-bit or x64-bit processor with SSE2 instruction set
* **Memory:** 2 GB RAM
* **Hard disk:** 3.0 GB of available disk space
* **Display PC:** Screen resolution of a minimum 1 280 × 800; graphics – graphics hardware acceleration requires a DirectX 10 graphics card.
* **Operating system:** Windows 10, Windows 8.1, Windows 8 or Windows 7 Service Pack 1
* **Browser:** Microsoft Edge, Safari, Google™ Chrome or Firefox.

Summary 6

1. Software is the general name given to all the programs (set of instructions) that computers use to perform different tasks and can be classified into application software and system software.

2. Application software programs carry out specific tasks or solve particular problems and can be categorised as general purpose software, integrated software, customised software and custom-written (tailor-made) software packages.

3. General-purpose software is software that is not written for any specific business or organisation but can be used or adapted to suit their specific needs.

4. An integrated software package is a set of related, specialised programs combined in a unified package that allows data to be transferred easily between the programs.

5. Specialised software is software that is written for a specific task rather than for a broad application area.

6. Customised software is general purpose software that has been modified to better meet the needs of an individual or organisation.

7. Custom-written (tailor-made) software is software written to meet the specific needs of a company.

8. System software manages and supports the resources and operations of a computer system, including the operating system and utility programs.

9. An operating system is a set of programs that governs the operation of a computer. It manages computer resources, files, memory and other tasks, and maintains security.

10. The user interface is the user-controllable part of the operating system that allows you to communicate or interact with it. The four types are command-driven, menu-driven, graphical and touch.

11. The command-driven interface requires you to enter a command by typing in codes or words. An example is MSDOS.

12. Menu-driven interfaces allow you to use either a mouse or cursor-movement (arrow keys) to make a selection from a menu. An example is the 'pull down' menus in Microsoft Word.

13. The graphical user interface, also called WIMP (windows, icons, menus and pointing devices), allows the use of graphics (icons), menus and simple key strokes to choose commands, start programs, see lists of files, and other options. The most popular example today is Windows.

14. The touch user interface lets users choose commands, start programs, see lists of files and other options by touching icons on a screen.

Questions 6

Copy and fill in the blanks questions

1. The general name given to all the programs that computers use to perform different tasks is _____.

2. _____ are programs developed to carry out specific tasks or solve particular problems.

3. An _____ software package is a set of related programs combined in a unified package that allows data to be transferred easily between the programs.

4. Software written for a specific task instead of a broad application area is called _____.

5. General purpose software that is modified to meet the needs of an individual or organisation is called _____ software.

6. _____ are short programs written to automate several steps in software such as databases, spreadsheets and word processors.

7. A/An _____ is a set of programs that governs the operation of a computer.

8 The term '_____' refers to the process of loading operating system software into a computer's main memory from disk.

9 A system that lets several users with online terminals interact with the same computer at the same time is called a _____ system.

True or false questions

1 An electronic encyclopaedia is an example of integrated software.

2 A payroll program that deals with all aspects of a company's payroll is an example of specialised software.

3 Custom-written software is written to meet the specific needs of a company.

4 System software enables the running of application software and the management of the system resources.

5 Firmware consists of RAM chips.

6 The operating system remains in main memory until you turn the computer off.

7 The operating system maintains security of a computer system.

8 A command-driven interface allows you to use either a mouse or cursor-movement (arrow keys) to make a selection from a menu.

Multiple-choice questions

1 Which is an example of application software?

   a Language translator

   b Operating system

   c Spreadsheet software

   d Utility program

2 Which is an example of system software?

   a Word-processing software

   b Device drivers

   c Entertainment software

   d Simulation software

3 Premier Programming is a software development company that writes programs that perform specific tasks. Which of the following software is most likely to be written by this company?

   a General-purpose software

   b Integrated software

   c Customised software

   d Custom-written software

4 Johnny wrote some macros to automate certain tasks in the accounting package to better meet the needs of his company. The software package can be referred to as:

   a general-purpose software.

   b integrated software.

   c customised software.

   d custom-written software.

Short-answer questions

1 Use examples to explain the difference between application software and system software.

2 State the name of an operating system that can be used with each of the devices in the table.

Device	Operating system
a Desktop PC	i
b Smartphone	ii
c Laptop	iii

3 a Define the term 'operating system'.

   b Give two functions of the operating system.

4 Name one example of operating system software used by personal computers.

5 A command user interface requires you to enter a command by typing in codes or words.

   a Name two other types of user interface.

   b Explain how each of the named user interfaces in (a) functions.

6 The ABC Bauxite company has bought a software package containing several applications to be used for different tasks within the company.

   a State the name of the type of package bought by the company.

   b Name an example of this type of package.

   c Give two advantages and one disadvantage of using this type of software.

7 The following is a list of software used in computers:

   i Microsoft Office

   ii Windows 10

   iii Utilities software

   Use the list above to identify each of the following:

   a An example of system software

   b An operating system.

   c General purpose software

   d An example of Integrated software

8 a Explain the difference between custom-written software and customised software.

   b Explain why it may be necessary for a company to customise certain types of software.

   c Give an example of a software that can be customised.

9 State the name of the type of software that can perform each of the tasks listed below:

   a Back-up data files and software

   b Translate programs written in a particular programming language into another programming language

   c Contains a number of applications that is packaged as a single software package

   d Control work-related machinery in a factory

   e Book flights (used by airline companies)

10 The operating system performs many functions in a computer. Use examples to explain how the operating system carries out the following functions:

   a Manages computer resources

   b Manages files and memory

   c Maintains security

11 Explain the difference between multitasking and multiprocessing.

Research questions

1 Copy the table below into your notebook. Then do research on the internet and complete the table by adding the names of two types of operating systems for each category.

Category	Example of operating system by category
Desktop	
Server	
Mobile	

2 Copy the table below into your notebook. Then do research on the internet and complete the table by filling in the most suitable current operating system.

Device	Operating system
Apple® iMac® desktop computer	
iPhone® Smartphone	
A named mainframe computer	
A named supercomputer	

3 Do research on the internet and then answer these questions in your notebook.

   a Name the operating system running on your cell phone or computer.

   b What are some reasons you may need to know the version of operating system that your computer is running?

   c What might happen if you attempt to install a program or app that is not designed for your operating system?

Crossword

Down

1 Refers to a computer system's ability to support more than one process (program) at the same time using multiple processors

2 Software that is written for a specific task rather than for a broad application area

6 Allows the transfer and sharing of information between applications

Across

3 Software that manages and supports the resources and operations of a computer system

4 Blocks of code that add features to the overall package

5 Small pictorial figures that represent programs, folders, files, tasks, procedures, and so on

7 Short programs written to automate several steps in software such as databases, spreadsheets and word processors.

STEM project

You are the substitute teacher for a group of Grade 9 (Form 3) information Technology students. They have started the topic 'Software', but some students are finding it difficult to understand how to differentiate between the two main types of software, and to explain the types of application software. You decide to create a computer walk-through presentation for your class. Your presentation will explain the two main types of software and help the students to differentiate between the types of application software. In the previous class, a student mentioned having viruses on her computer. Explain which functions of the operating system help to prevent computer viruses.

1 Write a clear and comprehensive name for your presentation.

2 Write brief notes on each step you plan to take in order to prepare your presentation. You should have at least three steps.

3 Write down the steps in your presentation. Do a practice run-through of your presentation for a group of classmates and obtain their feedback

4 From the feedback you received, describe how you can make your presentation more useful.

Hints

1 Revise the chapter and list the types of systems you must have in your presentation.
2 Think of strategies, such as acronyms or rhymes, to help you remember what the presentation has explained.

Data communications, networks and the internet (2)

Objectives

At the end of the chapter, you will be able to:

❏ define data communications

❏ explain the terms 'bandwidth', 'narrowband', 'voice-band' and 'broadband'

❏ define the terms 'simplex', 'duplex' and 'half-duplex'

❏ state the advantages and disadvantages of a cabled LAN and wireless LAN

❏ describe the three types of transmission cables (twisted pair, coaxial cable and fibre optic) used in a cabled LAN

❏ explain the functions of the NIC, access point, switch and router

❏ explain the terms 'wireless communication', 'bluetooth' and 'WiFi'

❏ explain the terms 'mail server', 'mail client', 'TCP/IP', 'network domain', 'latency', 'transfer rate' and 'file transfer protocol'

❏ explain the function of protocols for sending and receiving emails (POP3, IMAP4 and SMTP)

❏ use a search engine to search the internet using advanced syntax.

Data communications

Rapid developments in communications systems, computer use and multimedia technologies are changing the way people communicate and transmit data.

Data communication means the transmission of data from one location to another for direct use or for further processing.

Analogue and digital signaling methods

Information on a data network can be transmitted using one of two signaling methods: analogue or digital. The essential difference between analogue and digital signals is the way in which voltage creates the signal.

Voltage in analogue signals varies continuously and appears as a wavy line when graphed over time. Your speech, a siren and live music are all examples of analogue waves.

Digital signals are composed of pulses of precise, positive voltages and zero voltages. A pulse of positive voltage represents a 1. A pulse of zero voltage (in other words, the lack of any voltage) represents a 0. The use of 1s and 0s to represent information is characteristic of a binary system. Every pulse in the digital signal is called a binary digit, or bit. A bit can have only one of two possible values: 1 or 0. Eight bits together form a byte. In broad terms, one byte carries one piece of information.

Latency

Every network is subjected to a delay between the transmission of a signal and its eventual receipt. Although electrons travel rapidly, they still have to travel, and a brief delay takes place between the moment you send the message and the moment the message is received. This delay is called latency. Latency may be caused by factors such as the:

✱ length and type of the cable involved
✱ existence of any intervening connectivity device, such as a router.

Bandwidths

A data communication system is made up of hardware, software and communications facilities. Communications systems may be set up to serve a small area, or they may be set up on a global scale. Data in any communications system is moved from one location to another through data communication channels or links. These channels are classified according to **bandwidth**.

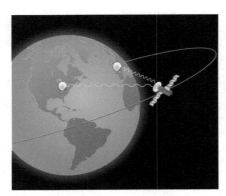

Figure 7.1 A communications satellite accepts signals beamed to it from one point and then reflects the signals to another point.

Did you know?

Did you know that there are currently over 4 600 satellites orbiting the Earth, of which the majority are used for communication and Earth observation?

Note!

The speed at which data is transferred from one device to another is called the transfer rate. The transfer rate or transmission rate is measured in bits per second.

Bandwidth determines the volume (amount) of data that can be transmitted in a given time. Wider bandwidths can transmit more data.

Bandwidths can be grouped into three classes of channels:

* **A narrow-band channel**, which is outdated and almost never used anymore, for example a telegraph system transmits data at slow speeds of between 10 and 30 bits per second (bps).
* **A voice-band channel** transmits data at the rate of up to 64 Kbps. A telephone line is voice-band, and is one of the most widely-used methods of transferring data.
* **A broadband channel** can transmit large volumes of data at speeds of over 45.48 Mbps (the global average). In some countries, the speeds are much higher while in others, they are much lower. For example, in Trinidad, the average fixed broadband download speed is 50 Mbps, while in Jamaica it is about 40 Mbps.

Communication satellites, coaxial cables, fibre optic cables and microwave links are commonly used to provide these channels. Microwave signals are very high frequency radio signals that can be transmitted through space. A communications satellite accepts signals beamed to it from a point on the Earth and then reflects those signals to another point, as shown in Figure 7.1. Communication satellites can transmit data that includes text, voice, pictures and video.

The lines that transmit data can also be classified according to the direction in which data flows through them.

* **A simplex line** permits data to flow in only one direction. You can send data or receive data, but not both.
* **A half-duplex line** can alternately send and receive data. This means that at any particular time you can either send data but not receive it, or receive data but not send it.
* **A full-duplex line** can simultaneously send and receive data.

Networks

In *Interact with IT* Book 1, you learned that a **network** is a group of two or more computers linked together so that they can share resources (hardware, software and data) and communicate with one another. You also learned that each network falls into one of these groups:

* Local area networks (LANs)
* Wide area networks (WANs)
* Personal area networks (PAN)
* Metropolitan area networks (MAN)
* The internet
* Mobile networks.

In this chapter, you will explore different aspects of networks.

Local area networks (LANs)

Figure 7.2 A LAN set up in an office allows users to share files.

A **LAN** consists of a collection of microcomputers, such as in an office building, department or school that can share peripherals, files and programs, as well as communicate with each other on the network. Each microcomputer that forms part of the network is connected to it either by cables or by a wireless link.

Cabled LAN

In a cabled LAN, all the computers and other peripheral devices on the network are attached to transmission cables. These cables fall into three types:

* **Twisted pair cable:** This type of cable is a convenient and cheap method of connecting computers and peripherals in a network. Twisted pair cable is usually used for home networking or on small sites where the distances between devices are small and there is no great need for speed.
* **Coaxial cable:** This type of cable is more expensive than twisted pair cable because it can transmit more data. Coaxial cable is used to transmit voice, video and data. It is used in medium-sized networks.
* **Fibre optic cable:** This type of cable is quite expensive. Fibre optic cable can transmit large volumes of digital data very quickly and with almost no errors. A single strand of a fibre optic cable is a hair-thin piece of glass tubing. The inside of the tube acts as a mirror, allowing pulses of light to travel along it. These pulses of light carry the data. A cable consists of thousands of these hair-thin strands.

Wireless communication

Wireless communication offers organisations and users the following benefits:

* Portability
* Flexibility
* Increased productivity
* Lower installation costs.

Wireless technologies, very simply, allow one or more devices to communicate with each other without physical connections, in other words, without cabling. Instead, they transmit data using radio frequency transmissions.

Twisted pair cable

Coaxial cable

Fibre optic cable

Figure 7.3 The three types of transmission cables

Figure 7.4 A TV remote control is a simple wireless device.

Wireless communications range from complex systems, such as wireless local area networks (WLANs) and cell phones, to simple devices such as wireless headphones, microphones and other devices that do not process or store information. These devices include infrared (IR) devices such as remote controls, some cordless computer keyboards and mice, and wireless hi-fi stereo headsets, all of which require a direct line of sight between the transmitter and the receiver to close the link.

Other types of wireless transmission media include broadcast radio, cellular radio, microwaves and communications satellites.

Infrared (IR)

Infrared (IR) is a wireless transmission medium that sends signals using infrared light waves. These signals are usually used for short-range communications and they do not pass through solid objects. Mobile computers and devices, such as mice, printers, cordless computer keyboards and smartphones, often have an Infrared Data Association (IrDA) port that enables the transfer of data from one device to another using infrared light waves.

Broadcast radio

Broadcast radio distributes radio signals through the air over long distances, such as between cities, regions and countries, as well as over short distances, such as within an office or home. WiFi and Bluetooth communications technologies use broadcast radio signals.

WiFi

WiFi is the most popular means of communicating data wirelessly, within a fixed location. Most modern devices support WiFi so that they can access a network to gain internet access and share network resources. The main requirement for WiFi is a device that can transmit the wireless signal, such as a router, **smartphone** or computer.

In a typical home, a router transmits an internet connection coming from outside the network, such as an internet service provider (ISP), and delivers that service to nearby devices that can reach the wireless signal.

Another way to use WiFi is a WiFi hotspot, whereby computers and mobile devices such as smartphones and tablets can share its wireless or wired internet connection to transfer files or carry voice messages.

Figure 7.5 Many coffee shops and shopping malls have WiFi hotspots to give their customers free access to the internet.

Bluetooth

Bluetooth is another type of technology that can be used to set up a wireless LAN (WLAN). Bluetooth is a standard developed by a group of electronics manufacturers that allows any sort of electronic equipment (computers, digital video cameras, cell phones, tablets, keyboards, cars, and so on) to automatically make their own connections without wires, cables or any direct action from a user.

The manufacturers program a Bluetooth radio transmitter into each unit with an address that falls into a range of standard addresses established for a particular type of device. When a device is turned on, it sends radio signals asking for a response from any unit with an address within a particular range. For example, if a computer and a printer are turned on and their addresses are within the established range, they will respond to each other and a tiny network (piconet) is formed. Once the networks are established, the systems begin communicating among themselves. Bluetooth networks are formed, broken up and reformed all the time, simply by switching on Bluetooth-enabled devices when they are in close proximity to each other.

Cellular radio

Cellular radio is a form of broadcast radio that is used widely for mobile communications – specifically wireless modems and cell phones.

Microwave transmission

Microwaves are radio waves that provide a high-speed signal transmission. The frequency of these radio waves varies from 300 MHz to 300 GHz. These signals are widely used for long-distance communications and are relatively less expensive. Microwave transmission involves sending signals from one microwave station to another. Microwave transmission is used in environments where installing physical transmission media is difficult or impossible, and where line-of-sight transmission is available. Current users of microwave transmission include universities, hospitals, cable television providers and telephone companies.

Communications satellites

A communications satellite is a type of spacecraft that receives microwave signals from an Earth-based station. The satellite receives and amplifies (makes bigger) the signals, and sends them back to the receiver antenna, which is located on the Earth's surface. Transmission from an Earth-based station to a satellite is called an uplink. Transmission from a satellite to an Earth-based station is known as a downlink. Communication satellites are used for air navigation, television and radio broadcasts, weather forecasting, video conferencing, paging, global positioning systems and internet connections.

Figure 7.6 A bluetooth headset connects wirelessly to a cell phone, so that the user can make or receive calls without having to hold the phone.

Note!

Table 7.1 shows the data transmission rates for wired and wireless communication media.

Table 7.1 Wired and wireless data transmission rates

Wired data transmission rates
Twisted pair cable – 10 Mbps to 1 Gbps
Coaxial cable – More than 10 Mbps
Fibre optic cable – More than 100 Gbps
Wireless data transmission rates
WiFi – More than 11 Gbps
Bluetooth – 128 Mbps
Communications satellite – 12 Mbps to 100 Mbps
Microwave – More than 274 Mbps

Wireless LAN (WLAN)

A WLAN can be used where it may be difficult or impractical to use a cabled LAN, for example in homes, large offices, warehouses and lecture halls. In a building with many rooms or large halls, a few **access points** (a networking hardware device that allows a WiFi device to connect to a wired network) may be needed. A user may take a laptop and walk from one room or from one end of a building to the next without losing network connectivity. This connection is possible because the laptop locks on to the strongest signal from an access point and will transfer its link to another access point if the signal there is stronger. WLANs have advantages and disadvantages.

Advantages

A WLAN has the following advantages:

* It has the same features that are available in a wired LAN.
* It provides more flexibility for obtaining information.
* It is more efficient because there is less wiring.
* It saves money because there is less wiring.

Disadvantages

A WLAN has the following disadvantages:

* It transmits data more slowly than a wired LAN.
* Interference from other users or devices using the same 2.4 GHz band can cause data corruption.
* There is a risk that someone can access your information illegally.

Devices needed to set up a WLAN

A WLAN can be set up in different ways. One of the most common methods uses two main sets of components: NICs (network interface cards) with radio transmitters and receivers and access points.

Before a PC can become part of a network, it must be fitted with a **network interface card (NIC)**. A network interface card is a device that enables wireless or wired capabilities on a device that did not previously support it. This card fits into an expansion slot in the motherboard and enables the computers on the network to send and receive messages.

In the case of a wired network, the card has an external outlet into which one end of the network cable is plugged. The other end of the cable plugs into a connection based on the configuration of the network. Most modern devices have a NIC already installed on the device's motherboard. This includes not only wired-capable devices such as desktops and laptops, but also tablets, cell phones, and other wireless devices. In cases where a wired-only desktop computer does not have a wireless NIC, a wireless network adapter can be used to interface with WiFi.

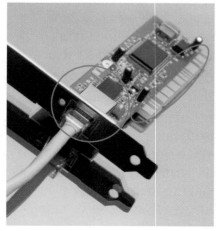

Figure 7.7 The two circled components together form the NIC.

An access point is a device attached to a LAN network, which contains a radio transmitter and receiver, an encryption facility and communications software. It translates computer signals into wireless signals, which it broadcasts to wireless NICs on the network. NICs equipped for wireless communications receive these signals, and can transmit back. They have a fixed or detachable radio antenna in place of the usual coaxial cable.

The access point and the NIC communicate with each other using a 2.4 gigahertz (GHz) radio band. The access point performs its role in reverse when transferring signals from a wireless NIC to the conventional network: it translates wireless signals received from NICs into wired signals.

The devices that form part of the network are connected to switches or hubs. A **switch** is a device that connects multiple devices on the same network to facilitate communication among the devices. A switch increases the overall performance of the devices on the network by sending data only to where it needs to go, thereby reducing the amount of data on the network. A switch also improves security, because data is not broadcast to every connected device, but only to the device for which it is destined. This prevents data from being monitored by other connected devices.

Figure 7.8 A network switch

Another device that forms part of a network is a **router**. This device acts as an interface between two networks. It helps facilitate communications between your home's network and the internet service provider's (ISP's) network. It takes information provided by the modem and routes it to the various devices that are connected.

Devices (such as computers, TVs, game consoles, digital picture frames, and so on) can be connected to a router in one of two ways – wired directly to the router or wirelessly. A router can also select the best route for packets to take in large interconnected networks. Routers also provide advanced functionality such as a built in firewall to help protect the network from unwanted attacks from hackers and some malware.

Figure 7.9 A router

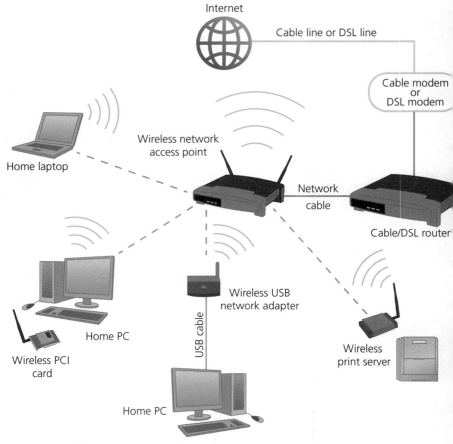

Figure 7.10 The components of a WLAN

The internet

In *Interact with IT* Book 1, we looked at the advantages and disadvantages of the internet, the services and applications available and different types of websites. We also discussed the function of a browser. In this section of the chapter, we will look at other types of software that are needed to send and receive information on the internet.

TCP/IP (Transmission Control Protocol/Internet Protocol)

All forms of communication, either electronic or other means, are based on some form of protocol. A **protocol** is a set of rules that defines how computers interact or communicate with each other. Computers connected to the internet use a computer network protocol called **TCP/IP**. This is a set of protocols used to transfer data from one computer to another over the internet. TCP/IP is a non-proprietary protocol suite (it is not designed for any specific type of computer) that enables hardware and operating systems software from different computers to communicate. For example, a PC computer can communicate with an Apple® Macintosh® or other type of computer.

Beside the Internet Protocol (IP) itself, other protocols such as TCP, HTTP and FTP all integrate with IP to provide additional capabilities.

TCP/IP is actually two protocols: the TCP portion divides the data that is to be transmitted into smaller pieces called **packets**.

This allows data to travel more easily, and therefore quickly, along communication lines. Each packet is numbered so that the data can be reassembled when it arrives at the destination computer. The IP protocol sends each packet by specifying the address of both the sending and the receiving computers.

Figure 7.11 TCP/IP allows computers with different operating systems to communicate.

Network domains

A network domain is a group of computers and devices on a network that are administered as a unit with common rules and procedures, and which share different types of data via network resources. A network domain is used to manage all user functions, including username and password, and shared system resource authentication and access. It is also used to assign specific resource privileges, such as user accounts. Within the network domain, all devices sharing a common part of the IP address are said to be in the same domain.

Domain names are used in URLs to identify particular web pages. For example, in the URL 'https://www.pcmag.com', the domain name is 'pcmag.com'. As the internet is based on IP addresses, and not on domain names, every web server requires a domain name system (DNS) server to translate domain names into IP addresses.

Email hardware and software requirements

The following process needs to take place for an email message to be sent and received:

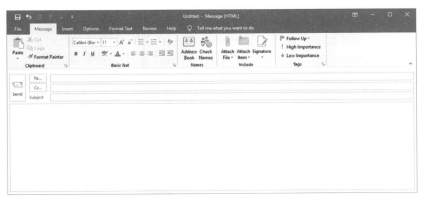

Figure 7.12 Microsoft Outlook Express email screen

* **Mail server:** This is a computer on the internet that operates like the traditional post office. The mail server receives incoming messages and delivers outgoing messages. It allocates a certain amount of storage to hold mail for registered users. The area of storage allocated to you is your mailbox. You retrieve your mail by supplying your username and password. This protects your email from unauthorised access.

* **Mail client:** This is a program that enables you to read and compose email messages, send email and access email from the server. If you are using Microsoft Office software, you may use the popular Outlook Express program as your mail client.

Figure 7.12 shows the Microsoft Outlook Express email screen for creating a new message; other email software uses a similar format.

Protocols for sending and receiving emails (POP3, IMAP4 and SMTP)

Different protocols are used to send and receive emails:

* Post Office Protocol 3 (POP3)
* Internet Message Access Protocol 4 (IMAP4)
* Simple Mail Transfer Protocol (SMTP).

Post Office Protocol 3 (POP3)

Post Office Protocol 3 (POP3) is used to receive mails sent from a remote server to a local email client. A POP3 mail server receives an email message and holds it for the user. The user can then download an email message on a local computer and even read it offline. When messages are downloaded to a local computer, they are removed from the email server. POP3 does not allow a mail client to send mail.

Internet Message Access Protocol 4 (IMAP4)

Internet Message Access Protocol 4 (IMAP4) works in the same way as POP3. An IMAP4 mail server receives an email message and then downloads it to an email client. Users can read their email messages locally in their email client, but they can't send an email message using IMAP4. When users access email messages via IMAP4, they have the option to view just the message header, including its title and the sender's name, before downloading the body of the message. Users can create, change or delete folders on the mail server, as well as search for and delete messages. Microsoft's Outlook Express email client applications support both POP3 and IMAP4.

Simple Mail Transfer Protocol (SMTP)

Simple Mail Transfer Protocol (SMTP) handles the sending of email from one SMTP server to another. When equipped for two-way communication, mail clients are configured with the address of a POP3 server to receive email and the address of an SMTP server to send email. SMTP can receive email messages, but its capabilities are limited. The most common implementations of SMTP are in conjunction with either POP3 or IMAP4. For example, users download an email message from a POP3 server, and then transmit a message via an SMTP server.

File Transfer Protocol (FTP)

File Transfer Protocol (FTP) is a set of rules for communicating over the internet. It enables you, through an FTP program, to upload and download files. The electronic files are stored on what are called FTP sites, which may be maintained by universities, government agencies and large organisations. Some of the sites are private, and you may have to pay to retrieve or store information on those sites.

Files in an FTP site are stored in directories. Each file has a name and an extension. The name labels the file contents and the extension indicates the file type, for example, text, sound, program, image or video.

Secure Hypertext Transfer Protocol (S-HTTP)

The Secure Hypertext Transfer Protocol (S-HTTP) is an extension to the Hypertext Transfer Protocol (HTTP). It was developed to protect commercial transactions by allowing the secure exchange of files on the World Wide Web. In this system, both the server and the client identify each other using a public key system. S-HTTP encrypts pages containing sensitive information such as credit card numbers that pass between the web server and the client. This means that anyone attempting to access the information by eavesdropping will only see the encrypted message. S-HTTP is usually when the server represents a financial institution and requires authentication from the user that is more secure than a user ID and password.

Internet Control Message Protocol (ICMP)

The Internet Control Message Protocol (ICMP) is a TCP/IP network layer protocol that provides troubleshooting, control and error message services. It provides feedback that the user can use for diagnostics or to report logical errors. ICMP is used most frequently in operating systems for networked computers, where it transmits error messages.

Transport Layer Security (TLS) protocol

Transport Layer Security (TLS) is a cryptographic protocol that is widely used for internet communications and online transactions. TLS provides privacy between communicating applications and their users on the internet. It is used to prevent eavesdropping, tampering and message forgery.

Finding information on the WWW using advanced search syntax

In Book 1 of this series, you learned that you can retrieve information by clicking on a direct link using your browser, or by using one of the many **search engines**. You also learned that you can access web pages by:

* searching through subject directories linked to organised collections of web pages
* entering an internet address or URL and retrieving a page directly
* browsing through pages and selecting links to move from one page to another
* entering a key word or a search statement at a search engine to retrieve pages on the topic of your choice.

Of the four options listed above, searching using key words is the most popular method of finding information on the WWW. However, this method usually returns a very large number of results, many of which may not be what you need. Performing an advanced search using advanced search **operators** can significantly narrow your searches and reveal more relevant pages.

The Advanced Search option in Google™ search simplifies the process by providing instructions for the user to input the search request (see Figure 7.13 on the next page).

Here are some tips for getting better search results.

Tip 1: Put some thought into your search terms

Do not start your search with a single word or broad term without first thinking about what it is you really want to find. For example, if you search for 'Jamaica', you will get approximately 591 million results (see Figure 7.13). However, if you search for 'tourist destinations in Jamaica', you will get about 26 million results (see Figure 7.14).

Figure 7.13 Google™ search engine

Figure 7.14 Google™ search engine

Tip 2: Adding more terms can narrow a broad search

As we mentioned earlier, using one word to conduct an online search can reveal a large number of results. To narrow the search to achieve better search results, it may be useful to include more information about the topic you are researching. For example, 'tourist destinations in Jamaica' will return more relevant results than simply 'Jamaica' if you are interested in a vacation in Jamaica.

Tip 3: Use synonyms

It may also be helpful to think of other similar words that could be used. For example, destinations can also be referred to as attractions or sites. Since different things are written using similar words (synonyms) for the same topic, it's a good idea to try searches with combinations of these various words (see Figure 7.15).

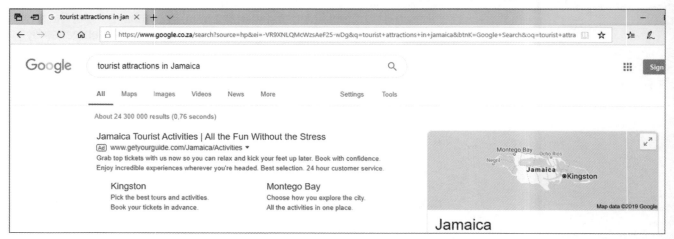

Figure 7.15 Google™ search engine

Tip 4: Use other search engines

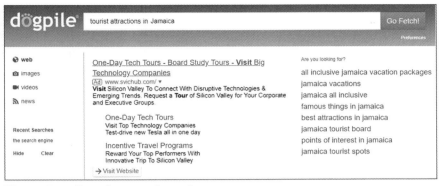

Figure 7.16 Dogpile search engine

©2018 Google LLC, used with permission. Google and the Google logo are registered trademarks of Google LLC.

Figure 7.17 Advanced Search option in Google™ search engine

©2018 Google LLC, used with permission. Google and the Google logo are registered trademarks of Google LLC.

Figure 7.18 Advanced Search dialog box in Google™ search engine

When doing research on the internet, be sure to try more than one search engine. Although Google™ search remains the most widely used, it is not the only search engine available on the internet. Each search engine has its own search formula, so you can get different results.

Other popular internet search engines are Yahoo!, Bing, Ask and Dogpile.

Figure 7.16 shows part of the search results of the phrase 'tourist attractions in Jamaica' using the Dogpile search engine.

Follow these steps to access the Advanced Search option in Google™ search:

1 Click the settings option on the bottom right of the Google™ search screen.

2 Select 'Advanced Search' from the menu, as shown in Figure 7.17.

3 The Advanced Search dialog box appears, as shown in Figure 7.18.

4 Key in your search word or phrase in the desired box.

Figure 7.19 shows the search results for the phrase 'The most popular tourist destinations in Jamaica', which was entered in the search box option 'all these words'. Figure 7.20 shows the search result of the phrase 'Popular tourist destinations in Jamaica', which was entered in the search box option 'this exact word or phrase'. Notice the search results were different. A more precise search phrase along with advanced operators can return better search results.

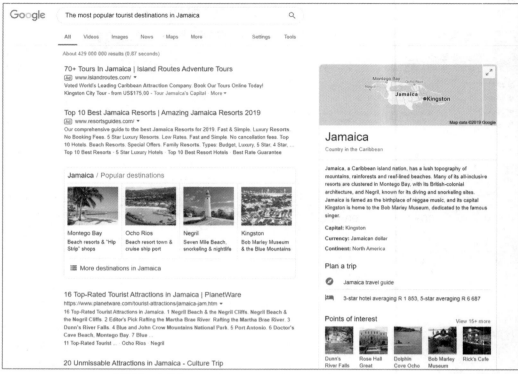

Figure 7.19 Search result for 'The most popular tourist destinations in Jamaica' entered in the search box option 'all these words'

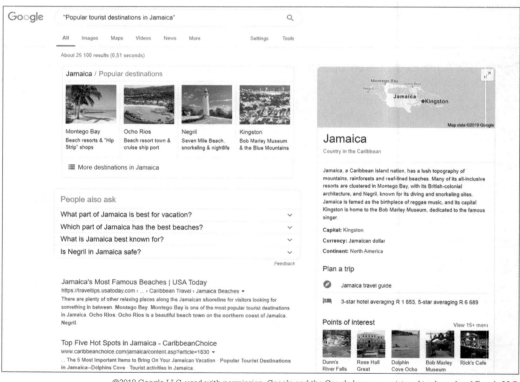

Figure 7.20 Search result for 'Popular tourist destinations in Jamaica' entered in the search box option 'this exact word or phrase'

Advanced searches

Not all search engines provide an advanced search page like Google™ search, but you can do an advanced search using operators. The operators used in this book work for Google™ search and other search engines. Here are some examples of the syntax commonly used when doing advanced searches in Google™ search and other search engines.

Phrase matching

Placing double quotes (" ") around a string of words usually tells a search engine that all search results must contain the string in the exact sequence. For example: "Tourist activities in the Blue mountains" will be far more likely to find that exact phrase, whereas searching without the quotes would lead to pages talking about Tourist activities in the Blue mountains, but not necessarily that exact phrase.

Required and specific search words

Placing a plus sign (+) in front of a word usually tells a search engine that the word must be included in all search results. Conversely, placing a minus sign (–) in front of a word specifies that the word must not be included in any of the search results.

If you want results with either (or any) of your words, use the OR keyword. It means that either (or any) of your search terms will be found, for example, "Konoko Falls" OR "Dunn's River Falls". This will find pages containing either the phrase "Konoko Falls" or the phrase "Dunn's River Falls". Some page results will contain both.

If you want your results to contain both phrases, you can replace the OR with AND. You use AND when you want to make sure that the topic you're researching is the topic you get in the search results, for example, "Konoko Falls" AND "Dunn's River Falls". This option will find pages containing both "Konoko Falls" and "Dunn's River Falls".

Parentheses

When you place search terms in a set of parentheses, they are treated as a single unit. For example, ("Water Falls" OR "Rivers") ("Jamaica" OR "Trinidad") will find pages containing both, either the phrase "Water Falls" or the word "Rivers", in Jamaica or Trinidad.

Dead link error codes

These error codes indicate a website with dead or broken links:

* **404 Page Not Found:** The external site is no longer available, is offline or has been permanently moved.
* **400 Bad Request:** The host server cannot understand the URL on your page.
* **Bad Host:** OR Invalid Host Name: The server with that name doesn't exist or is unreachable.
* **Bad URL:** The website owner has entered an improper URL for the link, (for example, a missing bracket, extra slashes, wrong protocol, and so on).
* **Timeout:** The HTTP requests constantly time out during the link check, which usually means that the user has software or is behind a firewall that blocks access to the destination website.

Figure 7.21 Error codes indicate websites with dead links.

Summary 7

1. Information on a data network can be transmitted using analogue or digital signals. The difference between analogue and digital signals is how voltage creates the signal.

2. Latency is the brief delay that takes place between the moment you send the message and the moment the message is received.

3. 'Data communication' refers to the transmission of data from one location to another for direct use or for further processing.

4. The data communication channels used to carry data can be classified into narrow-band, voice-band and broadband, depending on the volume of data that can be transmitted.

5. The transmission lines that carry the data are classified according to the direction of data flow: simplex, half-duplex or full-duplex.

6. The types of transmission cables used to connect a network are twisted pair cable, coaxial cable and fibre optic cable.

7. Wireless technologies enable devices to communicate without cabling.

8. WiFi is the most popular way to communicate data wirelessly, within a fixed location.

9. Bluetooth allows different types of electronic equipment (computers, smartphones, tablets, printers, cars and so on) to automatically make their own connections without wires, cables or any direct action from a user.

10. Other wireless transmission media include broadcast radio, cellular radio, microwaves and communication satellites.

11. A local area network (LAN) is a collection of microcomputers connected in a small geographical area that share information and peripherals, as well as communicate.

12. A network domain is used to manage all user functions, including username and password, and shared system resource authentication and access.

13. An ISP is a company that has a direct connection to the internet and gives users access to it, usually for a fee.

14. To transfer data from one computer to the next, computers must follow a set of rules called protocols. The protocol used over the internet is TCP/IP (Transfer Control Protocol/Internet Protocol), which allows operating systems software from different computers to communicate. Each computer on the internet has a unique address called the IP address.

15. A mail server is a computer on the internet that receives incoming messages and delivers outgoing messages.

16. A mail client is a program that enables you to read and compose email messages, send email and access email from the server.

17. Protocols used to send and receive email include POP3, IMAP4 and SMTP.

18. Searches on the internet can be refined using advanced search syntax.

19. Error codes occur when you try and retrieve a website with dead or broken links.

Questions 7

Copy and fill in the blanks questions

1. _____ can be broadly described as the process by which information is transmitted or exchanged.

2. _____ determines the volume of data that can be transmitted in a given time.

3. A _____ channel can transmit large volumes of data at a rate of over 45 Mbps.

4. You can send data or receive data, but not both when you use a _____ line.

5 A _____ runs the networking software that allows resources to be shared with the other computers on the network.

6 The networking hardware device that allows a WiFi device to connect to a wired network is a/an _____.

7 A _____ is a set of rules that defines how computers interact or communicate with each other.

8 When using a search engine to conduct a search on the WWW, search terms placed within _____ are treated as a single unit.

True or false questions

1 A narrow band channel can transmit data at the rate of up to 64 Kbps.

2 Wireless communication uses radio frequency transmissions to transmit data.

3 A switch increases the overall performance of the devices on the network.

4 A router is an interface that enables communication between two networks.

5 A WLAN can only be wireless.

6 Simple Mail Transfer Protocol (SMTP) is the standard protocol for sending emails across the internet.

7 A mail client receives incoming messages and delivers outgoing messages.

Multiple-choice questions

1 Which of the following allows data to flow in both directions simultaneously?

a Full duplex   **b** Half duplex

c Simplex   **d** None of the above

2 Which of the following is a benefit of a LAN?

a Hardware such as printers can be shared.

b Storage facilities can be shared.

c Software and data files can be shared by many users

d All of the above.

3 In a cabled LAN, which of these cables provides the fastest transmission speed?

a Unshielded twisted pair cable

b Shielded twisted pair cable

c Coaxial cable

d Fibre optic cable

4 A network that involves a computer, smartphone, printer and other device set up for personal use is called a:

a MAN.   **b** PAN.

c LAN.   **d** WAN.

Short-answer questions

1 **a** Define the term 'data communication'.

b Explain the term 'bandwidth'.

c Give the speed and an application for each of the three bandwidth channels available.

2 **a** Explain the term 'wireless LAN (WLAN)'.

b State two advantages and two disadvantages of using a WLAN.

c What devices are necessary to create a WLAN?

3 Explain the purpose of the following devices in a WLAN:

a Access point   **b** Switch   **c** Router

Research questions

You are an intern at a local manufacturing company that has patents for several products. The company wants to set up a WLAN, but some people have raised concerns about the use of a WLAN. The manager has asked you to answer some of the concerns raised.

1 Which hardware is required for a WLAN?

2 Would thick walls in the building affect the network? If yes, how can it be resolved?

3 What security concerns exist for a WLAN? What steps can be taken to protect the network?

4 Is a wireless network a health hazard?

5 What advantages does a wireless network have over a wired network for a company?

Crossword

Down

1 Determines the volume of data that can be transmitted in a given time

2 A transmission line that permits data to flow in only one direction

5 Acts as an interface between networks

Across

3 The most popular means of communicating data wirelessly

4 A protocol for sending email messages over the internet

6 Allows any sort of electronic equipment to automatically make their own connections without cables or any direct action from a user

STEM project

Revon is a new employee at VideoCel Inc. – a start-up communications company in a small Caribbean country. His daily duties include monitoring the company's network and data communication channels to ensure that they are working smoothly. Revon left university many years ago and that was the last time he interacted with these topics. He is currently doing a refresher course via the internet. What advice can you give to Revon, to help him do his job correctly?

Your teacher will divide the class into an even number of groups. Each group must do the activity separately, and then your teacher will place the groups in pairs to present to each other.

1 What are the three most important problems Revon is likely to experience? What are your reasons for selecting these problems?

2 Write short revision notes on the relevant topics to guide Revon and prevent him from experiencing the problems that you identified.

3 Present your notes to your partner group and record the feedback you receive.

4 What improvements can you make to your analysis of the problems and corresponding notes?

Hints

1 Do research at a local communications company to find out the main skills of the current staff.

2 List all the possible problems that a new staff member at a communications company could face. Then arrange these problems in order of importance according to the functions of the job.

8 Multimedia (PowerPoint)

Objectives

At the end of the chapter, you will be able to:

- define 'multimedia', 'multimedia authoring' and 'tools'
- explain how multimedia developed historically
- name and describe the elements of multimedia
- identify input devices used to enter media elements
- identify some file formats used to store media files
- give some advantages and disadvantages of multimedia
- state some uses of multimedia in education, business, law enforcement, medicine and entertainment
- understand the uses of PowerPoint
- start a presentation using the three options
- create a basic PowerPoint presentation, and:
  - navigate through the different views
  - understand and use a placeholder
  - add a new slide
  - change the slide layout
- work with the design template.

Multimedia

Multimedia is a combination of media elements (text, images, audio, video and animation) used to present a message or information to the user. Multimedia is used in journalism, films and television, as well as on mobile devices, computers, the internet, and signs and displays.

A computer is used to create multimedia presentations. The process of creating, enhancing or editing a multimedia presentation or application is called **multimedia authoring**. This process allows you to create, save, make changes, specify sequence, and add media elements, effects, interactivity and navigation to the presentation or application. **Authoring tools** (also called **authorware**) are programs that programmers use to write code to create these multimedia presentations or applications. Examples of authoring tools include Macromedia Flash, Adobe® Captivate®, PowerPoint, Authorware and IconAuthor.

Multimedia software combines multimedia elements to produce a single presentation. Some multimedia software includes desktop publishing software such as Microsoft Publisher and presentation software such as PowerPoint.

A brief history of multimedia

Long ago, books and newspapers were printed only as text on paper using printing presses. They became the first type of media. Later, newspapers could print pages with text and images or pictures. In the early 1900s, the radio was invented and audio broadcasts became popular (for example, news on the radio). Television (TV) then combined audio, images and video, first in black and white (in the late 1920s) and then later in colour (in the 1940s). In the 1980s, due to the rapid advancement in computer technology, computer programmers started creating software to produce and deliver multimedia on computer, the Web and now on mobile devices.

Figure 8.1 Multimedia can be produced and viewed on computers, the Web and mobile devices.

✳ Objectives

- ❏ move slides to change their sequence
- ❏ add sound, video clips, photos and graphics to a presentation
- ❏ make an effective presentation
- ❏ add a transition
- ❏ animate your presentation
- ❏ add sound to animations by:
  - ❏ recording your own sound files
  - ❏ adding sound files to your presentation
  - ❏ attaching sound files to objects
  - ❏ adding music from CDs and other sources.

Note!

Here are the meanings for these file extension abbreviations:

txt – text

doc, docx – Microsoft Word document

pdf – portable document format

MP3 – Media Player 3

WMA – Windows Media Audio

MP4 – Media Player 4

FLV – Flash Video

WMV – Windows Media Video

AVI – Audio Video Interleave

JPG – Joint Photographic Group

PNG – Portable Network Graphic

TIF – Tagged Image Format

BMP – BitMap

GIF – Graphic Interchange Format

Multimedia elements

A multimedia presentation consists of different types of information called multimedia elements, which include the following:

- ✳ **Text:** Characters typed on the keyboard, for example, letters, numbers and symbols (* / @ and $)
- ✳ **Audio:** The spoken word, music, sound or anything you can hear
- ✳ **Graphics/Still images:** Still pictures, drawings or images selected from a collection in a program
- ✳ **Video:** A recording of moving visual images, with background sound or added audio that plays on a visual display unit with speakers
- ✳ **Animation:** Several drawings of an image in slightly different positions, so that when recorded and speeded up, it looks as if the content is moving (for example cartoons and animated movies)
- ✳ **Interactivity:** The ability of an area or object on a presentation to respond to a user's action, such as to click on a button, add text to a textbox, touch an area or object, drag a bar or even speak to the device or into a microphone
- ✳ **Navigation:** This allows the presentation to move on after a few seconds, with a click on the area or on navigation buttons labelled 'Next', 'Back', 'Home', 'Previous', 'First', 'Last' or the names of certain sections. These buttons all have links to the desired locations.

Input devices for capturing multimedia

When you create a multimedia presentation, you need to capture the different media elements using specific input devices suitable for each one. Text is captured and stored in a computer from a keyboard or by using a document scanner or an optical character recognition (OCR) device. Audio is captured using a microphone or created using a synthesiser. Many devices have small built-in microphones.

Graphics can be entered using a document scanner, a digital camera or a graphic pad (or digitiser). You can also use your cell phone's digital camera to capture the graphic. Video can be entered using a webcam, digital camera or video camera. You can also use the video camera on your cell phone. Animation requires a graphic pad or tablet, a microphone and a digital camera.

Software for capturing multimedia

This software can capture and/or combine multimedia elements:

- ✳ **Text:** Microsoft Word and iWork® (for Apple® PCs)
- ✳ **Audio:** Audacity, Sound Forge and GarageBand(for Apple® PCs)
- ✳ **Video:** QuickTime, CamStudio, Windows 10 Gamebar and Filmora Scrn
- ✳ **Images:** Windows Scan, PaperScan, Screenshot Captor, Adobe® Acrobat® and Lightshot
- ✳ **Animation**: Cinema 4D, MakeHuman, Pencil 2D and Keyshot.

Multimedia is saved in different file formats, with these extensions:

* **Text:** txt, doc, docx and pdf
* **Audio:** MP3 and WMA
* **Video:** MP4, FLV, WMV and AVI
* **Images:** JPG, JPEG, TIF, BMP and PNG
* **Animation:** GIF and FLV.

Advantages and disadvantages of multimedia

Table 8.1 shows the advantages and disadvantages of multimedia.

Table 8.1 The advantages and disadvantages of multimedia

Advantages of multimedia	Disadvantages of multimedia
It can be used for work and play. It is suitable for all ages and different audience types and sizes.	It uses many items of equipment, so device failure or poor quality output is a possibility.
It uses multiple sensors to capture your attention.	It can be expensive to produce and purchase.
It makes messages interesting or entertaining.	File sizes are large and take up a lot of storage space.
Many apps are being developed that are useful to the public, for example, online banking apps.	Elements such as background music may distract from the real message being shared.
It plays a big role in the rapid growth of the internet.	It takes time to put a presentation together.

The use of multimedia in various fields

Multimedia is used in many different fields.

Education
Multimedia is used:

* in presentations to teach or present topics
* in computer-aided learning CDs and DVDs
* on websites used for research
* in downloadable content for distance learners
* in video conferencing.

Business
Multimedia is used:

* in advertisements of products and services
* to create company websites or online stores
* in presentations at conferences and seminars
* in video conferencing
* in the creation of apps.

Law enforcement
Multimedia is used:

* when detectives look at video recordings taken at or near a crime scene while working on a case
* by the police using surveillance cameras or CCTV cameras to monitor crime hot spots
* by the police saving or retrieving files on criminals (text, photos, fingerprints, interrogation videos)
* in police or legal fraternity training, conferencing or accessing witness testimonies from offsite
* in the analysis and presentation of forensic evidence.

Medical

Multimedia is used:

* in presentations, lectures and real-life simulations to train doctors and nurses
* in ultrasound, heart monitors and surgical procedures
* in endoscopy, where a long thin tube with a tiny camera is inserted into the body through the mouth or a small hole to view what is happening inside an organ.

Entertainment

Multimedia is used:

* in producing computer games and video games
* in creating films for the cinema and on DVDs, including sound effects
* in music video productions and for sharing messages, pictures and audio on social media
* in TV programming and podcasting.

Microsoft PowerPoint

Microsoft PowerPoint is an application that lets you create, print and show presentations. It is a multimedia tool that combines all media elements (text, images, audio, video and animation) in its presentation. Presentations can pass on information quickly to a group of people in classrooms, lecture theatres, or at your desk. When you give a presentation, your main aim is for your audience to understand your key points quickly.

PowerPoint presentations help you to do this by showing information concisely (briefly in summary format), on a page-by-page basis. Each page of information is called a **slide**. PowerPoint's special features let you create imaginative and concise slides easily. Related slides can be viewed in sequence as a **slide show**. PowerPoint is a dynamic way of presenting slides, because a click of the mouse lets you move easily from one slide to the next, and back again.

You can show your presentation in different ways:

* **On-screen presentation:** A small group of people views the presentation on a PC screen. Large (24 inch) screens make this a convenient way of presenting. Sometimes, several screens are linked together for larger audiences.

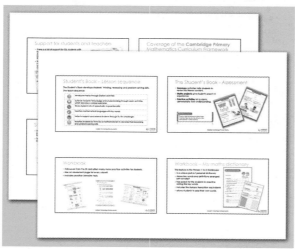

* **Digital projection:** For large groups of people, it is more convenient to project the presentation onto a large screen. The projector has an interface to the computer so that what you see on the PC screen is transmitted to the projector as a video signal, and then converted by the projection engine into light. The three digital projection technologies are LCD (liquid crystal display), LED (light emitting diode) and DLP (digital light processing™).
* **Printed handouts:** These are copies of the slides printed onto paper, with each sheet containing between one and nine slide images. In this way, the audience attending your presentation can take home a copy of it to review the information that you presented in their own time.

Figure 8.2 An example of printed handouts of four PowerPoint slides

Microsoft PowerPoint 2016

Similar to Word and Excel, PowerPoint 2007, PowerPoint 2013, 2016, 2019 and Office PowerPoint 365 use a single ribbon with tabs at the top of the screen. Most functions and icons are present in the different versions of PowerPoint, and most are in the same location with slight variations. You should find it easy to navigate and find the icons in whichever version you have. In this chapter, however, we will use PowerPoint 2016.

Commands are organised in logical groups, which are collected together under tabs. Each tab relates to a type of activity, such as Home (deals mostly with **formatting** of slides) or Insert (tables, graphics, movies, sounds, and so on). The ribbon design makes it easier to find the commands that you need to complete a task quickly.

PowerPoint allows you to choose from different options for creating a presentation. These include the following:

* **Design Template:** This option allows you to choose from a number of backgrounds and colour schemes that are available before you develop your new presentation.
* **Blank Presentation:** This option gives you a blank page with no background or colour schemes.
* **Open an existing Presentation:** This option displays a list of recently opened PowerPoint presentations from which you can choose to reopen one of the displayed files. You can also choose **More Files …** If the file you want is not displayed, this allows you to select the location of the file by browsing through other folders on your system.

In this chapter, we will look at creating a presentation using the Design Template and Blank Presentation features.

Figure 8.3 Selecting PowerPoint 2016

Starting PowerPoint 2016

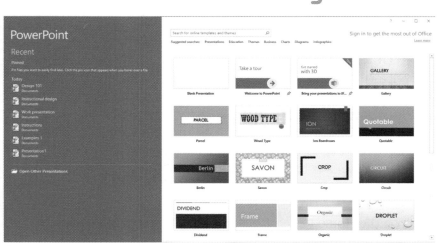

Figure 8.4 Getting Started task pane

Follow these steps to start PowerPoint:

1   Click on the **Start/ Windows** button.

2   Select **PowerPoint 2016** from the menu (see Figure 8.3).

3   The **Getting Started** task pane appears, as shown in Figure 8.4.

4   You can select and create a **Blank Presentation** (see Figure 8.4).

Creating a new presentation

Once you have chosen a new presentation option either from Design Template or Blank Presentation, a Slide Layout task pane containing several layouts appears. This is called the **AutoLayout**. It consists of several predefined layouts, depending on what you want to illustrate. Once the mouse cursor is placed over a layout the name of that particular layout appears.

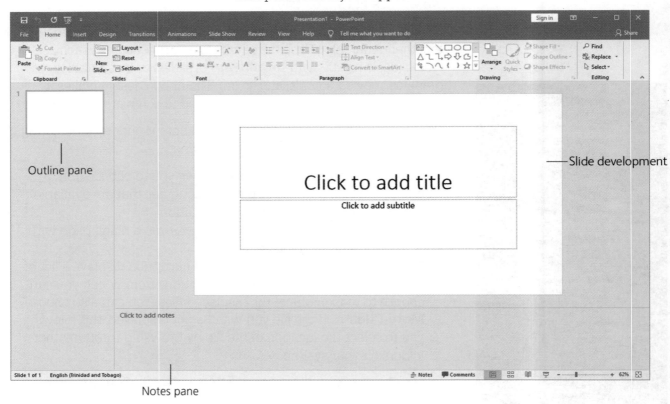

Figure 8.5 Initial PowerPoint screen (Normal view)

When you click on a particular layout, PowerPoint opens this layout in its Normal view, which shows three panes with development areas (see Figure 8.5) as follows:

* An **Outline** pane on the left contains the title of each slide, as well as the information typed into the placeholders.
* A **Slide Development** pane on the top right, contains **Placeholders**, which are pre-selected boxes with dotted or hatched borders used to hold titles and other text or objects, such as charts, tables and pictures, within the slide.
* A **Notes** pane is located on the bottom right.

Slide layout

Click on the Home tab and select Layout from the Slides group (see Figure 8.6).

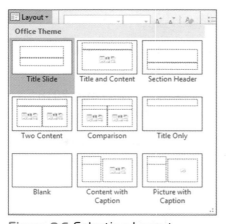

Figure 8.6 Selecting Layout

Views

The Views toolbar is located in the bottom left-hand corner of the Outline pane (see Figure 8.7). It allows you to move through the different views of your presentation.

* **Normal view:** This is the default view and consists of the three panes (Outline, Slide Development and Notes).
* **Reading view:** This expands Slide Development to fill most of the screen and allows you to develop the slides of your presentation.
* **Slide Sorter view:** This view shows a small picture of all your slides (a **thumbnail** – a miniature image of a graphic, document or slide) thus allowing you to move or rearrange the slides in the order that you would like them to appear. You can select a particular slide to view by double clicking on that slide.
* **Slide Show view:** This option allows you to view an on-screen production of your presentation. Clicking the mouse button will change the slides.

Figure 8.7 The Views toolbar

Placeholders

PowerPoint uses the information within placeholders to help you know where you are within your presentation document. The titles as well as text in these placeholders appear in the Outline pane of the Normal view. It allows you to move to that particular slide in your presentation by clicking on these titles in the Outline pane.

Entering data into a placeholder

Click anywhere within the dotted borders and begin typing (see Figure 8.8). If, however, you do not need to use a particular placeholder, you do not need to delete it – unused placeholders do not show up in a presentation.

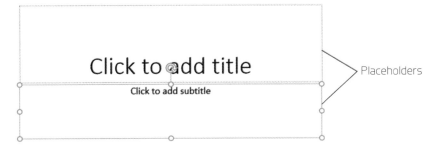

Figure 8.8 A blank PowerPoint placeholder

Moving a placeholder

Follow these steps to move a placeholder:

1   Click on the dotted border to select the placeholder.

2   Place the cursor on or near the border or box until a four-headed arrow appears.

3   Drag the placeholder to a new location.

Adding a new slide

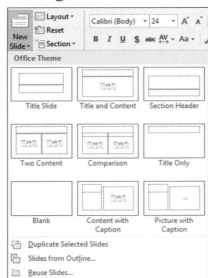

Click on the Home tab and select New Slide from the Slides group (see Figure 8.9).

Figure 8.9 New Slide drop-down menu

Activity 1

You are going to create a new presentation. Follow these steps.

1 Choose Blank Presentation from the PowerPoint dialogue box.

2 Select the Title Slide from the AutoLayout dialogue box.

3 Click in the Title placeholder box and enter the following title:

'Our school trip'.

4 In the Sub-title placeholder, enter the name of the place you visited on your school trip, for example, 'The museum'.

5 Insert a new slide by selecting New Slide from the Insert Menu.

6 Select the AutoLayout with the bulleted list from the New Slide dialog box that appears.

7 Type the following heading in the Title placeholder of this layout: 'Interesting facts about ....' (where '....' represents the place you visited on your school trip).

8 Enter at least four interesting facts about the place you visited on your school trip in the Bulleted List placeholder.

9 Insert a third slide from the Insert menu, choosing the same layout as the previous slide.

10 Enter the following text In the Title placeholder: 'A little about XXX' (where 'XXX' represents the place you visited on your school trip).

11 Enter the following information about the place you visited on your school trip in the Bulleted List placeholder:

❑ Where is the place located?

❑ What are the opening hours?

❑ Who is allowed to visit?

❑ What is the cost of visiting?

12 Save your presentation as 'My school trip'.

13 Display your presentation as a slide show using the Slide Show view in the lower left-hand corner of your screen, or choosing Slide Show from the Slide Show menu.

Changing the slide layout

You can change your slide layout or apply a different format to an existing slide by clicking on the **Home** tab. Then, select **Layout** from the **Slides** group.

The design template

Changing or applying a new design template

Each slide in your presentation can have a different design or it can use the same design template. You can choose a Slide Design template from the Design tab. The Design tab appears as shown in Figure 8.10. This pane allows you to select from a variety of designs, as shown in Figure 8.11.

The background and other selections available in the Slide Design task pane have two options: **Apply to All** and **Apply**:

* **Apply to All** will apply your changes to each slide in the presentation, both the existing slides and any slides that will be created in the future for that particular presentation.
* **Apply** will cause the change to occur only in the slide that you are currently viewing.

Figure 8.10 Design tab

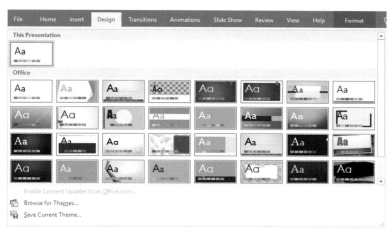

Figure 8.11 Slide designs available from the Design tab

Activity 2

You are going to apply a design template to the slides in your presentation. Follow these steps:

1 Retrieve the presentation 'My school trip' that you created in the previous activity.

2 Choose a design from the Themes group of the Design tab.

3 Save your presentation.

4 Display your presentation as a slide show using the Slide Show view in the lower right-hand corner of your screen, or by choosing From Beginning from the Start Slide Show group of the Slide Show tab.

Activity 3

You are going to change the background to the slides in your presentation. Follow these steps:

1 Retrieve the presentation 'My school trip' that you created in Activity 1.

2 In the Outline pane of the Normal view, or in the Outline view, select your second slide.

3 Select Format Background from the Customise group of the Design tab. The Format Background pane appears to the right of your slide, as shown in Figure 8.12.

4 Select your background choices from the options listed.

5 Save your presentation.

6 Display your presentation as a slide show using the Slide Show view in the lower right-hand corner of your screen, or by choosing From Beginning from the Start Slide Show group, as shown in Figure 8.13.

Figure 8.12 Format Background pane

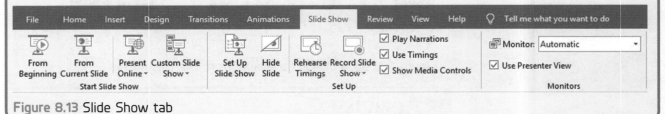

Figure 8.13 Slide Show tab

Activity 4

You are going to rearrange the order of your slides. Follow these steps:

1 Retrieve the presentation 'My school trip'.

2 In the Slide Sorter view, move the third slide to the second position.

3 Save your presentation.

4 Display your presentation as a slide show using the Slide Show view at the lower left-hand corner of your screen or choosing Slide Show from the Slide Show menu.

Working with sound, video clips, photographs and graphics

Sound, video clips and photographs are inserted in your slide in the same way as you would insert a clipart image (a graphic). Once these images are inserted, they appear in the middle of your slide. You can then move or reposition them by dragging them to any location. There are specially designed layouts that allow you to include video clips, sound, charts, tables and photographs in the slide by clicking on the icons on the slide itself (see Figure 8.14 and Figure 8.15).

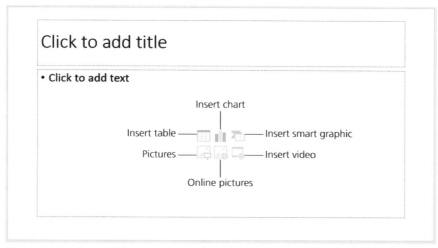

Figure 8.14 Inserting a graphic, table, picture or video by choosing icons from inside the slide

Figure 8.15 Selecting sound clips

Did you know?

The later version of Microsoft 2013, 2016, 2019 no longer has the clip art organiser library built into the program. Instead, you have to search online for the Microsoft clip art library through Bing Image Search.

Figure 8.16 Online search for clip art using Bing Image Search

Activity 5

You are going to add graphics to your slides. Follow these steps:

1 Retrieve the presentation 'My school trip'.

2 Add a new slide to your presentation.

3 Choose the layout Two Content from the New Slide drop-down menu in the Slide group of the Home tab.

4 Click on the placeholder to add a clip art.

5 Choose a map of your country for your presentation. (Hint: You can download the map from Google™ Maps.)

6 Enter the title 'Make your trip a memorable one'.

7 Enter some additional information about your school trip.

8 Save your presentation.

9 Display your presentation as a slide show using the Slide Show view in the lower right-hand corner of your screen, or by choosing From Beginning from the Start Slide Show group of the Slide Show tab.

Moving slides – changing the sequence of slides

Once you have created a sequence of slides, you may want to change their order a little, in order to make the flow of the presentation clearer and more logical. You can move slides around easily within PowerPoint, in either the Outline view or Outline pane of the Normal view, or in the Slide Sorter view (see Figure 8.17).

Follow these steps to change the sequence of slides:

1   Drag the slide to the position where you want it.

2   A grey vertical line indicates the slide's position as you are dragging when you are in the Slide Sorter view, and a horizontal line indicates the same when you are in the Outline view.

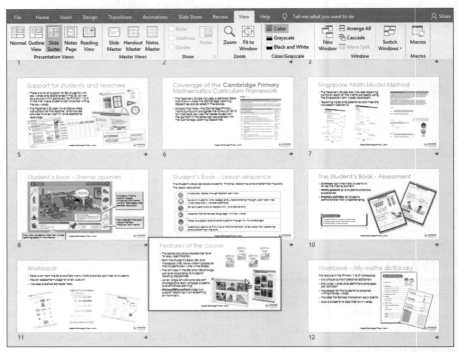

Figure 8.17 In this sequence of slides, you may want to move the slides around for a better order of presentation.

Activity 6

You are going to rearrange the order of your slides. Follow these steps:

1 Retrieve the presentation 'My school trip'.

2 In the Slide Sorter view, move the third slide to the second position.

3 Save your presentation.

4 Display your presentation as a slide show using the Slide Show view in the lower right-hand corner of your screen, or by choosing From Beginning from the Start Slide Show group of the Slide Show tab.

Transitions and animations

Animation is the simulated movement of objects, graphics and text on the screen. Animation in PowerPoint makes our presentations more unforgettable to the audience. However, if there is too much animation it can also be very distracting and your audience may not pay attention to the actual content of the presentation.

Transitions are animations that add movement to the slides themselves rather than the objects on the slides. They affect how the slides appear or disappear as you change or move from one slide to the next during a presentation.

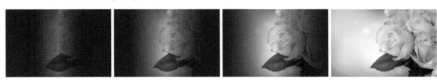

Figure 8.18 An example of a split transition special effect on a slide

Adding a transition

You can choose a special effect to introduce a slide in your presentation. This special effect is known as a transition.

Follow these steps to add a transition to a slide:

1   Select the slide to which you want to apply the transition effect.

2   Select the effect or transition you want from the **Transition to this slide** group of the **Transition** tab (see Figure 8.19).

Figure 8.19 Transitions tab

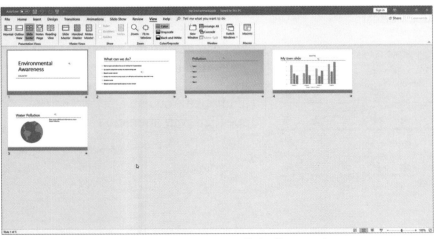

Figure 8.20 Checking your transition in Slide Sorter view

3   You can apply the effect or transition to that slide or click the **Apply to All icon** in the Timing group of the Transition tab.

4   You can add a sound by selecting the **Sound** drop-down arrow from the Timing group on the Transitions tab.

5   You can check your transition by going to the Slide Sorter view and clicking on the **star** icon at the bottom of the particular slide (see Figure 8.20).

Activity 7

You are going to add transitions to your slides. Follow these steps:

1 Retrieve the presentation 'My school trip'.

2 Fill in the data based on your school trip's information.

3 Add two different transitions, one to slide 2 and another to slide 3.

4 Save your presentation.

5 Display your presentation as a slide show using the Slide Show view in the lower right-hand corner of your screen, or by choosing From Beginning from the Start Slide Show group of the Slide Show tab.

Animating your presentation

As mentioned earlier, animation is the simulated movement of objects, graphics and text on the screen. We will look at how to:

* animate a single object (graphic or image)
* animate more than one object on a slide
* animate text
* add sound to a slide.

Animating a single object (graphic or image) on a slide

Follow these steps to animate a single object on a slide:

1   Select the object you want to animate by clicking on it in the Slide Development pane.

2   Select an animation effect from the Animation group on the Animations tab (see Figure 8.21 and Figure 8.22).

3   View as a slide show.

Figure 8.21 Animations tab with animation effects

Figure 8.22 Animation effects

You can choose whether you want your animation to start by either a mouse click or after a previous animation. You can also choose the speed of your animation.

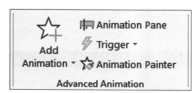

Figure 8.23 Advanced Animation group on Animation tab

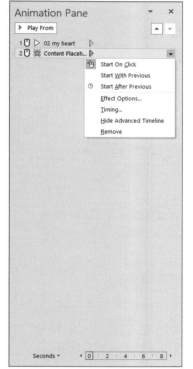

Figure 8.24 Animation pane

Animating more than one object on a slide

Follow these steps to animate more than one object on a slide:

1 Choose **Animation** Pane from the Advanced Animation group on the Animation tab (see Figure 8.23).

2 The Animation pane (Figure 8.24) will appear.

3 Click on the object you want to animate.

4 Click on the **Add Animation** button, a drop-down list will appear. Select the animation effect you want (see Figure 8.22).

5 The object you animated will appear in a list in the Animation pane.

6 You can preview your animation by clicking the **Play** button in the Animation pane.

Activity 8

You are going to animate an object. Follow these steps:

1 Retrieve the presentation you saved earlier as 'My school trip'.

2 Select the first slide of your presentation.

3 Click on the Title placeholder.

4 Choose Animation Pane from the Advanced Animation group on the Animation tab and choose an effect.

5 Save your presentation.

6 Display your presentation as a slide show using the Slide Show view in the lower right-hand corner of your screen, or by choosing From Beginning from the Start Slide Show group of the Slide Show tab.

Animating text

You can animate text by using Animation effects. Choosing Animation effects will automatically animate your text one paragraph at a time.

Follow these steps to animate text:

1 Select the slide.

2 Choose the type of animation from the Animation group on the Animations tab.

3 Click on the down arrow next of the **Effect Options**. The Effects Option drop-down menu will appear.

4 Select one of the available options (see Figure 8.25 on the next page).

You can also choose to have a special sound effect by clicking on the **Effects** tab of the same dialog box (see Figure 8.25).

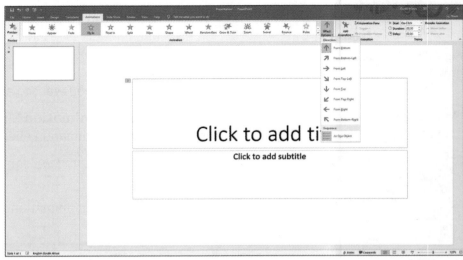

Figure 8.25 Effects Option dialog box

Adding sound to an animation

Adding sound to an animation can make your presentation more appealing, fun or even humorous for your audience.

Recording your own sound files

Follow these steps to record your own sound files:

Figure 8.26 Audio icon

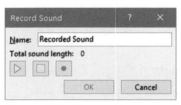

Figure 8.27 Recording sound

1   Plug your microphone into the microphone jack into your computer or use the built-in microphone on your laptop.

2   Select **Audio** from the Media group of the Insert tab (see Figure 8.26).

3   Select **Record Audio**, the Record Sound dialog box appears (see Figure 8.27).

4   Enter the name of the recording.

5   Click the **Record** button and talk into the microphone.

6   Click the **Stop** button when you finish recording.

7   You can play back your recording by pressing the **Play** button.

If you want to add another segment to your recording, you can simply click the **Record** button and continue talking. Click the **Stop** button when you are finished. The new segment will be added to your previous recording.

If you are unsatisfied with your recording, you can simply click the **Cancel** button, and re-record your sound. If you are satisfied with it, click the **OK** button. The Record Sound dialog box will close and a speaker icon will appear in the middle of your slide. You can drag and position the icon anywhere on your slide.

Playing sound files in your presentation

Double clicking the speaker icon will play the sound that you recorded. Clicking anywhere on the slide will stop the sound before it finishes.

Adding music from CDs and other sources

You can add music to your presentation, such as your MP3s and other music formats from CDs or other sources. The music can be attached to your objects, transitions or animations within your presentation.

Follow these steps to add music from CDs and other sources to your presentation:

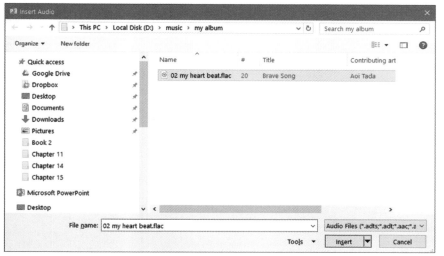

Figure 8.28 Selecting sound from a file

Figure 8.29 Playback tab

1 Select **Audio** from the Media group of the Insert tab.

2 Select **Audio on My PC**.

3 Search for the sound on your PC (see Figure 8.28).

4 After selecting the sound, a **Playback** tab appears (see Figure 8.29). You can choose to select if you want the music or sound to automatically play in your presentation, or only when the icon is clicked. In the Audio Options group, Start drop-down list, choose either **On Click** or **Automatically**.

5 A speaker icon will appear in your slide (see Figure 8.30).

6 You can choose to hide the sound icon during the slide show by clicking the check box **Hide During Show** icon (see Figure 8.29).

Figure 8.30 Sound icon

Activity 9

You are going to add sound to your slides. Follow these steps:

1 Retrieve the presentation 'My school trip' you saved from the earlier activity.

2 Add a voice recorded sound to one slide in the presentation.

3 Add a music file from an audio CD or MP3 file to the last slide in your presentation (if possible).

4 Save your presentation.

5 Display your presentation as a slide show to check the sounds.

Summary 8

1. Multimedia is a combination of media elements used to present a message or meaning to the user. Multimedia elements consist of text, images, audio, video, animation and interactivity.

2. Multimedia is all around us. It is on our computers, cell phones, the TV and internet, and at school, work or play.

3. Input devices used in multimedia presentations include keyboards, document scanners, microphones, digital cameras, graphic pads, webcams, OCRs and synthesisers.

4. Several file types or formats are used for different multimedia elements, including 'docx', 'jpg', 'MP3', 'MP4', 'txt' and 'pdf'.

5. Multimedia authoring is the process of creating, enhancing or editing a multimedia presentation or application. Authoring tools are programs that programmers use to write code to create multimedia presentations or applications.

6. Using multimedia has advantages and disadvantages.

7. Multimedia is used in various fields, such as education, media, law enforcement, business, medical and entertainment.

8. PowerPoint is an application that allows you to create, print and show presentations.

9. PowerPoint allows you to include sound, animation, videos, photos and graphics in your presentations.

10. PowerPoint presentations are shown on a page-by-page basis, where each 'page' of information is called a slide.

11. Presentations can be shown as on-screen presentations, digital projections or printed handouts.

12. PowerPoint has four presentation options: AutoContent Wizard, Design Template, Blank Presentation and Open an Existing Presentation.

13. PowerPoint opens a predefined layout in its Normal view, which has a three-pane development area (an Outline pane with the slide titles and the placeholder information; a Slide Development pane; and a Notes pane).

14. Placeholders are boxes used to hold titles and other text or objects.

15. The View toolbar lets you move through the different presentation views. Normal view is the default view, while Outline view lets you develop the text of your presentation, Slide view lets you develop your presentation slides, Slide Sorter view shows you small pictures of all your slides and the Slide Show view shows you an on-screen production of your presentation.

16. The sequence of slides in a presentation can be changed in the Outline pane of the Normal view or in the Slide Sorter view, by dragging the slide to the required new position.

17. Sound, video clips and photos are inserted into your slide in the same way that you would insert a clip art graphic image.

18. A transition is a special effect that introduces a new slide in a PowerPoint presentation, when moving from the previous slide.

19. PowerPoint allows you to animate the objects on your slides.

20. You can add sound from a file, CD or your own recording to objects, transitions or animations within your presentation.

Questions 8

Copy and fill in the blanks questions

1 PowerPoint is a/an _____ application. It allows you to _____ and present a lecture in several different ways.

2 A presentation allows you to view a _____ on the PC screen.

3 Each page of information in your presentation is known as a _____.

4 _____ add movement to the slides themselves rather than the objects on the slides.

5 Double clicking the _____ icon will play the sound that you recorded.

Matching questions

Match each icon to its correct view.

1 Slide Sorter view   2 Reading view

3 Normal view   4 Slide Show view

a   b   c   d

True or false questions

1 PowerPoint does not allow you to include sound and animation in your presentation.

2 The blank presentation start-up option of PowerPoint gives you a blank page with no background or colour scheme.

3 The New Slide dialog box consists of a number of different layouts.

4 There are four panes of development in the Normal view of PowerPoint.

5 You cannot change the colour and background of a slide once you have selected them.

6 Both text and graphics can be animated.

7 You can preview your animations after making changes.

8 Transitions cannot be added to PowerPoint presentations.

Multiple-choice questions

Choose the best option for each question.

1 Which one of the following is not a means of delivering a presentation using PowerPoint?

   a Slide show on a PC   b Printed handout

   c Digital projection   d Handwritten notes

2 Which of the following are start-up options?

   a Open an existing presentation

   b Open a blank presentation

   c Design Template

   d All of the above.

3 Which one is not a pane in the Normal view?

   a Outline pane

   b Slide Development pane

   c Slide Show pane

   d Notes pane

4 Moving slides can take place in:

   a Normal view.   b Slide Sorter view.

   c Outline view.   d all of the above.

5 To animate an object, you must choose:

   a Slide Show from the File tab.

   b Animation Effects from the Insert tab.

   c Custom Animation from the Slide Show tab.

   d Animation from the Animations tab.

6 Which of the following is a special effect?

   a Fly in   b Notes

   c Frame   d Outline

Short-answer questions

1 What is a placeholder? Explain its use in PowerPoint.

2 List three situations in which PowerPoint presentation software can be used.

3 What is a thumbnail?

4 Explain how sound can enhance your presentation.

Crossword

Across

3 A view that shows small graphics of all slides and allows you to rearrange them (2 words)

5 Normal view has three of these

6 This lets you choose from several backgrounds and colour schemes (2 words)

8 This view expands to fill most of the screen

Down

1 Animations that add movement to the slides themselves

2 A view that lets you look at an on-screen production of your presentation (2 words)

4 Pre-selected boxes with dotted line borders that can hold text and other objects

7 Simulated movement of objects, graphics and text on screen

Project

Create a ten-slide presentation on one of these topics:

1 Personal safety during carnival time

2 Dangers of texting and driving

3 Schools should ban unhealthy snacks.

4 Reduce, reuse, recycle: Going green at my school

5 Movies affect our perception of how things are.

6 Peer pressure, both good and bad

7 Piracy affecting our local artists

8 Certain types of music influence our behaviour.

9 Safety on the internet

10 Childhood obesity on the rise: Children do not play outside anymore

11 How this new or emerging technology (choose one) will affect our lives in the future.

12 Computers have changed how we do things

13 The pros and cons of wearing a school uniform

14 A day in the life of a tomato plant

15 The benefits of visual and performing arts

16 Earthquake preparedness

17 Interact Club helps families in need

18 Teenage driving is the cause of most major road accidents. Agree or disagree?

19 How to stop bullying or cyberbullying

20 Advertise an event at your school.

Scenarios

1 This year, you went to the beach to see the leatherback turtles nesting. You noticed that a man lifted his child and placed him on the back of the turtle. You were very shocked, so you approached the man and explained to him that what he was doing was wrong. He apologised and said that he was unaware that what he was doing was wrong. When you returned to school the next day, you decided to create a presentation to educate your classmates about the do's and don'ts of interacting with nesting leatherback turtles.

2 You noticed that your neighbour, Mr Smith, lit a pile of garbage in his backyard. After a few minutes the fire started to get larger and larger and started to spread. Mr Smith became panicky and ran for a bucket of water. Realising that the fire was out of control, Mr Smith rang the fire station. They arrived quickly and put out the fire. Mr Smith received a stern lecture about setting fires particularly during the dry season. Create a presentation to show the dangers of setting fires during the dry season.

3 In an effort to earn some money, you have co-opted your siblings, cousins and close friends into your 'We cut lawns' business. You have a few customers to who you provide lawn-cutting services, but you want to expand your business. You have been given 15 minutes at the weekly church meeting to present your start-up business to the people in your neighbourhood. Create a presentation to showcase your 'We cut lawns' business.

4 Your mother complains weekly about the rising price of vegetables in the market. You have learnt in school how easy it is to start a garden. You want to encourage your mother to start her own kitchen garden to reduce the cost of buying vegetables every week. Select a few herbs and vegetables, and create a presentation to explain to your mother how easily she can start a kitchen garden.

STEM project

A parent, Steffion, and a few other parents have been asked to prepare a presentation for their children's kindergarten class. This presentation is to highlight the importance of good behaviour. Steffion was elected as the leader of the team of parents. The team wants to make the presentation as interesting and interactive as possible using visual, aural and print media. The presentation must not be longer than ten minutes because of the short attention span of the kindergarten students. You can play the role of Steffion and your classmates can play the roles of the other parents on the team.

1 What do you want to achieve with your presentation?

2 List and explain three major components of your presentation.

3 Write the steps you plan to take for preparing your presentation. Give each classmate at least one task to do.

4 Produce your presentation and ask a parent of a kindergarten-aged child to evaluate it. What feedback did you receive?

5 From the feedback you received, explain how you an make your presentation more impactful.

Hints

1 Revise all that you have learned about input and output devices before starting this project.

2 Is your PowerPoint presentation presented simply and with vocabulary that is appropriate for kindergarten students?

3 Did you obtain input from your classmates? If not, what can you do to improve this for future project work?

9 Advanced word processing

In *Interact with IT* Book 1 of this series, you learned to use some of the key aspects of word processors, especially Microsoft Word. In this chapter, we will look at more features and operations of this powerful application package.

Editing and proofing text

A word processor provides many editing features that let you make quick changes to a document, which would have taken a long time to do manually. Some editing features include:

* cutting, copying and pasting
* finding and replacing text.

Cutting, copying and pasting text

Figure 9.1 Cutting and pasting is easier on a computer.

To **cut** means to delete or remove a piece of text such as a character, word, phrase, line or block of text. To use the Cut feature, you must first select the piece of text, as discussed in Book 1.

* You can use the Select option in the Editing group of the Home tab (see Figure 9.2) to select an entire document or the mouse keys to select words or sections of text.
* To delete the selected text, press the Delete key. If you want to move the text from one part of the document to another part, you need to cut and paste.

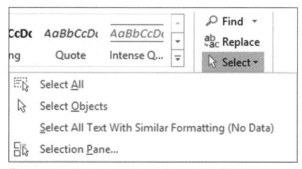

Figure 9.2 Select options from the Editing group

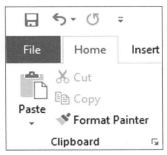

Figure 9.3 Cut, Copy and Paste icons from the Clipboard group

Did you know?

You can use the cut and paste or copy and paste instructions to move data from one application to another. For example, you can copy and paste a graph created in the Microsoft Excel application to a word-processing document.

Follow these steps to cut, copy and paste:

1 Select the text that you want to copy or cut.

2 Select the **Copy** or **Cut icon** from the Clipboard group in the Home tab (see Figure 9.3).

3 Click where you wish to copy or move the text.

4 Select the **Paste** icon.

When the **Cut** command is used, the piece of document that is removed is placed in a temporary storage area called the **Clipboard**. A copy of the contents of the clipboard can be inserted anywhere in any active document and as many times as you like. The process is called **pasting**.

Finding and replacing text

The **Find** feature allows you to search a document for a particular word or string of characters that you may want to change or edit. Follow these steps to find a word or phrase:

1 Select **Find** from the **Editing group** in the **Home tab**.

2 Enter the word or phrase in the 'Navigation pane' that appears on the left of the window.

3 Word automatically gives the results.

The **Replace** feature allows a user to search for a word or string of characters and replace it with another word or string of characters. Follow these steps to replace a word or phrase:

1 Select **Replace** from the **Editing group** in the **Home tab**. The Find and Replace dialog box appears (see Figure 9.4).

2 Enter the word or phrase you wish to replace in the 'Find what:' box.

3 Enter the word or phrase you wish to replace it with in the 'Replace with:' box.

4 Click the **Find Next** button to find the first occurrence of the word or phrase.

5 Click the **Replace** button to replace the word or phrase, or the **Replace All** button to make the change throughout the entire document.

Figure 9.4 Find and Replace dialog box

Spelling and grammar checks

Spelling and grammatical errors can make a document look unprofessional. To help create a more accurate and professional-looking document, Word identifies those words that are spelled incorrectly or not recognisable with a jagged red underline. If the Word spelling checker believes that it has spotted a word spelled incorrectly, you can right click on the word with the mouse, and it will display a list of possible suggestions or alternative words from which you can choose.

When Word spots a phrase or sentence that does not follow grammatical rules or when there is a problem with the spacing between characters, it identifies this text with a green jagged underline. If you right click on any part of the green underline with the mouse, the grammar checker displays possible grammatical errors and suggests corrections. You can choose to ignore the suggestions or accept the suggestions, which then changes the text.

Checking grammar and spelling

Follow these steps to check grammar and spelling.

1   Select the word or text for which you would like to check the spelling and grammar.

2   Select **Spelling & Grammar** in the Proofing group from the Review tab (see Figure 9.5).

3   Word checks the selected text and gives you the option to make changes based on a list of suggestions, as shown in Figure 9.6. Table 9.1 provides details of each option.

Figure 9.5 Select Spelling & Grammar in the Proofing group from the Review tab

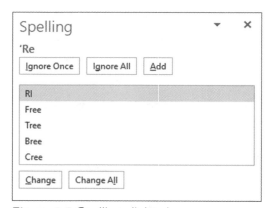

Figure 9.6 Spelling dialog box

Table 9.1 Spelling options

Ignore Once	If you do not want to change the word or this occurrence of the word.
Ignore All	If you do not want to change all occurrences of the word throughout the document.
Change	Choose the correct word in the 'Suggestions:' box and click the Change button.
Change All	If you want to change all occurrences of the word in the document.
Add to Dictionary	If the computer has detected a word that it does not recognise and is not in the computer's dictionary you can choose to add the word to the dictionary.

Undoing and redoing document changes

Do not be scared to make changes to your document. The **Undo** ↶ ▾ and **Redo** ↻ ⇌ features allow users to undo mistakes or changes made during editing, formatting or drawing. For example, if you deliberately or by accident make changes to a document, you can reverse these changes using the **Undo** button.

Generally, most actions can be reversed right after you discover the problem. You can also undo more than one previous action. A list of the most recent actions that can be undone is displayed when you check the arrow next to the Undo button in the standard toolbar.

The **Redo** button allows you to undo and redo, if you later decide you do not want to undo the change.

Formatting

Changing the appearance of the text in a document is called formatting.

Character formatting

Character formatting involves applying attributes such as font type, size, style and colour, as well as different effects, to characters, which can be letters, numbers, symbols, punctuation marks and spaces.

In Book 1, you explored different character formatting functions. In this book, we will look at applying effects such as Superscript, Subscript, Strikethrough, Double strikethrough, All caps (capital letters), Small caps and Hidden characters. You can access all these effects in the Font dialog box by clicking the Dialog box launcher in the Font group of the Home tab.

Applying superscript and subscript

A superscript character is one that is raised above the normal line. For example 3rd, $100°C$, $4x^3 + 5x^2$ have the characters 'rd', '°', '3' and '2' raised above the normal line and are superscript characters.

Subscript characters are placed below the normal line. For example, the chemical representation of water is H_2O or a number in base 2 can be written 1101_2. The number 2 in each of these cases are subscript characters.

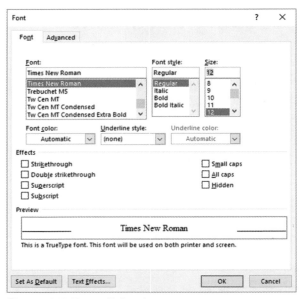

Figure 9.7 Font dialog box

> Shortcut: Select or type the character(s) you want to format as superscript or subscript. Click the superscript icon $\mathbf{x}^2$ or the subscript icon $\mathbf{x}_2$ from the Font group in the Home tab.

Follow these steps to apply superscript and subscript:

1 Select the **Font group** from the Home tab.

2 Click the **Dialog box launcher** in the Font group. The Font dialog box appears as shown in Figure 9.7.

3 Check the **Superscript** or **Subscript** box in the Effects section and click the **OK** button.

4 Select or type the character(s) you want to format as superscript or subscript.

5 Change back to normal typing mode by going back to the dialog box and unchecking the **Superscript** or **Subscript** box.

6 Apply the other effects, such as Strikethrough, Double strikethrough, All caps (capital letters), Small caps and Hidden characters by checking the appropriate box, using the same process as for Superscript and Subscript.

Paragraph formatting

A paragraph in Microsoft Word can consist of any number of characters. It can include text, graphics, objects (for example, charts), blank lines and other items. A document can have a number of paragraphs. Click the **Home tab** to access the Paragraph group. The Paragraph group appears as shown in Figure 9.8a.

Alignment

Alignment is the process of aligning a block of text, a paragraph or an entire document within the text margins. The default setting for Word is left aligned. These are the alignment options:

* **Align Left** means that the text is flush on the left margin, but the text at the right margin is uneven.
* **Align Right** means that text is flush with the right margin, but text at the left margin is uneven.
* **Center** means that the text is centred along the middle of the document or frame. Text at both margins is uneven.
* **Justify** means that the text is flush with both left and right margins, except in the last line of a paragraph where there are not enough words to meet the margin.

Follow these steps to change the alignment using the options in the Paragraph group:

1 Select the text.

2 Select **Paragraph group** from the Home tab (Figure 9.8b).

3 Click on the alignment you desire from the options provided in the Paragraph group.

Figure 9.8a Paragraph group in the Home tab

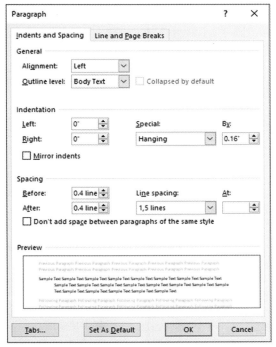

Figure 9.8b Paragraph dialog box

Shortcut: A user can change the indent using buttons in the Paragraph group of the Home tab.

Aligning text using the Paragraph dialog box

Follow these steps to change the alignment using the Paragraph dialog box:

1 Select the text for which you would like to change the alignment.

2 Click on the **Dialog box launcher** in the Paragraph group. The Paragraph dialog box will appear as shown in Figure 9.8b.

3 Select the alignment from the 'Alignment:' drop-down box by clicking on the **down arrow** and choosing the desired alignment (Left, Centered, Right or Justified).

Indentation

In word processing, the word 'indent' refers to the distance, or number of blank spaces, used to separate a paragraph from the left or right margins. For many documents, a **First line indent** is the most common way to show the start of a new paragraph. These are the indent options:

* The **First line indent** is one in which the first line is shorter than the rest of the paragraph.
* The **Hanging indent** occurs when the first line of a paragraph is left indented less than the rest of the lines in the paragraph. The first line will therefore be hanging to the left of the rest of the lines in the paragraph. It is used in bulleted lists, numbered lists, numbered paragraphs and bibliographies.
* The **Increase Indent** button moves the left indent marker to the right, the distance of one tab stop at a time.
* The **Decrease Indent** button moves the left indent marker back (to the left) one tab stop at a time.

Indenting text using the Paragraph dialog box

Follow these steps to indent text using the 'Paragraph dialog box'.

1 Place the insertion point in a paragraph or select the required paragraphs.

2 Click the **Dialog box launcher** from the Paragraph group. The Paragraph dialog box is displayed as shown in Figure 9.8b.

3 Specify the indentations in the **Right**, **Left**, and/or **Special Indent** boxes. (The Preview box at the bottom will show the effect of the changes on the text.)

4 Click **OK**.

You can press the Enter key to maintain the indent settings when starting each new paragraph.

Bullets and numbering

Bullets and numbers can be added to already typed text or to text that is being typed. Several different bullets and numbering lists are available.

Examples of numbering are shown in Table 9.2.

Table 9.2 Examples of numbering

1. Monday	I. Monday	(a) Monday	A. Monday
2. Tuesday	II. Tuesday	(b) Tuesday	B. Tuesday
3. Wednesday	III. Wednesday	(c) Wednesday	C. Wednesday

Examples of bullets are shown in Table 9.3.

Table 9.3 Examples of bullets

⏴ Monday	❖ Monday	■ Monday	✦ Monday
⏴ Tuesday	❖ Tuesday	■ Tuesday	✦ Tuesday
⏴ Wednesday	❖ Wednesday	■ Wednesday	✦ Wednesday

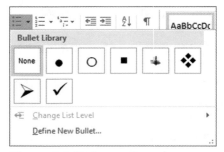

Figure 9.9 Bullet options

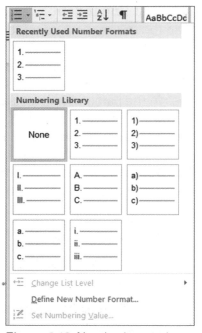

Figure 9.10 Numbering options

Adding bullets and numbers to a list

Follow these steps to add bullets or numbers to a list:

1 Select the list to which you want to add bullets or numbers.

2 Click the down arrow in the Bullet or Numbering options in the Paragraph group of the Home tab.

3 Select the desired bullet (see Figure 9.9) or numbering style (see Figure 9.10) by clicking on one of the boxes shown.

4 Click **OK**.

Removing bullets or numbers from a list

Follow these steps to remove bullets or numbers from a list:

1 Select **Bullets and Numbering** from the Paragraph group. The Bullets and Numbering options appear.

2 Select the **None** box from the options shown.

▶Activity 1

Open Microsoft Word and type the following document as accurately as possible.

1 Bold and centre the headings ('Important' and 'Grilling Guidelines').

2 Number the guidelines.

3 Increase the font size of the heading 'Important' to 20 points.

4 Increase the font size of the 'Grilling Guidelines' to 16 points.

5 Double underline 'Grilling Guidelines'.

6 Apply the Outline character effect to the heading 'Important'.

7 Save the document as 'Grilling Guidelines' in the 'Recipes' folder on your USB drive.

Important
Grilling guidelines
To prevent drying, food must be coated in oil/fat.
Preheat grill to red hot.
Reduce heat after initially placing food on grill.
Vary cooking time depending on type of food, thickness and quality.
Turn food frequently.
Avoid pricking surface of food, as it may result in loss of nutrients.

Here is how it is done.

1 Bold and centre the headings ('Important' and 'Grilling Guidelines').

 a Select the headings.
 b Select the Bold option (B) from the Font group in the Home tab.
 c Click the Centre alignment (≡) option from the Paragraph group in the Home tab.

2 Number the guidelines.

 a Select the guidelines.
 b Click on the **down arrow** in the 'Recently Used Number Formats' (½≡ ▾) option from the Paragraph group in the Home tab.
 c Select the desired numbering style.

3 Increase the font size of the heading 'Important' to 20 points.

 a Select the heading.
 b Click the **down arrow** in the Font size box from the Font group in the Home tab.
 c Select **20** from the options provided.

> ## Activity 1 continued
>
> 4 Increase the font size of the 'Grilling guidelines' to 16 points.
>
> 5 Select the heading.
>
> 6 Click the **down arrow** in the Font size box from the Font group in the Home tab.
>
> 7 Select **16** from the options provided.
>
> 8 Double underline 'Grilling Guidelines'.
>
>   a Select the words 'Grilling Guidelines'.
>   b Click the **down arrow** next to the Underline option (**U** ▾) from the Font group in the Home tab.
>   c Select the Double underline option (══════).
>
> 9 Apply the Outline character effect to the heading 'Important'.
>
>   a Select the word 'Important'.
>   b Click the **down arrow** next to the 'Text Effects and Typography' (Ⓐ) option.
>   c Select the first option 'Outline' from the options provided.
>
> 10 Save the document as 'Grilling guidelines' in the 'Recipes' folder on your flash drive.

Shortcut: Place the insertion point in a paragraph or select multiple paragraphs. Click on the Line spacing icon (‡≡ ▾) in the **Paragraph group** of the **Home tab**. Then, select from the options provided, as shown in Figure 9.11.

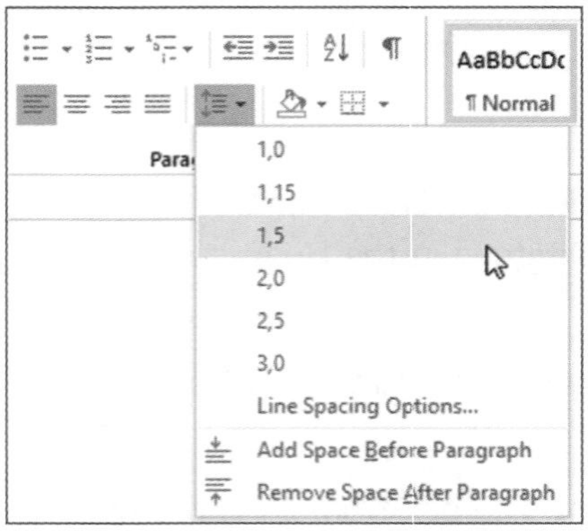

Figure 9.11 Line spacing drop-down menu

Page layout

We will look at the following aspects of page layout:

* Line spacing
* Page size and orientation
* Page margins.

Line spacing

Line spacing is the distance between lines of text. Suitable line spacing makes a document look better and easier to read. The line spacing options available are Single, Double, 1.5 lines, At least, Exactly and Multiple. The default line spacing for Word is single. You may need to change the line spacing depending on the type of document.

Changing line spacing using the Paragraph dialog box

Follow these steps to change the line spacing using the Paragraph dialog box:

1 Place the insertion point in a paragraph or select multiple paragraphs.

2 Select the **Home tab**. Click the **Dialog box launcher** in the Paragraph group. The Paragraph dialog box appears (see Figure 9.8).

3 Select the required spacing by selecting the option from the Line spacing box.

Page size and orientation

You may need to select the paper size and page orientation (portrait or landscape) before you begin to type your document.

Selecting the paper size using the Page Layout tab

Follow these steps to select the paper size:

1 Select the **Page Layout tab**.

2 Click the down arrow in the Size option from the Page Setup group (see Figure 9.12).

3 Choose the paper size from the drop-down menu provided.

Selecting the page orientation using the Page Layout tab

Follow these steps to select the paper orientation:

1 Select the **Page layout tab**.

2 Click the down arrow in the Orientation option from the Page Setup group (see Figure 9.12).

3 Choose from the two options: **Portrait** or **Landscape**.

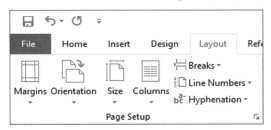

Figure 9.12 Page Setup group

Figure 9.13 Page Setup dialog box

Selecting paper size and page orientation using the Page Setup dialog box

Another way to select the paper size and page orientation is by clicking the Page Setup dialog launcher to access the Page Setup dialog box (see Figure 9.13). You can change the margins, orientation, paper size and layout using this dialog box.

Activity 2

Retrieve the document 'Tourist Destination' from the 'Tours' folder in Documents.

1 Centre align the heading.

2 Delete the last paragraph.

3 Double space the entire document.

4 Full justify the remaining two paragraphs.

5 Replace '22 miles north-east' with '357 km north'.

6 Replace the word 'Tobago' with the words 'Saint Lucia' throughout the document.

7 Save the document as 'Destination St Lucia' in the 'Tours' folder.

Here is how it is done.

1 Centre align the heading.

    a Select the heading 'Tobago'.
    b Select **Paragraph group** from the Home tab.
    c Click on the Centre alignment option in the Paragraph group.

2 Delete the last paragraph.

    a Select the entire paragraph.
    b Press the **Delete key** on the keyboard or select **Cut** from the Clipboard group in the Home tab.

3 Double space the entire document.

    a Select the entire document.
    b Select the **Home tab**.
    c Click the **Dialog box launcher** in the Paragraph group. The Paragraph dialog box appears.
    d Select the **2.0** spacing from the Line spacing box.

4 Full justify the remaining two paragraphs.

    a Select the two paragraphs in the document.
    b Click the **Centre alignment icon** (☰) from the Paragraph group in the Home tab.

5 Replace '22 miles north-east' with '357 km north'.

    a Click the **Replace option** from the Editing group in the Home tab. The Find and Replace dialog box appears.
    b Type in '22 miles north-east' in the 'Find what: box'.
    c Type in '357 km north' in the 'Replace with: box'.
    d Click on the **Replace option**.

Activity 2 continued

6 Replace the word 'Tobago' with the words 'Saint Lucia' throughout the document.

    a Click the Replace option from the Editing group in the Home tab. The Find and Replace dialog box appears.

    b Type in 'Tobago' in the Find what: box.

    c Type in 'Saint Lucia' in the Replace with: box.

    d Click on the Replace All option.

7 Save the document as 'Destination St Lucia' in the 'Tours' folder.

Page margins

Margins are the blank spaces around the work area of a sheet of paper or the distance between the text and the edge of paper. The different margins are:

* top
* bottom
* left
* right
* gutter.

The **gutter margin** is the space selected for binding. This space is needed so that work will not be hidden if the document is bound. A blank document in Word has a default setting of one inch for the top, bottom, left and right margins.

> Shortcut: With the document opened, click the down arrow in the **Margins** option of the **Page Setup group** of the **Page Layout tab**. Select from the **Margin** options shown in the drop-down menu.

Changing margins using the Page setup dialog box

Follow these steps to change margins using the Page setup dialog box:

1 Click the **Dialog box launcher** from the Page Setup group of the Page Layout tab. The Page Setup dialog box appears as shown in Figure 9.14.

2 Change any or all of these values by selecting the up arrows to increase the size, the down arrows to decrease the size of the respective margins, or by typing in the values. As the values are changed, a preview of how the document will change appears in the preview section.

3 You can change the margins for the whole document or from a particular point by selecting:

    a **Whole document**

    b **This point forward** in the 'Apply to:' drop-down box of the Dialog box.

Figure 9.14 Page Setup dialog box

Page numbering

If a document is longer than a few pages, you may want to number the pages. You can add page numbers using the Page Number option and the Header and Footer options in the Header & Footer group of the Insert tab.

Inserting page numbers

Follow these steps to insert page numbers:

1   Click on the **Insert tab**. Select **Page Number** from the Header & Footer group. The Page Number options drop-down menu appears as shown in Figure 9.15.

2   Select from the options provided.

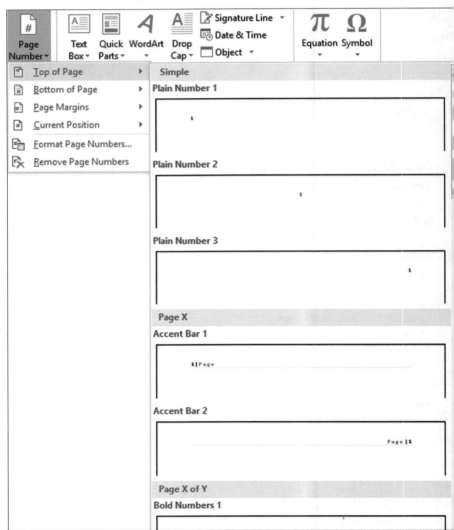

Figure 9.15 Position of Page Number options menu

Columns in newspapers and newsletters

I HAVE A DREAM

Speech by Dr Martin Luther King

In 1963 Martin Luther King gave a speech that has become a defining moment in the history of the United States. Facing oppression for being black, Dr King headed a rally in Washington D.C. to campaign for equality between citizens of the USA, regardless of the colour of their skin.

The Speech

I am happy to join with you today in what will go down in history as the greatest demonstration for freedom in the history of our nation.

Five score years ago, a great American, in whose symbolic shadow we stand today, signed the Emancipation Proclamation. This momentous decree came as a great beacon light of hope to millions of Negro slaves who had been seared in the flames of withering injustice. It came as a joyous daybreak to end the long night of captivity.

But one hundred years later, the Negro still is not free. One hundred years later, the life of the Negro is still sadly crippled by the manacles of segregation and the chains of discrimination. One hundred years later, the Negro lives on a lonely island of poverty in the midst of a vast ocean of material prosperity. One hundred years later, the Negro is still languished in the corners of American society and finds himself in exile in his own land. So we have come here today to dramatize an shameful condition.

In a sense we've come to our nation's Capital to cash a check. When the architects of our republic wrote the magnificent words of the Constitution and the Declaration of Independence, they were signing a promissory note to which every American was to fall heir.

This note was a promise that all men, yes, black men as well as white men, would be guaranteed the unalienable rights of life, liberty, and the pursuit of happiness.

It is obvious today that America has defaulted on this promissory note insofar as her citizens of color are concerned. Instead of honoring this sacred obligation, America has given the Negro people a bad check; a check which has come back marked "insufficient funds."

But we refuse to believe that the bank of justice is bankrupt. We refuse to believe that there are insufficient funds in the great vaults of opportunity of this nation. So we have come to cash this check- a check that will give us upon demand the riches of freedom and the security of justice.

Figure 9.16 Document with three columns

Newspapers and newsletter documents are produced using the column feature. When the first column is filled, the text flows over and continues in the next column. The document in Figure 9.16 is divided into two sections. The first section has one column and the second section has three columns.

Creating columns

Follow these steps to create columns:

1 Click the **Page Layout tab** and choose **Columns** from the Page Setup group. A drop-down menu will appear, allowing you to select the number of columns, as shown in Figure 9.17.

2 Click **More Columns** to open the Columns dialog box as shown in Figure 9.18.

3 The Columns dialog box allows you to specify the spaces between the columns and also to indicate to Word if the columns will be on one sheet or the entire document.

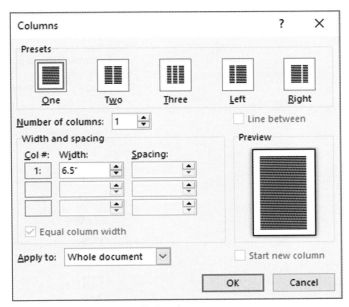

Figure 9.18 Columns dialog box

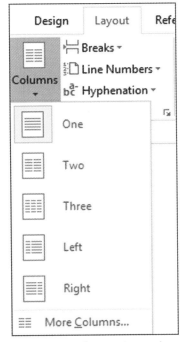

Figure 9.17 Accessing columns options from Page Layout

Borders

You may often need to place a border around your page or around a paragraph. A border can make a document look more professional. It can also create a visual separation between different areas of a document, making it easier to read.

Creating a border around a page

1   Select the **Design tab**. Click on **Page Borders** from the Page Background group. The Borders and Shading dialog box will appear as shown in Figure 9.19.

2   Click the **Page Border tab**.

3   Select whether you want a **Box**, **Shadow**, **3D** or **Custom border**.

4   Select either a line style from the Style box, or art from the Art drop-down menu.

5   You can change the colour of the border by clicking the **Colour drop-down menu**.

6   You can change the width of the border by clicking the **Width drop-down menu**.

7   Click **OK**.

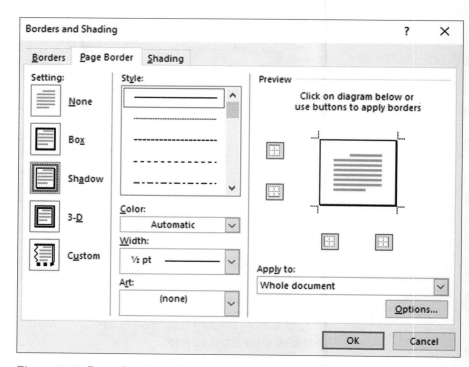

Figure 9.19 Page Border tab selected in the Borders and Shading dialog box

Creating a border around a paragraph

1 Select or highlight the paragraph.

2 Select the **Design tab**. Click on **Page Borders** from the Page Background group. The Borders and Shading dialog box will appear as shown in Figure 9.20.

3 Click the **Borders tab**.

4 Select whether you want a **Box**, **Shadow**, **3D** or **Custom border**.

5 Select the line style from the **Style box**.

6 Select the colour from the **Colour drop-down menu**.

7 Select the width of the border from the **Width drop-down menu**.

8 Click **OK**.

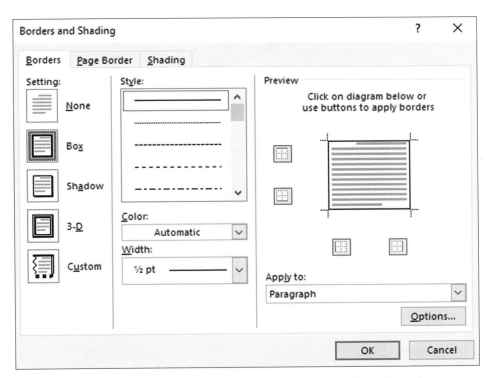

Figure 9.20 Borders tab selected in the Borders and Shading dialog box

Mail merges

The mail merge feature allows you to produce large volumes of personalised letters, mailing labels, memos and emails without having to type each one individually for each recipient. For example, many companies send standard letters to customers in which the body of the letter is the same, but the name, address and a few pieces of additional information may be different. This type of multi-recipient correspondence can be produced easily using mail merge.

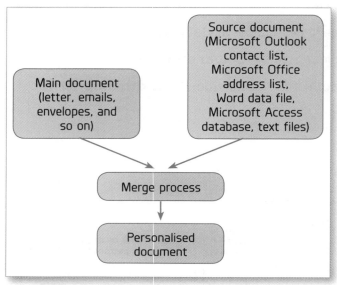

Figure 9.21 The mail merge process

Merging requires the use of two files:

* a main document (primary file)
* a data source (secondary file).

Data from the data source is inserted into the main document to produce personalised documents. Figure 9.21 shows the merging process.

The **main document** (or **primary file**) contains the letter or other document that is meant for each recipient. It also contains the merge fields, which are positioned at the points where the information from the data source is to be inserted. When the mail merge begins, the merge fields are replaced with the information from the data source.

The **data source** (or **secondary file**) contains the personalised information that would vary in each document, such as names and addresses of individuals. The data source can be an existing data source, or you can create a new data source by using the 'Mail Merge Helper'.

The information stored in the data source is organised in the form of a table. The first row, known as the **header row**, contains the merge fields. A **merge field** is the name of a data item that will be stored in the data source and later be merged into the main document. Some common field names are 'Title', 'First name', 'Address' and 'Phoneno'.

When creating merge fields, you must ensure that each merge field:

* is unique
* begins with a letter
* contains no more than 40 characters
* does not contain any blank spaces.

Each row after the header row contains the information that is unique to each document, and is known as a **data record**. The collection of data records is called a **data file**.

Creating a main document

You can create a main document before you access the 'Mail Merge Wizard 'task pane'. The areas designated to hold the data that will be unique to each recipient could be indicated as blank spaces, or by typing dummy field names enclosed in double angle-brackets, for example: << Name >>. This is necessary so that the field codes will be inserted in the correct positions, even though the actual codes will not be available to be inserted into the main document until you have created the data source document.

Follow these steps to create a mail merge document:

1 Decide on the type of document you are going to create, for example, a letter, an email message, a label, an envelope or a directory.

2 Decide on the starting document: either use the current active document or open a document from storage.

3 Change the document layout if necessary (for envelopes and labels only).

4 Decide on the recipients: decide what data source to use, that is whether to create it or to use an existing one.

Using the Mail Merge Wizard to do a mail merge

Follow these steps to do a mail merge using the Mail Merge Wizard:

1 Select the **Mailings tab**.

2 Click on the **Start Mail Merge** option in the Start Mail Merge group. A drop-down menu appears, as shown in Figure 9.22.

3 Click on **Step-by-Step Mail Merge Wizard** from the drop-down menu.

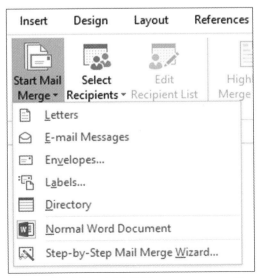

Figure 9.22 Start Mail Merge menu options

4 The Mail Merge Wizard task pane appears on the right side of the Word document window, as shown in Figure 9.23. Select the document type by clicking the **Radio** button. Click the blue arrow at the bottom to move to the next step.

5 Select the starting document. Choose the appropriate option by clicking on the **Radio** button (see Figure 9.24).

   * The option **Use the current document** allows you to use the current active or open document.
   * The option **Start from a template** allows you to choose one of the Word templates to use to create your letter.
   * The option **Start from existing document** allows you to choose an existing file to work with.

6 Click on **Next: Select recipients** at the bottom of the task pane. The Select recipients task pane appears (see Figure 9.25).

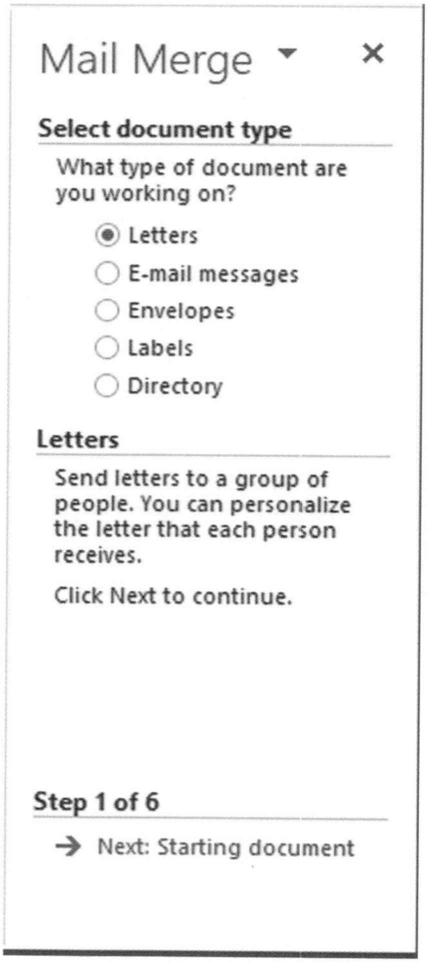

Mail Merge ▼ ✕

Select document type

What type of document are you working on?

⦿ Letters
◯ E-mail messages
◯ Envelopes
◯ Labels
◯ Directory

Letters

Send letters to a group of people. You can personalize the letter that each person receives.

Click Next to continue.

Step 1 of 6

→ Next: Starting document

Figure 9.23 Step 1 of the mail merge process – Select document type

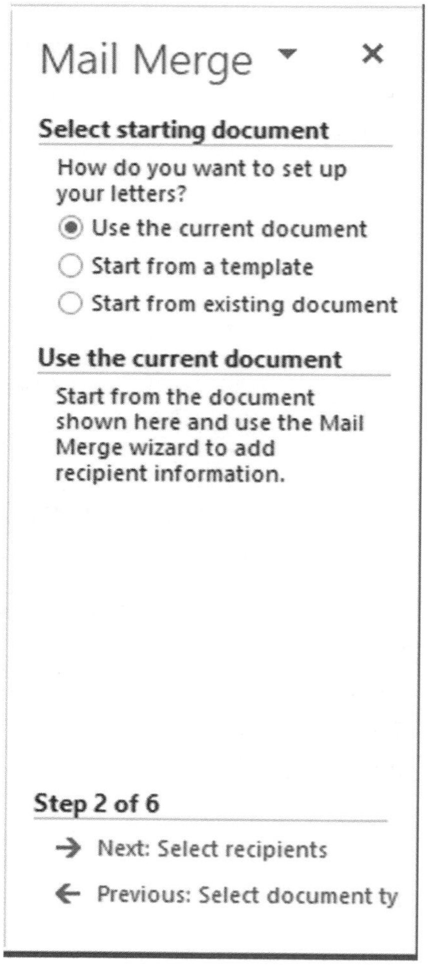

Mail Merge ▼ ✕

Select starting document

How do you want to set up your letters?

⦿ Use the current document
◯ Start from a template
◯ Start from existing document

Use the current document

Start from the document shown here and use the Mail Merge wizard to add recipient information.

Step 2 of 6

→ Next: Select recipients

← Previous: Select document ty

Figure 9.24 Step 2 of the mail merge process – Select starting document

Mail Merge ▼ ✕

Select recipients

⦿ Use an existing list
◯ Select from Outlook contacts
◯ Type a new list

Use an existing list

Use names and addresses from a file or a database.

🗔 Browse...

🗎 Edit recipient list...

Step 3 of 6

→ Next: Write your letter

← Previous: Starting document

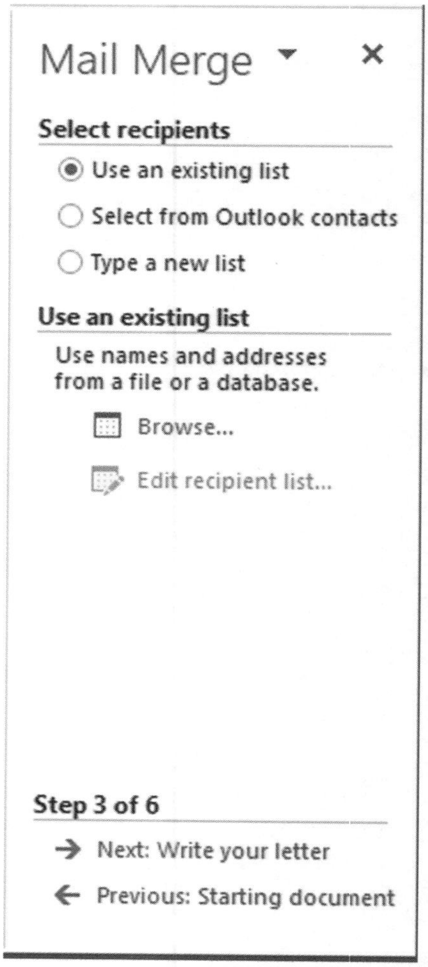

Figure 9.25 Step 3 of the mail merge process – Select recipients

7 Choose **Use an existing list**; this allows you to use a document you already created.

8 Click **Browse**. The Select Data Source dialog box appears as shown in Figure 9.26.

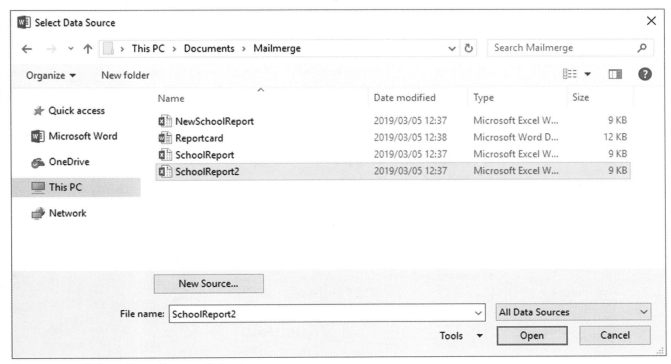

Figure 9.26 Select Data Source dialog box

9 Select the name of the data source and click **Open**. If the data source is a spreadsheet file, the Select Table dialog box will appear, as shown in Figure 9.27.

10 Select the sheet that contains the data from the list of sheets in the Microsoft Excel workbook. Click **OK**.

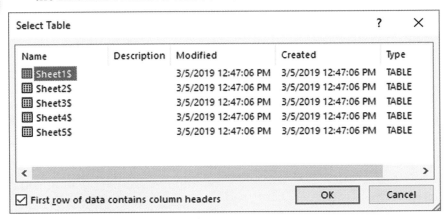

Figure 9.27 Select Table dialog box

11 A list of the recipients that will be used in the mail merge appears in the Mail Merge Recipients dialog box shown in Figure 9.28. Click **OK**.

12 Click **Next: Write your letter** to move to the next step in the process.

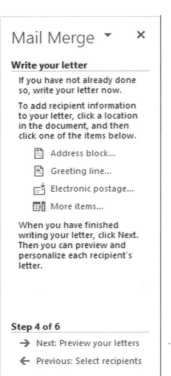

Figure 9.29 Step 4 of the mail merge process – Write your letter

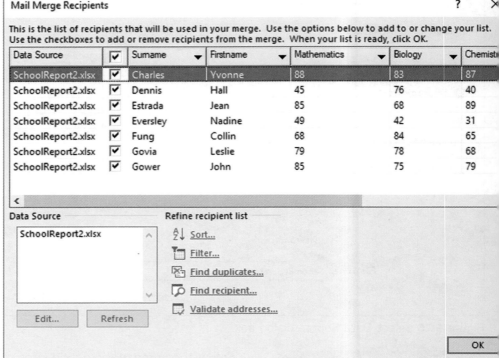

Figure 9.28 Mail Merge Recipients dialog box

13 The Write your letter option appears. Click on **More items**, as shown in Figure 9.29. The Insert Merge Field dialog box appears, as shown in Figure 9.29.

Inserting the merge fields

Follow these steps to insert the merge fields:

1 Position your insertion point where the first merge field is to be inserted into the document.

2 Click on the **Insert Merge Field** button. The 'Insert Merge Field' dialog box appears (see Figure 9.30).

3 Select the desired field and click the **Insert** button. The field appears in the position you indicated (see Figure 9.30).

4 Place all the other fields in their respective positions.

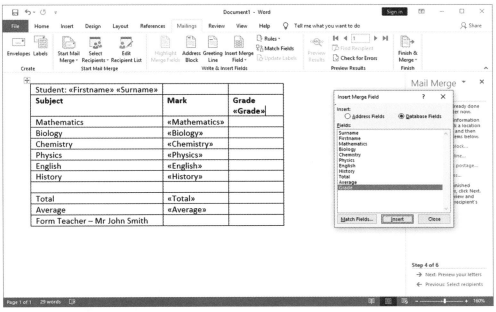

Figure 9.30 Inserting merge fields from the Insert Merge Field dialog box into the main document

5   After inserting all the fields into the source document, click **Next: Preview your letters**.

6   The Preview your letters dialog box appears showing the first merged document (see Figure 9.31).

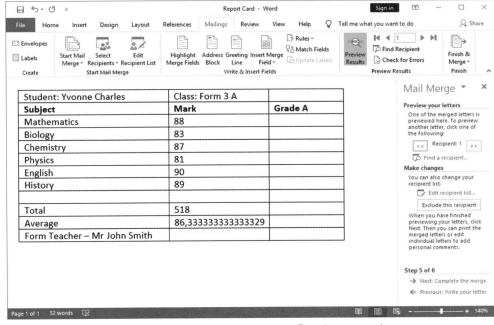

Figure 9.31 Step 5 of the mail merge process – Preview your letters

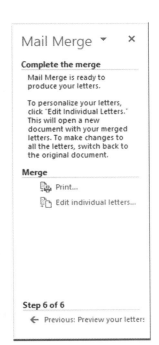

Figure 9.32 Step 6 of the mail merge process – Complete the merge

7   Click **Next: Complete the merge** to move on to the last step of the process. This option gives you the opportunity to print out all the letters or edit individual letters (see Figure 9.32).

Copying data and graphs from a spreadsheet into a Word document

It may become necessary when writing a report to display information such as the data and graphs produced in a spreadsheet. Moving data and graphs from a spreadsheet to a Word document involves copying or cutting and pasting.

Copying data or graphs from an Micorsoft Excel worksheet into a Word document

Follow these steps to copy data or graphs from an Excel worksheet into a Word document:

Figure 9.33 Being able to create and move graphs and data from a spreadsheet to a Word document is useful when preparing business documents such as reports.

1 Open the Word document.

2 Open the Excel workbook.

3 Click the appropriate worksheet and select the data/chart required.

4 Select **Copy/Cut** from the Clipboard group in the Home tab of Excel.

5 Click the Word document on the task bar to make it active.

6 Position the cursor in the Word document where you would like to insert the data or chart.

7 Select **Paste**. The data/chart will be inserted into the Word document.

Extracting a page

On occasion, you may need to take the contents of one or more pages in a document and create a new document. Follow these steps to extract a page:

1 Move to the page that you want to use to create a new document.

2 Select the contents of the page and select **Copy/Cut**.

3 Open a new blank document.

4 Paste the selected content into the new blank document.

5 Save the document using a different file name.

Summary 9

1 A word processor contains many editing and proofing features that enable you to make changes to a document quickly and easily. Some of the editing features include the following:

- **Delete:** Characters, words and blocks of text can be easily deleted.
- **Insert:** Characters, words and blocks of text can be easily inserted.
- **Cut, copy and paste:** Characters, words and blocks of text can be removed or copied from one part of a document and placed in another part of the same document or in another document that is currently on the desktop.

2 Formatting determines the final appearance of a document. Formatting can be carried out at three levels – character, paragraph and page.

3 Pages can be formatted by adjusting the margins and changing orientation (portrait or landscape).

4 The Find and Replace functions allow a user to search for a word or string of characters and replace it with another word or string of characters.

5 The Undo and Redo functions allow users to undo mistakes or redo changes made during editing, formatting or drawing.

6 Character formatting attributes can be applied to letters, numbers, symbols, punctuation marks and spaces.

7 A number of effects can be applied to characters, such as Strikethrough, Superscript, Subscript, Shadow, Outline, Emboss, Engrave and Caps.

8 A superscript effect is one in which characters are raised above the normal line.

9 A subscript effect is one in which characters are placed below the normal line.

10 The Change Case function allows us to change lower case (common letters) to upper case (capitals letters) and vice versa.

11 You can indent a line or a paragraph by pushing them away from the left or right margins.

12 Bullets and numbers can be added to an already typed list or to text that is being typed.

13 Margins are the blank spaces around the work area of a sheet of paper or the distance between the text and the edge of paper.

14 Pages can be formatted by adjusting the margins and by including page numbers.

15 The column feature in Word allows you to produce newspapers and newsletter-type documents with single, double, triple column layouts, and so on.

16 Borders can be placed around a page or around a part of a page to enhance a document.

17 The mail merge feature, allows you to produce large volumes of personalised letters, mailing labels, memos and emails without having to type each one individually for each recipient.

18 Word has a number of preset designs called templates that you can use to create a letter when doing a mail merge.

19 Data and graphs from a spreadsheet can be moved to a Word document by copying or cutting and pasting.

Questions 9

Copy and fill in the blanks questions

1 _____ allows you to change the appearance of the text in a document.

2 When the Cut command is used, the piece of document that is removed is placed in a temporary storage area called the _____.

3 The _____ feature allows you to search a document for a particular word or string of characters that you may want to change or edit.

4 The _____ feature allows a user to search for a word or string of characters and replace it with another word or string of characters.

5 A _____ effect is one in which characters are raised above the normal line.

6 _____ are the blank spaces around the work area of a sheet of paper or the distance between the text and the edge of paper.

7 The _____ margin is the space allotted for binding.

8 The _____ feature, allows you to produce large volumes of personalised letters, mailing labels, memos and emails without having to type each one individually for each recipient.

9 In the mail merge process, the _____ file contains the personalised information that would vary in each document, such as names and addresses of individuals.

10 A _____ field is the name of a data item that will be stored in the data source and later be merged into the main document.

True or false questions

1 Editing determines the final appearance of a document. Formatting can be carried out at three levels – character, paragraph and page.

2 The Find and Replace functions allow a user to search for a word or string of characters and replace it with another word or string of characters.

3 The Undo and Redo functions allow users to undo mistakes or redo changes made during editing, formatting or drawing.

4 A subscript effect is one in which characters are raised above the normal line.

5 Bullets and numbers can be added to an already typed list or to text that is being typed.

6 Borders can only be placed around a page of a Word document.

7 The mail merge feature allows you to produce large volumes of personalised letters, mailing labels, memos and emails without having to type each one individually for each recipient.

Multiple-choice questions

1 From which group would you find the functions to apply effects to characters?

a Clipboard   b Font

c Paragraph   d Styles

2 Which of the following happens when a document is left aligned?

a Text at the right margin is uneven

b Text at the left margin is uneven

c Text at both margins are even

d Text at both margins are uneven

3 What happens to a piece of text that is cut from a document?

a It is deleted forever.

b It is placed on the clipboard.

c It is moved to a section of the document.

d It is placed in a blank document.

4 All of the following are text effects that can be applied to text except:

a italics.   b superscript.

c subscript.   d strikethrough.

5 The space allotted for binding is known as the:

a left margin.   b right margin.

c gutter margin.   d top margin.

6 Borders can be placed around:

    a a page.   **b** a paragraph.

    c a graphic.   **d** all of the above.

7 Two files are needed to perform a mail merge. The file that contains the letter or other document that is meant for each recipient process is known as the:

    a primary file.   **b** secondary file.

    c merged file.   **d** original file.

Application questions

1 Type out the following and save as 'Effects' in the folder named 'Practice' on your flash drive.

    a $40 x^3 + 20 x^2 - 5 x + 25$

    b $C_6H_{12}O_6$

2 Enter the following text and save it as 'Notes:fd'

> Direct variation between non-linear quantities
>
> Expressions stating the relation between quantities which vary directly are not always in linear form. For example, the mass, m, of a cardboard square is directly proportional to its area, A.
>
> $m \, \alpha \, A$
>
> However, $A = x^2$
>
> Here, x is the length of a side of a square, so it follows that $m \, \alpha \, x^2$. Therefore, $m \, \alpha \, x^2$ is an example of direct proportion in which one variable is a quadratic form.

Carry out the following operations on the document 'Notes'.

    a Bold and underline the heading.

    b Fully justify the text.

    c Add the following piece of text as a new paragraph.

> Similarly, the volume of a sphere is directly proportional to the cube of its radius:
>
> $V = {}^4/_3 \, \pi r^3$
>
> So that $V \, \alpha \, r^3$, since π is a constant.

    d Delete the sentence starting with the words, 'Here, x ...'

    e Re-save the document as 'Variation'.

3 Here is a recipe for the Jamaican dish of ackee and saltfish.

> **Ackee and saltfish**
>
> Ackee and saltfish is the most famous dish in Jamaica and is recognised as the national dish. This dish is very popular with locals and with tourists who visit the island. It is usually served at breakfast, but can be eaten at any time.
>
> What is Ackee?
>
> Ackee is a pear-shaped fruit that is found in tropical climates. When the fruit ripens, it turns from green to bright red to yellow-orange. The fruit has a buttery, creamy texture and a mild taste. The Ackee and saltfish dish is usually served with ground provisions such as yams, green bananas or breadfruit. It is also eaten with boiled or fried dumplings, green or ripe plantains, hard-dough bread or even crackers.
>
> Ingredients required for preparing the ackee and salt fish dish
>
> Salt fish
> Fresh ackee soaked, or tinned ackee
> A chopped onion
> Sweet pepper (yellow, red or green)
> Chopped tomato
> Minced garlic
> Scotch bonnet pepper, chopped finely
> A chopped scallion
> Extra virgin olive oil
> Salt and pepper to taste

You are required to:

    a Type out the text and save it as 'National Dish'.

    b Change the left and right margins to 5.08 cm.

    c Change the font size of the heading to a size larger than that of the rest of the document.

    d Make bold, underline and centre justify the heading.

    e Indent the first line of each paragraph.

    f Change the line spacing of the entire document to 1.5 spacing.

    g Add bullets to the ingredients required.

    h Cut the last two lines of the first paragraph and place it at the end of the document.

    i Place a border around the entire document.

    j Re-save the document.

4 Customers who do not pay their monthly instalment by the fifteenth day of the following month are sent the following reminder letter by Top Brand Furniture Store:

Top Brand Furniture Store
Hope Road Kingston
Jamaica

18-01-2019
<<Title>> << First name>> << Surname>>
<< First line of address>>
<<Second line of address>>

Dear <<Title>> <<Surname>>

Please be informed that our accounts are showing that you have not paid your monthly instalment of <<amount>> towards your purchase on <<date>>. Kindly pay the aforementioned amount to your account number <<account number>>, to avoid any inconvenience.

Yours truly,

_____

Lenore Brown

Credit Manager

---

a Type out the letter to be used as a mail merge document. Save it as 'Overdue' on your flash drive.

b Create a secondary document (data file) called 'Defaulters', with the following data:

Title:	Mr
First name:	Conrad
Surname:	Lewis
First line of address:	10 Wilson Avenue
Second line of address:	Kingston
Amount:	$75 000
Date:	15-10-2019
Account number:	OCT256

Title:	Mr
First name:	Kelvin
Surname:	Harry
First line of address:	3 Hibiscus Lane
Second line of address:	Kingston
Amount:	$125 000
Date:	18-10-2019
Account number:	OCT275

Title:	Ms
First name:	Sherry
Surname:	Roach
First line of address:	18 Railroad Street
Second line of address:	Kingston
Amount:	$185 000
Date:	20-10-2019
Account number:	OCT274

c Add two records of your own.

d Merge the two documents to produce letters to be sent to defaulting customers. Save the letters as 'Owing'.

e Add a new field called 'Item'.

f Fill in possible names of items for each customer.

g Change the amount owing for Ms Roach from $185 000 to $158 000.

h Save all changes.

Research questions

Do research on the internet and then answer these questions in your notebook:

1 What are the differences between a word processor and desktop publishing software?

2 For a named task, explain why desktop publishing software would be more appropriate to use than a word processor.

Crossword

Down

1 A character that is raised above the normal line

2 Blank spaces around the work area of a sheet of paper or the distance between the text and the edge of paper

3 Preset designs in Microsoft Word that you can use to create a letter for a mail merge

4 Means that the text is flush with both left and right margins

7 Can give a document a more professional look, or create a visual separation between different areas of a document, making it easier to read

Across

3 The form in which the information stored in the data source is organised

5 A file that contains the letter or other document that is meant for each recipient in a mail merge

6 A file that contains the personalised information that would vary in each document, such as names and addresses of individuals in a mail merge

8 The first row that contains the merge fields in the data source

STEM project

Better Care Barber Shop (BCBS) has been experiencing a rapid drop in its clientele since Best Care Barbers (Best C) opened up close by. This competition has affected BCBS financially in a bad way. So, to try and improve business, the BCBS manager has developed an advertising campaign and a series of activities, which include special monthly discounts to all clients in the database, group discounts and mass media advertisements. As most of the students in your class are clients, the BCBS manager has asked your class to create a range of suitable advertisements. Your teacher will divide the class into groups and each group will work on a different type of advertisement.

1 What do you and your group have to do? Write a detailed statement.

2 Write a complete list of all the necessary content that should be in your advertisement.

3 Write a paragraph to explain why you and your group decided on this list of content.

4 List at least five steps that you and your group will take to produce your advertisement.

5 Work together as a group and produce an electronic version of your advertisement. Then ask another group of classmates to review it. Record their comments and feedback.

6 Do you need to re-examine any parts of the advertisement before you show the final version to the BCBS manager? What improvements do you intend to make?

Hints

1 What are the key features of an advertisement?

2 What makes an advertisement appealing? Are these elements evident in your advertisement?

10 Spreadsheets (Excel)

Objectives

At the end of the chapter, you will be able to:

- define a spreadsheet
- give examples of where spreadsheets can be used
- identify elements of the Excel application window
- state what is meant by a row, column, cell, label, value and formula
- navigate to specified locations within a spreadsheet
- format a worksheet, including:
  - align cells
  - change orientation of cells
  - modify the layout of cells by adding borders and colours
  - resize columns and rows
  - format values as currency with decimal values
- perform editing, including:
  - edit and delete contents of cells
  - insert and delete rows and columns
  - copy and move data within a worksheet and among applications
  - insert, delete and rename worksheets

People have used spreadsheets for a very long time. Traditionally, a spreadsheet was, and still is, a grid of rows and columns for showing on a sheet of paper all the number data for a business or other organisation. A spreadsheet package is an application package that enables you to carry out numerical work easily. It is a way of showing how numerical data items relate to each other (see Figure 10.1).

Figure 10.1 A spreadsheet

A spreadsheet enables you to store not only numerical data, but also **formulae** to carry out operations on the numerical data. These formulae are applied to the data in the sheet whenever you make a change to it. For example, if you change any data values, the entire worksheet is automatically recalculated, updating other numbers as necessary.

One of the most important features of a spreadsheet is **automatic recalculation**. Another important advantage is its ability to represent the numerical data quickly and easily in one of many graphical forms (such as pie charts, bar graphs, histograms, and so on).

A spreadsheet package is a flexible modelling tool that can be used in any job that involves repetitive numerical calculations. This is because it allows you to obtain answers to what are called 'what-if scenarios'. Suppose your cricket club wants to predict the income it would earn from fundraisers based on last year's income. Using a spreadsheet program such as Microsoft Excel, you can set up the appropriate model and then test various assumptions. For example, 'What if the raffle sales increased by 10%?' or 'What if the Bar-B-Que sale made 15% less?'

Objectives

- ❏ develop formulae using different arithmetic operators (+, −, *, / and ^) to create worksheets

- ❏ use functions to create a worksheet (SUM, MIN, MAX, IF, COUNT)

- ❏ sort data

- ❏ use spreadsheet data to produce charts, (for example, column charts and pie charts)

- ❏ explain the importance of importing and exporting data between and among software applications

- ❏ use the options in the 'Print' dialog box to print a worksheet.

Note!

Can you think of other examples of where spreadsheets can be used?

Spreadsheets can also be used for:

- ✳ statistics, for example, finding averages or calculating the standard deviation of a set of values
- ✳ loan calculations
- ✳ financial plans, for example budgeting
- ✳ stock-keeping in a supermarket
- ✳ payrolls
- ✳ company accounts
- ✳ schools to prepare the end-of-term school reports.

Features of Excel equivalent or similar to Word

Excel is one of the applications in the Microsoft office suite. As such, many of the operations are the same for all the applications. In Excel, all the basic commands such as Open, New, Close, Save and Save As, work in the same way as they do in Word. The only difference to note is that when you save an Excel file, it is given the file extension **.xls**.

Other features that are similar are Spell Check, Find and Replace, Page Setup for margins, Page Orientation and many of the formatting features.

Software note

The entire Chapter 10 focuses on Excel 2016. Most of the features of Excel 2016 are exactly the same as Excel 2010 or 2013. Therefore, if the computers at your school have Excel 2010 or Excel 2013 installed, you have no need to worry as the differences between these versions will not affect your ability to complete the requirements of your curriculum.

Starting Excel

Excel is started in a similar way to any other program. You can also start Excel using these steps.

1. If the Windows taskbar includes a Microsoft Office Excel 2016 shortcut icon, double-click on the **Excel icon** ▓ to start the program.

2. You can also access Excel by performing a search using the search box. Simply type the name of the program 'Excel' and it will be displayed, as shown in Figure 10.2 on the next page. Then click on the **Excel icon** to start the program.

Figure 10.2 Starting Excel 2016 in Windows 10 using the search box

3 You can click on the **Start button** and search the menu displayed. The programs are stored in alphabetical order. Scroll down until you see the Excel program.

The Excel application window

The initial Excel application window (see Figure 10.3) includes the following elements:

* **Title bar:** This displays the name of the program, as well as the name of the current **workbook** if it has been saved. (If the workbook has not been saved, it is identified by a number; for example, 'Book1'.)
* **Ribbon tabs:** These are usually found at the top of a **worksheet** and have key words that represent a group of closely-related commands.
* **Vertical and horizontal scroll bars:** These are used to scroll the workbook window vertically and horizontally through a worksheet.
* **Worksheet tabs:** These identify the various worksheets in a workbook, and allow you to move from one worksheet to another. Worksheets are therefore sub-parts of workbooks.
* **Status bar:** This displays helpful information as you use the program. The 'Ready' indicator that currently appears lets you know that the program is ready for data input.
* **Name box:** This identifies the active cell.
* **Formula bar:** This displays the contents of the active cell, if any.
* **Workbook window:** This window, which occupies the majority of the screen, displays an Excel workbook.

A workbook initially contains three worksheets, which are saved in a single file. A spreadsheet can be thought of as an electronic version of an accountant's columnar pad. It is a large grid divided into rows and columns. The rows run up and down and are numbered, while the columns run left to right and are lettered. As an entire Excel worksheet can contain 1 048 576 rows and 16 384 columns of data, only a small part appears in this window at one time. A typical screen display may contain 39 rows and 29 columns.

The intersection of a row and a column is called a **cell**. Each cell in the spreadsheet can be identified by its **cell reference (cell address)**. The cell reference is simply the column position and the row position combined. For example, the address F6 means that the cell is in column F and row 6. Notice that cell A6 in Figure 10.3 is currently surrounded by a border. This border, or **cell pointer**, identifies the **active cell**, which is the cell in which any information entered from the keyboard will be stored.

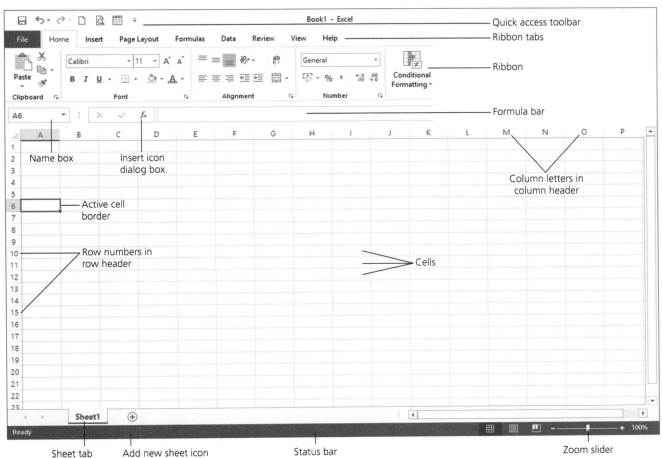

Figure 10.3 Some elements of the Excel 2016 window

Basic concepts

A cell can contain one of three types of information: label (text), value (number) or formula.

* A **label** can be used as a title or heading to describe an aspect of the worksheet. Although a label can contain any string of characters (letters or numbers), it must start with a character that does not indicate a formula or number. A label cannot be used in a calculation.
* A **value** is a piece of data that can be used in a calculation.
* A **formula** is an instruction to perform operations on values. Depending on the package you are using, a formula must start with one of these special symbols: +, −, @, = to identify it as a formula. All formulae in Excel start with an equal sign (=).

Navigating around worksheets

Table 10.1 shows some short-cut keys to help you navigate around a worksheet.

Table 10.1 Short-cut keys to help you navigate around a worksheet

Mouse click	Click any cell with your mouse
Cursor keys on keyboard	Use the cursor keys to move in the direction of the arrow one cell at a time
Enter	Moves one cell down
Tab	Moves one cell to the right
CTRL+HOME	Moves back to cell A1
HOME	Moves to the first cell in a row
CTRL+END	Moves to the last cell in the worksheet
PgDown	Moves one screen down in a worksheet
PgUp	Moves one screen up in a worksheet
F5	Moves to a designated cell

Entering data

Before you can place data in a cell, you need to select the cell. You can do this by simply moving the cursor to the cell and clicking the left mouse button or by using the arrow keys. Notice that when you type data, it is displayed in the entry line of the formula bar, as well as in the cell itself, as you enter it. The data enters the cell when keys such as the Enter key or arrow keys are pressed.

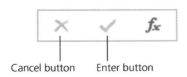

Cancel button   Enter button

Figure 10.4 Excel formula bar

Once you start entering data, the formula bar buttons (Cancel and Enter) are activated (see Figure 10.4).

After you have typed all the data you need into a cell, you need to confirm the data entry. This means that you have to say the data should stay in this cell. You can do this in various ways. One way is to click on the Enter formula bar button. If you make a mistake while you are entering data, click the Cancel button on the formula bar to discard the entry and clear the cell. This will also switch off the formula bar buttons. Alternatively, press the ESC key on the keyboard.

Confirming data entry

As you learned earlier, you can click the Enter button on the formula bar to confirm entry. However, there are also other ways to do this. The method that you use will depend on where you wish to type next. Table 10.2 summarises the different methods of confirming data entry and to where the position of the active cell will move in each instance.

Table 10.2 Methods of confirming data entry

Method of confirming entry	Position of active cells
Enter button on formula bar	Active cells remain the same
Enter key on keyboard	Cell below original becomes active
Tab key on keyboard	Cell to right of original becomes active
One of four cursor keys on keyboard	Cell in direction of cursor key becomes active
Click any other cell in worksheet (do not use this method when entering formulae)	New cell clicked becomes the active cell

Activity 1

Entering labels and values

Table 10.3 shows the names of the top five cricketers in the Hitters Cricket Club, along with their total scores in each of the five matches they played against other teams. Enter the data shown in Table 10.3 in a worksheet.

Table 10.3 Data for Activity 1

	A	B	C	D	E	F
1				Hitters Cricket Club		
2						
3				Top 5 Cricketers		
4	Players	Match 1	Match 2	Match 3	Match 4	Match 5
5	Vinai Birbal	45	60	59	109	85
6	Damian Small	65	75	120	84	20
7	Jason Brown	85	62	75	56	95
8	Gordon King	55	94	76	103	51
9	Cameron Gayle	90	56	45	78	165

Here is how it is done.

1 Select **D1** and type 'Hitters Cricket Club'.

2 Select **D3** and type 'Top 5 Cricketers'.

3 Select cell **A4** and type 'Players'.

4 Now that you know what to do, enter the remaining labels and the values in the appropriate cells.

5 Save the worksheet as 'Top Cricketers' on your flash drive. Use the same method you used to save documents in Word.

Figure 10.5 shows the completed worksheet for Activity 1.

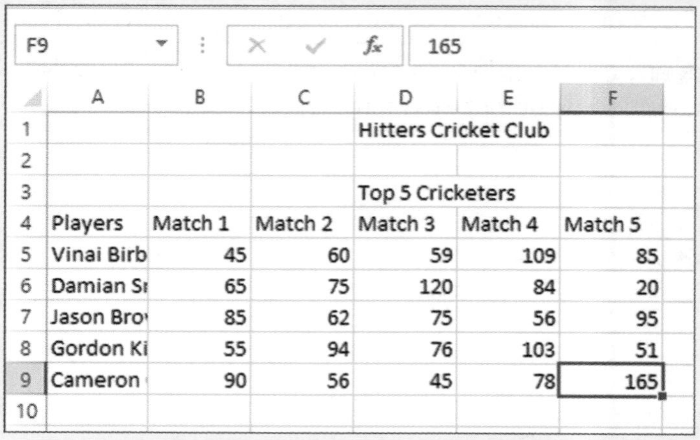

F9 | 165

	A	B	C	D	E	F
1				Hitters Cricket Club		
2						
3				Top 5 Cricketers		
4	Players	Match 1	Match 2	Match 3	Match 4	Match 5
5	Vinai Birb	45	60	59	109	85
6	Damian Sı	65	75	120	84	20
7	Jason Bro	85	62	75	56	95
8	Gordon Ki	55	94	76	103	51
9	Cameron	90	56	45	78	165
10						

Figure 10.5 Completed worksheet for Activity 1

Formatting

After entering the data, notice that the numbers move to the right of the cells, and the labels (text) move to the left. These alignments occur automatically (by default), but you can change them if needed.

Default formatting

Excel applies the following defaults to data that is entered:

* Text is automatically left aligned; 'text' includes a string of numerical characters that includes hyphens or spaces, such as telephone numbers.
* Numbers are automatically right aligned.
* Text is 11-point Calibri by default. If you type text that exceeds the width of a column it will appear to flow into the next cell if that cell is empty. If the next cell is not empty the text that does not fit into the cell will be hidden.

Changing the alignment of a cell or cells

Follow these steps to change the alignment of a cell or cells.

1 Select the cell(s).

2 Click the **Home tab**.

3 Select the option you require from the **Alignment group**. The Alignment group has many options to change the way text is displayed in a cell (see Figure 10.6).

4 More options are available from the Alignment launcher (bottom right-hand arrow in the Alignment group), which will display the Format Cells dialog box (see Figure 10.11).

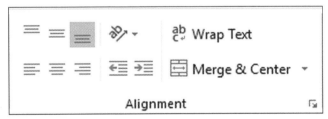

Figure 10.6 Excel Alignment group

Using formatting, you can control the appearance of cells and of the worksheet in general. We have already looked at one aspect of formatting – the alignment of the contents of cells. We will now look at other aspects of formatting.

Resizing columns and rows

Columns and rows may be resized in the following ways:

* Click and drag
* Autofit
* The cells group.

Resizing with click and drag

You can change the height of each row and width of each column in a worksheet using the mouse. When you move the mouse pointer between the row and column headings, it changes shape to a two-way arrow, as shown in Figure 10.7. When the two-way arrow appears, click and drag to the desired position. For example, to increase or decrease the width of column A, click between the A and B column headings and drag either to the right or left to the position you require.

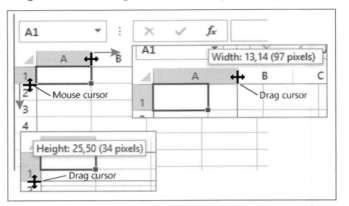

Figure 10.7 Resizing a column/row using click and drag

Resizing with autofit

You can double-click the right boundary of the column heading to **autofit** a column. To autofit a row, you can double-click on the lower boundary of the row heading. Excel then 'looks' at all the entries in the column or row and resizes the column or row to match the width or height of the longest or tallest entry.

Resizing using the cells group

From the **Home tab**, select **Format** from the **Cells group** then select **Width** (or **Height**) from the drop-down menu (see Figure 10.8). When the Column Width dialog box appears (see Figure 10.9), enter an exact measurement. Note that only a value between 0 and 255 will be accepted.

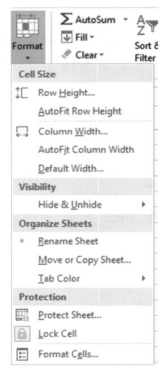

Figure 10.8 Options to change row height and column width

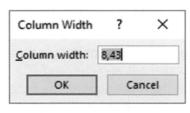

Figure 10.9 Column Width dialog box

To retrieve a worksheet

Follow these steps to retrieve a worksheet from a USB device or hard disk:

1   Pull down the **File** menu.

2   Select **Open**. The 'Open' dialog box appears.

3   Choose the appropriate location where the document is stored. For example, 'Recent' appears in the far right column and shows a list of recent worksheets you may have worked on. Other options include 'One drive' or 'Computer' where you can access your hard disk (C:), USB (E:) – from the window.

4   Double-click the icon of the selected worksheet or click the icon once and then click **Open**.

Wrapping text

The 'Wrap text' option allows a label that is more than one word and that exceeds the width of a cell to move to another line in the same cell. For example, the label in cell D1 in Figure 10.12 on page 161 is wrapped.

How to wrap text

Follow these steps to wrap text:

1   Select the cell or cells.

2   Click the **Home tab**.

3   Select the **Wrap Text icon** from the Alignment group.

Basic editing

If you make a mistake when entering data into a cell, you can easily change the data or remove it entirely.

Changing the contents of cells

Follow these steps to change the contents of a cell by editing inside the cell or formula bar:

1   Click once in the cell requiring the edit.

2   Click inside the text in the formula bar (a cursor or insertion point appears in the formula bar). Edit the contents.

3   Confirm the entry using any of the methods outlined earlier.
    Or:
    Double-click on the cell to open it for editing and edit directly in the cell, and then confirm the entry.

Deleting the content of cells

Follow these steps to delete the content of cells:

1   Select the cell or cells.

2   Click **Delete** from the Cells group in the Home tab (see Figure 10.10).

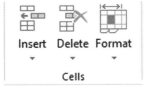

Figure 10.10 Cells group

Activity 2

Retrieve or create the spreadsheet shown in Figure 10.5. You are required to do the following:

1 Resize column 1 so that the names of all the players are fully displayed.

2 Change the contents of cell B6 from 65 to 75. Perform the edit within the cell.

3 Centre align all the values.

4 Change the orientation of the labels in cells B4, C4, D4, E4 and F4 to 45 degrees.

5 Wrap the label in cell D1.

6 Re-save the worksheet.

Here is how it is done.

1 Place the cursor between columns A and B (wait until the cursor changes into a double arrow pointing left and right (←|→) and double-click.

2 Double-click on cell **B6**. The cursor appears in the cell. Edit the number.

3 Select the cells B5 to F10. Select the **Centre align shortcut icon** on the Alignment group of the Home tab.

4 Select the cells **B4** to **F4**.

5 From the Home tab click on the **Alignment launcher** (bottom right-hand arrow in the Alignment group), which will display the Format Cells dialog box (see Figure 10.11).

6 Click the **Up-arrow** in the Degrees box in the Orientation pane until you reach 45 degrees. Click **OK**.

7 Select the cell **D1**. Click the **Wrap text box** in the Text control pane on the Alignment group. Click **OK**.

8 Click the **Save icon** or select **Save** from the File menu.

Activity 2 continued

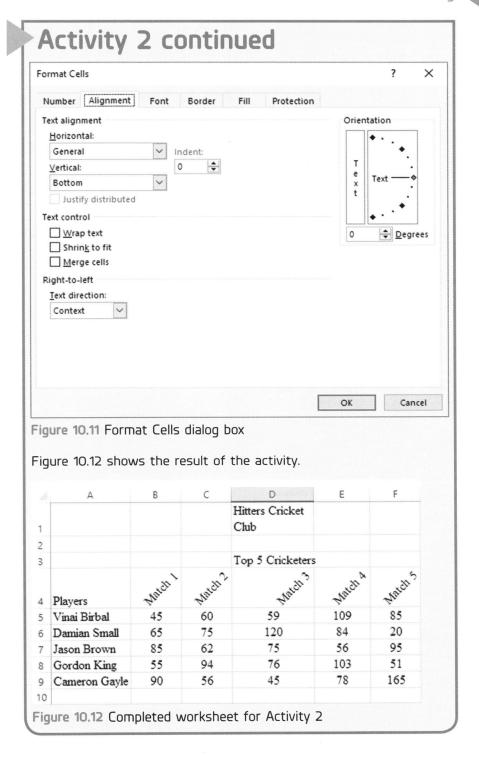

Figure 10.11 Format Cells dialog box

Figure 10.12 shows the result of the activity.

	A	B	C	D	E	F
1				Hitters Cricket Club		
2						
3				Top 5 Cricketers		
4	Players	Match 1	Match 2	Match 3	Match 4	Match 5
5	Vinai Birbal	45	60	59	109	85
6	Damian Small	65	75	120	84	20
7	Jason Brown	85	62	75	56	95
8	Gordon King	55	94	76	103	51
9	Cameron Gayle	90	56	45	78	165
10						

Figure 10.12 Completed worksheet for Activity 2

Inserting and deleting rows and columns

A row or column can be inserted between existing rows or columns. You can also delete rows and columns.

Inserting a row

Follow these steps to insert a row:

1   Click on a cell in the row below the row where you want the new row to go.

2   **Home tab / Cells group / Insert Sheet Rows**.

Inserting a column

Follow these steps to insert a column:

1   Click on a cell in a column to the right of the column where you want the new column to go.

2   **Home tab / Cells group / Insert Sheet Columns**.

3   If you wish to insert more than one row or column, for Step 1 select the exact number of rows or columns you require and then carry out Step 2.

OR use this alternative method:

Click on the column. Right click and click **Insert**. Choose the entire column from the dialog box.

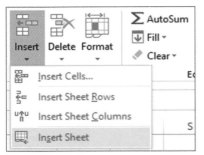

Figure 10.13 Inserting cells, rows or columns

Deleting a row or column

Follow these steps to delete a row or column:

1   Click on a cell or cells in the row or column that you want to delete.

2   **Home tab / Cells group / Delete Sheet Rows** or **Delete Sheet Columns**.

OR use this alternative method:

Click on the row column. Right click. Click **Delete**.

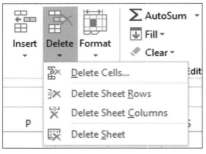

Figure 10.14 Deleting cells, rows or columns

Figure 10.15 Insert dialog box

Inserting rows and columns using the right-click method

Follow these steps to insert rows and columns using the right-click method:

1   Select the whole row(s) or column(s) to the right, or below, of where you want to enter the new one.

2   Right-click anywhere in the selected area.

3   The 'Insert' drop-down menu shown in Figure 10.15 appears. Select **Entire row** or **Entire column** as desired.

4   To delete a row or column, follow the same procedure as above and click **Entire row** or **Entire column** when the 'Delete' dialog box appears.

Activity 3

Retrieve the 'Top Cricketers' worksheet and do the following:

1 Insert a column between column A and B.

2 Delete the content of cell A4 and replace with the label 'Surname',

3 Insert the label 'First Name' in cell B4.

4 Delete row 7.

5 Place the surnames of the players in column A and their first names in column B.

6 Insert the following details for a new player between rows 5 and 6. Hall Gary 65, 45, 76, 124, 87

7 Re-save the worksheet.

Here is how it is done.

1 Click on any cell in column B. Select **Home tab / Cells group / Insert Sheet Columns.**

2 Move to cell A4. Double click the cell. Delete 'Players' and type in 'Surname'.

3 Move to cell B4 and type 'First Name'.

4 Click on a cell or cells in row 7.

5 Select **Delete Sheet Rows** from the Cells group in the Home tab.

6 Click on a cell in row 6.

7 Select **Home tab / Cells group / Insert Sheet Rows**.

8 Type in the required data for Gary Hall.

9 Re-save the spreadsheet.

Figure 10.16 shows the completed worksheet for Activity 3.

	A	B	C	D	E	F	G
1					Hitters Cricket Club		
2							
3					Top 5 Cricketers		
4	Surname	First Name	Match 1	Match 2	Match 3	Match 4	Match 5
5	Birbal	Vinai	45	60	59	109	85
6	Hall	Gary	65	75	120	84	20
7	Small	Damian	85	62	75	56	95
8	King	Gordon	55	94	76	103	51
9	Gayle	Cameron	90	56	45	78	165
10							

Figure 10.16 Completed worksheet for Activity 3

Formatting numbers

Another aspect of formatting relates to the way in which numbers are represented. For instance, some standard formats as shown in Figure 10.17 are the following:

* **General:** Used if you want no specific number format
* **Number:** Used for general display of numbers (decimal places and negative)
* **Currency:** Used to represent monetary values (for example, $5 810.54)
* **Accounting:** Used for lining up currency symbols and decimal points.
* **Percentage:** The percentage formats display the number multiplied by 100 with a percentage sign (%) to the right of the number. For example, .407 is displayed as 40.7%.
* **Date and time:** Dates and times in Excel can be displayed in various ways. Use this option to insert the date and time from the different formats available into your worksheet.

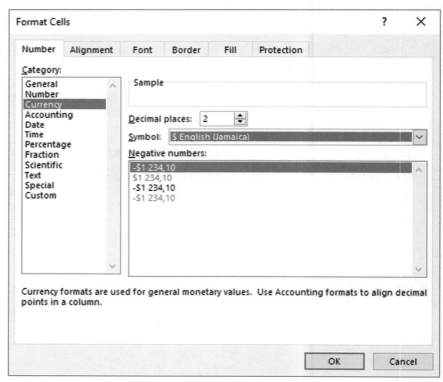

Figure 10 .17 Format Cells dialog box

Formatting cells for currency data

Follow these steps to format cells for currency data:

1   Highlight the cell or cells to be formatted.

2   If your chosen currency is not shown in the Number group of the Home tab, click the **Number group dialog box launcher**. The Format Cells dialog box will appear, as shown in Figure 10.17.

Shortcut: Highlight the cell or cells that you want to format as currency data, and click the **Currency icon ($)** in the Number group of the Home tab shown in Figure 10.18.

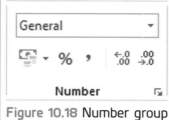

Figure 10.18 Number group

3 Select the **Number tab**, and then select **Currency** from the displayed list categories.

4 Choose the number of decimal places and the currency symbol you want to use.

Changing the font style or size in a worksheet

Follow these steps to apply another font style or size to your entire worksheet:

1 Click the first cell in the worksheet (cell **A1**).

2 Press **Ctrl+Spacebar**, and then press **Shift+Spacebar**.

3 Click the arrow next to the font name and select another font type.

4 Click the arrow next to the font size and select another font size.

Adding borders and colour to a cell

Adding borders and colours can make it easier to show the differences between different sets of data in a spreadsheet. Follow these steps to add colour to a cell:

1 Select the cell(s) to which you would like to add colour.

2 Select **Home tab** / **Font group** / **Fill colour**. Choose from the options available.

Follow these steps to add border(s) to a cell:

1 Select the cell(s) to which you would like to add the border(s).

2 Select the **Home tab** / **Font group** / **Borders** option. Choose from the border options provided.

Merging and centring a heading

Follow these steps to merge and centre a heading:

1 Select the heading and the cells in which you would like to centre the heading.

2 Select the **Home tab** / **Alignment group** / **Merge & Centre** option.

Editing

As part of editing a worksheet, you can copy data using several different methods:

Copying data

It is possible to copy data from cell(s) to cell(s) within a worksheet, across to a different worksheet or even to a different workbook. There are different ways in which you can do this.

Note!

* When you Copy, and then use the Paste command, the data remains on the clipboard so that you can repeat the paste many times. The cell containing the original data will have a broken line around it indicating that the data is still on the clipboard. To get rid of the broken lines around the cell containing the original data and remove the data from the clipboard, press the ESC key.

* If you use the Cut command when moving data, or if you use the Enter key to paste data you have copied, you will find that you can only paste once, as the data does not remain on the clipboard. If you want to paste again, you will have to copy or cut again.

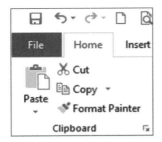

Figure 10.19 Commands in the Clipboard group

Cutting, copying and pasting commands

Follow these steps to cut, copy and paste data.

1   Select the cell or cells you want to cut or copy to other cells.

2   Select the **Cut** or **Copy icon** from the Clipboard group of the Home tab (see Figure 10.19).

3   Select the cell or the first cell of the cells where you wish to copy the data.

4   Select the **Paste icon**.

Filling down

Follow these steps to fill down:

1   Select the cell that has the data you wish to copy.

2   Click on the bottom right-hand corner of the cell (fill handle), as shown in Figure 10.20 and drag down or across as desired. The value in the first cell will be copied to all the cells selected.

	A	B	C	D
1	Surname	Firstname	Health Surcharge	
2	Ali	Imam	20	
3	Blake	Keron		
4	Boldon	Tony		
5	Crater	Ian		
6	Dalton	Kerry		
7				20
8				

Figure 10.20 Spreadsheet cells selected to be filled using the fill handle

Working with worksheets

By default, each new workbook is provided with three worksheets (Sheet 1, Sheet 2 and Sheet 3) of which the active worksheet is always white. These sheets allow you to keep varied and large amounts of information together in one workbook. To move from worksheet to worksheet, click on the worksheet tab at the bottom of the screen for the worksheet you require.

Inserting, deleting and renaming worksheets

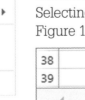

Figure 10.21 Worksheet drop-down menu

Right-click one of the worksheet tabs and then select the command you require from the drop-down menu shown in Figure 10.21. Any inserted worksheet will be given a default name, for example, Sheet 4. Selecting **Rename** allows you to change the name of the worksheet. Figure 10.22 shows Sheet 1 renamed as '1st Quarter Report'.

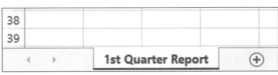

Figure 10.22 Renamed worksheet

Activity 4

Create the worksheet shown in Figure 10.23.

1 Insert the details of a new employee between rows 4 and 5:
Surname – McLoclanding, First name – Johnathan,
Position – Mason

2 Insert a column to the left of column A.

3 Type the label 'Worker ID' in cell A1.

4 Input the following worker ID numbers for the nine workers.
Starting from the first worker: 10, 11, 12, 13, 14, 15, 16, 17, 18.

5 Resize all columns to make all the data visible.

6 Insert the label 'Health Surcharge' in cell E1.

7 Input the value 20 for each worker in the Health Surcharge column.

8 Format the Health Surcharge values as currency.

9 Delete row 4.

10 Change the name of the worksheet to 'Salary'.

11 Save the worksheet as 'Payroll'.

	A	B	C
1	Surname	Firstname	Position
2	Abbot	John	Supervisor
3	Alexis	Mark	Carpenter
4	Brown	Kerry	Carpenter
5	Berch	Tom	Mason
6	Cameron-Brown	Phillip	Labourer
7	Hugh-Bailey	Shane	Mason
8	Dobson	Jonny	Labourer
9	Henry	Lelsie	Labourer

Figure 10.23 Worksheet for Activity 4

Here is how it is done.

1 Place the cursor anywhere in row 5. Click **Home tab** and then click **Insert** from the Cells group. Click the **Insert Sheet Rows** option. Enter the data in the appropriate cells. (**Home tab / Cells group / Insert menu / Insert Sheet Rows option**).

2 Select any cell in column A. Click **Home tab** and then click **Insert** from the **Cells group**. Click the **Insert Sheet Columns** option. Enter the data in the appropriate cells. (**Home tab / Cells group / Insert menu / Insert Sheet Columns option**).

3 Select cell **A1** and input the label 'Worker ID'.

4 Select cell **A2**. Type '10' and press **Enter**. Continue entering the other Worker ID numbers.

5 Place the cursor between column B and column C. Double-click the mouse.

6 Select cell **E1**. Type in the label 'Health Surcharge'.

7 Select cell **E2** and enter the number '20'. Using the fill handle at the bottom right corner of the cell, drag to fill the cells for each worker.

8 Select the cells **E2** to **E10**. Click on the **dollar sign ($)** in the formatting toolbar or click **Home tab / Number group / click the down arrow / Currency**.

9 Place the cursor anywhere in row 4. Click **Home tab** then click **Delete** from the **Cells group**. Click the **Delete Sheet Rows** option. (**Home tab / Cells group / Delete menu / Delete Sheet Rows option**).

10 Right-click **Sheet 1**. Select **Rename**. Type 'Salary'.

Figure 10.24 shows the completed worksheet for Activity 4.

	A	B	C	D	E
1	Worker ID	Surname	Firstname	Position	Health Surcharge
2	10	Abbot	John	Supervisor	$ 20.00
3	11	Alexis	Mark	Carpenter	$ 20.00
4	13	Mc Loclanding	Jonathan	Mason	$ 20.00
5	14	Berch	Tom	Mason	$ 20.00
6	15	Cameron-Brown	Phillip	Labourer	$ 20.00
7	16	Hugh-Bailey	Shane	Mason	$ 20.00
8	17	Dobson	Jonny	Labourer	$ 20.00
9	18	Henry	Lelsie	Labourer	$ 20.00

Figure 10.24 Completed worksheet for Activity 4

Formulae

Formulae are used to perform calculations using data contained in the cells and to display the results. Some features of a formula include the following:

∗ A formula is entered in the cell in which the result is to be displayed.

∗ A formula begins with an equals sign (=).

∗ A formula includes **arguments** (such as cell references, text or numbers) and **operators**. Operators are mathematical symbols that are used in formulae. Here are some examples of operators used in formulae.

Addition	+	Division	/
Subtraction	–	Exponentiation	^ (raising to a power)
Multiplication	*		

∗ After a formula has been confirmed in a cell, only the calculation result is displayed in that cell; the formula will be displayed in the formula bar. If you double-click on a cell containing a formula, the full formula will be displayed and will be ready for you to edit.

BODMAS rule

An expression in a formula in a spreadsheet package follows the same order of precedence as for normal arithmetic. This means that whatever is within brackets is performed first, followed by exponentiation, and then multiplication and/or division, and then addition and/or subtraction.

Figure 10.25 shows examples of various formulae applied to the values in the cells A3 to B7. Figure 10.26 shows the results of applying the formulae.

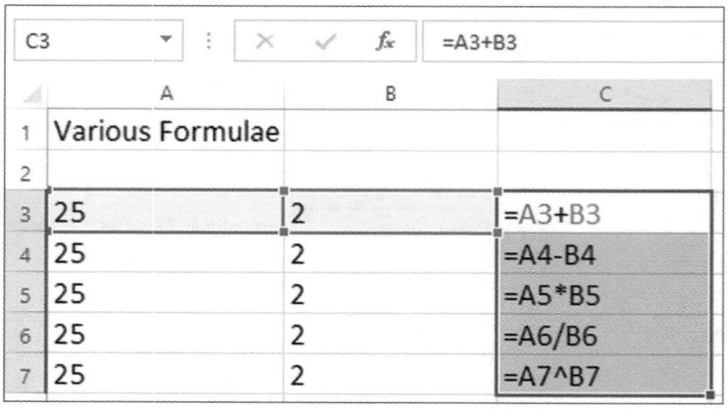

Figure 10.25 Examples of various formulae

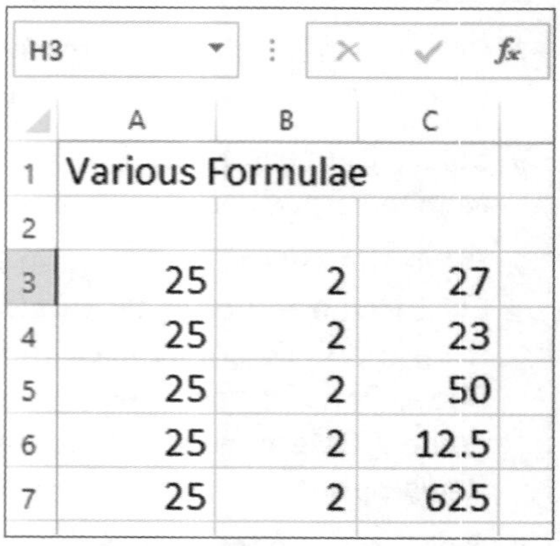

Figure 10.26 Results of applying various formulae

▶Activity 5

The worksheet in Figure 10.27 on the next page shows the sales and expenditure for the first quarter of 2018 for the Optimum Trading Company. You are required to calculate the following:

1 The profit before tax for each month

2 The tax on the profit, which is set at 15%

3 The profit after tax

4 The percentage of profit (profit %) made each month

5 The total for sales, expenditure, profit before tax, tax, profit after tax and profit percentage

6 Format the cells B5:F8 as currency and G5:G8 as %.

Here is how it is done.

1 Select cell **D5** and type the formula =B5–C5. Copy this formula to cells D6 and D7.

2 Select cell **E5** and type the formula =.15*D5. Copy this formula to cells E6 and E7.

3 Select cell **F5** and type the formula =D5–E5. Copy this formula to cells F6 and F7.

4 Select cell **G5** and type the formula =F5/B5. Copy this formula to cells G6 and G7.

5 Select cell **B8** and type the formula =B5+B6+B7. Copy the formula to cells C8, D8, E8, F8 and G8.

6 a Select the cells **B5:F8**, Click on the **dollar sign ($)** in the Number group from the Home tab or click **Home tab / Number group / Currency** (click the down arrow in the combo box).
   b Select the cells **G5:G8**.
   c Select **percentage (%)** sign in the Number group from the Home tab or click **Home tab / Number group / Percentage** (click the down arrow in the combo box).

Did you know?

To calculate the formula for the percent profit in cell G5 of Figure 10.27, we did not write the formula as you would do in mathematics, namely:

=F5/B5 * 100

If you wrote the formula like this, the result would be expressed in the cell just as a number without a percentage symbol. If you format it to 'per cent' at this point, it would be multiplied by 100. Therefore, when you write your formula to calculate percentages, you must remember to leave the formula expressed just as a fraction and not multiply by 100.

Activity 5 continued

Figure 10.27 shows the formulae used to create the worksheet.

	A	B	C	D	E	F	G
1				Optimum Trading Company			
2	Quarterly Sales Report						
3							
4		Sales	Expenditure	Profit before Tax	Tax (15%)	Profit after Tax	Profit %
5	January	456852	154275	=B5-C5	=0.15*D5	=D5-E5	=F5/B5
6	February	654587	256478				
7	March	554587	268975				
8	Corporate	=B5+B6+B7					

Figure 10.27 Worksheet showing formulae for Activity 5

It is important to note that the formula includes the *cell addresses* and not the values that are currently in the cells. If you type the values themselves, the re-calculation feature of the spreadsheet package would not work.

For example, typing the formula =456852 + 654587 + 554587 in cell B8 would give the correct answer for the 'Corporate' sales but the re-calculation feature would not work. If any of the values in the cells were changed, the total in cell B8 would remain the same. If the value in cell B5 were changed from 456852 to 556852, the formula =456852 + 654587 + 554587 in cell B8 would remain unchanged, which would result in the wrong total for the new value in cell B5.

However, when we use cell addresses in a formula, any changes to the content of a cell that forms part of a formula results in immediate adjustments to any cell that depends on the value that was changed.

Figure 10.28 shows the completed worksheet for Activity 5.

J15			fx				

	A	B	C	D	E	F	G
1				Optimum Trading Company			
2	Quarterly Sales Report						
3							
4		Sales	Expenditure	Profit before Tax	Tax (15%)	Profit after Tax	Profit %
5	January	$ 456,852.00	$ 154,275.00	$ 302,577.00	$ 45,386.55	$ 257,190.45	56%
6	February	$ 654,587.00	$ 256,478.00	$ 398,109.00	$ 59,716.35	$ 338,392.65	52%
7	March	$ 554,587.00	$ 268,975.00	$ 285,612.00	$ 42,841.80	$ 242,770.20	44%
8	Corporate	$ 1,666,026.00	$ 679,728.00	$ 986,298.00	$ 147,944.70	$ 838,353.30	

Figure 10.28 Completed worksheet for Activity 5

Functions

There are easier and faster methods to find the total of a group of cells. The **SUM** function could do the same task as the formula we used in Activity 4 to calculate the total sales for the first quarter. A **function** is a *predefined* formula in Excel that can:

* automatically calculate results
* perform worksheet actions
* assist with decision-making based on the information provided in your worksheet.

Functions fall into several categories, including the following:

* **Math and Trig:** This category includes functions for computing totals, square roots, tangents, and so on.
* **More Functions:** This category includes functions for statistical analysis, engineering, cube, and so on.
* **Financial:** This category includes functions for computing loan repayments, rates of return, depreciation, and so on.
* **Date and Time:** This category includes functions for computing the number of days in a specific date interval, the number of hours in a specific time interval, and so on.

The SUM function

The **SUM** function starts with an equals (=) sign, followed by the word '**SUM**', an open bracket, the arguments and a closing bracket. An argument is the information passed to a function, on which it operates. The general form of the **SUM** function is as follows:

Function   Arguments

=SUM(first cell:last cell)

The worksheet in Figure 10.30 on the next page shows the first-quarter sales figures for the five branches of Home Makers Furniture Store in North, South, Central, East and West branches. To find the total sales for the North branch for the period January to March, we need to find the total of cells B5, C5 and D5. The formula would be =B5+C5+D5 or, using the **SUM** function, the formula to put into cell E5 will be =**SUM**(B5:D5). Whenever we want to add up the values of a column or row of continuous cells, we can use the **SUM** function. Every time cell E5 is highlighted, the content box will show the formula.

If we wanted to find the total for the South branch for the period January to March, we would now have to go to cell E5 and type out another formula. The formula would be =B6+C6+D6 or =**SUM**(B6:D6). The formula to calculate the total for the Central branch would be =**SUM**(B7:D7) and for the East branch would be =**SUM**(B8:D8) and for the West branch it would be =**SUM**(B9:D9). Notice that the formula is almost the same for each branch except that the cell addresses are different. So instead of making us type out five different formulae, the package lets us copy the original formula to the other cells. The structure of the formula remains the same, but the addresses of the cells used in the formula will change relative to the position of the formula. This feature is called **relative cell referencing (addressing)**.

AutoSum button

Another way to easily sum a row or column of cells is to use the AutoSum button (see Figure 10.29). You can use the AutoSum function in either of these ways:

1 Click in the cell where you want the result to appear: in this case, the first vacant cell under the five cells we are summing (B10).

2 Click the **AutoSum** button [Σ].

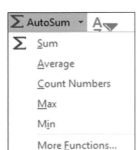

Figure 10.29 AutoSum and options

Using the AutoSum function

Follow these steps to use the AutoSum function.

1 **Home tab/Editing group/Click on the Σ AutoSum icon**.

2 Figure 10.29 shows the other functions available if the arrow in the icon is clicked.

3 Check the formula entered by Excel, to ensure that the correct cell or cells have been chosen. If Excel has selected an incorrect cell or cells, simply click and drag to select the correct cells.

4 Confirm the entry.

Or:

1 Select the cells or cells to be added and also the cell where you wish to place the formula. In this case it will be cells B5:B10, as shown in Figure 10.30.

2 Click the **AutoSum** button. In this case, the formula is entered and confirmed automatically.

	A	B	C	D	E	F	G
1				Home Makers Furniture Store			
2							
3		First Quarter Report					
4		January	February	March			
5	North	26500	22442	23456			
6	South	45600	23246	67543			
7	Central	34568	29687	46578			
8	East	78540	98755	65981			
9	West	53546	94786	65847			
10	Corporate	238754					

Figure 10.30 Worksheet showing the use of AutoSum

Using the Insert Function button

Follow these steps to use the Insert Function button.

1   Click in the cell where you want the result to appear. Using the worksheet in Figure 10.30, this is the first vacant cell under the five cells we are summing (B10).

2   Click the **Formulas tab**.

3   Click the **Insert Function** button in the Function Library group. The 'Insert Function' dialog box appears as shown in Figure 10.31.

4   Select the **SUM** function from the 'Insert Function' dialog box and click **OK**. The 'Function Arguments' dialog box appears.

5   Check that the correct cell or cells are selected for summing. Here, the cells B5:B9 should be displayed.

6   If an incorrect cell has been selected, move the 'Functions Arguments' dialog box out of the way if necessary, select the correct cells with your mouse, and then click **OK** on the dialog box.

The resulting formula will appear identical to the formula constructed by the previous methods.

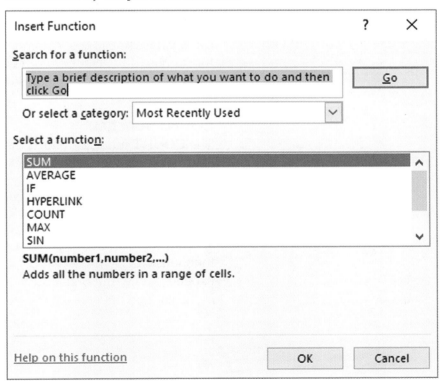

Figure 10.31 Insert Function dialog box

Other functions

Other functions include the:

* AVERAGE function
* MAX function
* MIN function
* COUNT function.

AVERAGE function

The **AVERAGE** function is used to find the mean of a set of values. The general form of the function is =AVERAGE(first cell:last cell). For example, if you want to find the average of the cells A2 to A9, the formula would be =AVERAGE(A2:A9). You can enter the AVERAGE function into a worksheet either manually or by expanding the AutoSum button and selecting the AVERAGE option in the list that appears.

MAX function

The **MAX** (maximum) function is used to find the largest value in a set of values in a row or column. The general form of the maximum function is =MAX(first cell:last cell). For example, if you want to find the largest value in the cells A2 to A9, the formula would be =MAX(A2:A9).

MIN function

The **MIN** (minimum) function is used to find the smallest value in a set of values in a row or column. The general form of the minimum function is =MIN(first cell:last cell). For example, if you want to find the lowest value in the cells A2 to A9, the formula would be =MIN(A2:A9).

COUNT function

The **COUNT** function returns the number of entries in its argument list that represent numbers. For example, if you want to count the amount of number values in the cells A2 to A9, the formula would be =COUNT(A2:A9). The COUNT function does not count blank cells or labels.

As with the AVERAGE function, the MAX, MIN and COUNT functions can be entered into a worksheet either manually or by expanding the AutoSum button and selecting the appropriate option in the list that appears.

Interpreting formula error messages

Error messages will appear when you use incorrect syntax or try to do something that prevents Excel from calculating the formula. Some common examples of error messages are shown in Table 10.3.

Table 10.4 Some common formula error messages

#####	This means that the column is not wide enough to display the value. Use any of the methods described earlier to widen the column to allow the value to display.
#DIV/0!	The formula is attempting to divide by zero. Check the values of the cell in the formula.
#NAME?	Excel does not recognise text in a formula. Check the spelling of your function or check that a name exists.
#NUM!	This appears when Excel encounters a problem with the number in the formula, such as the wrong type of argument in an Excel function or a calculation that produces a number too large or too small to be represented in the worksheet.
#REF!	This appears when Excel encounters an invalid cell reference, such as when you delete a cell referred to in a formula or paste cells over the cells referred to in a formula.
CIRCULAR	The formula is referencing itself. The cell reference containing the formula is also part of the formula.
#VALUE!	Occurs when the wrong type of operand or argument is used.

Whenever an error message appears, you will also see a green marker in the top left of the cell (see Figure 10.32). If you click on the cell to select it, an information symbol will appear. Click on this symbol to display a drop-down menu, which offers you many choices including a 'Help on this error' option that will take you to a help file explaining the message error in detail.

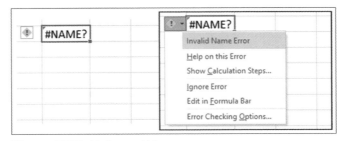

Figure 10.32 Help on this error menu

Activity 6

Retrieve or create the worksheet 'Home Makers' (Figure 10.30).

1 Change the label 'First Quarter Report' to 'First Quarter Sales Report'.

2 Insert the label 'Expenditure' in cell F4.

3 Enter the following expenditure for each branch:

Branch	Expenditure
North	25000
South	32056
Central	30123
East	54345
West	45632

4 Calculate the following:

a The amount of tax paid if the profit is taxed at 15%
b The after-tax profit
c The corporate totals for every column
d The greatest after-tax profit, that is, the store that performed best
e The lowest after-tax profit, that is, the store that performed worst
f The mean after-tax profit across all the stores
g The number of branches processed.

5 Format all monetary values as currency.

Here is how it is done.

1 Retrieve the worksheet 'Home Makers'.

2 Select cell **B3**. Change 'First Quarter Sales' to 'First Quarter Sales Report.

3 Select **F4**. Enter the label 'Expenditure'.

4 Enter the expenditure data in the appropriate cells.

5 Select cell **G4**. Enter the label 'Profit before tax'.

6 Change the width of the cell to accommodate the label.

7 Select cell **G5**. Enter the formula =E5-F5. Copy the formula down to G10.

8 Select cell **H4**. Enter the label 'Tax on Profit' and change the column width.

9 Select cell **H5**. Enter the formula =G5*.15. Copy the formula down to H10.

Activity 6 continued

10 Select cell I4. Enter the label 'Profit after Tax' and change the column width.

11 Select cell I5. Enter the formula =G5-H5. Copy the formula down to I10.

12 Select cell **B10**. Enter the formula =Sum(B5:B9). Copy the formula across to I10.

13 Highlight or mark off the cells B5 to I10. Change the number format to currency.

14 Select cell **A10**. Enter the label 'Maximum Profit'.

15 Select cell **B10**. Enter the formula =Max(I5:I9).

16 Select cell **A14**. Enter the label 'Minimum Profit'.

17 Select cell **B14**. Enter the formula =Min(I5:I9).

18 Select cell **A15**. Enter the label 'Average Profit'.

19 Select cell **B15**. Enter the formula =Average(I5:I9).

20 Select cell **A16**. Enter the label 'Branches Processed'.

21 Select Cell **B16**. Enter the formula =Count(I5:I9).

22 Highlight B9 to B15. Change the number format to currency.

23 Save the worksheet.

After completing steps 1 to 23, the worksheet should look like Figure 10.33.

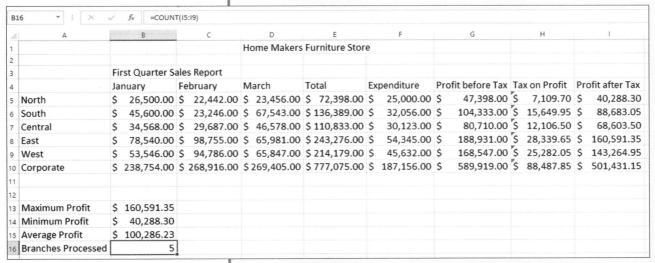

B16		✗ ✓ fx	=COUNT(I5:I9)						
	A	B	C	D	E	F	G	H	I
1				Home Makers Furniture Store					
2									
3		First Quarter Sales Report							
4		January	February	March	Total	Expenditure	Profit before Tax	Tax on Profit	Profit after Tax
5	North	$ 26,500.00	$ 22,442.00	$ 23,456.00	$ 72,398.00	$ 25,000.00	$ 47,398.00	$ 7,109.70	$ 40,288.30
6	South	$ 45,600.00	$ 23,246.00	$ 67,543.00	$ 136,389.00	$ 32,056.00	$ 104,333.00	$ 15,649.95	$ 88,683.05
7	Central	$ 34,568.00	$ 29,687.00	$ 46,578.00	$ 110,833.00	$ 30,123.00	$ 80,710.00	$ 12,106.50	$ 68,603.50
8	East	$ 78,540.00	$ 98,755.00	$ 65,981.00	$ 243,276.00	$ 54,345.00	$ 188,931.00	$ 28,339.65	$ 160,591.35
9	West	$ 53,546.00	$ 94,786.00	$ 65,847.00	$ 214,179.00	$ 45,632.00	$ 168,547.00	$ 25,282.05	$ 143,264.95
10	Corporate	$ 238,754.00	$ 268,916.00	$ 269,405.00	$ 777,075.00	$ 187,156.00	$ 589,919.00	$ 88,487.85	$ 501,431.15
11									
12									
13	Maximum Profit	$ 160,591.35							
14	Minimum Profit	$ 40,288.30							
15	Average Profit	$ 100,286.23							
16	Branches Processed	5							

Figure 10.33 Worksheet after Activity 6 is complete

Absolute cell references

As we saw earlier, you can copy a formula to other cell(s) in a row or column and let Excel change the formula relative to the position of the cell(s) (relative cell reference).

However, there are situations where you do *not* want Excel to adjust the cell references when a formula is copied from one location to another. To prevent the cell references in a formula from changing, place a dollar ($) sign before and after the column. These are called **absolute cell references**.

In Figure 10.35, the values of B1 and B2 remain unchanged no matter where they are copied or moved in the worksheet.

▶ Activity 7

A store owner would like to build a worksheet to calculate the final selling price of each item in his store. First, he first adds a mark-up of 20% to the cost price, to produce the marked-up price. Then he adds on 15% value-added tax (VAT) to the marked-up price to get the final selling price.

	A	B	C	D	E
1	**Mark UP**				
2	**VAT**				
3					
4	**Item**	**Cost Price**	**Marked-Up**	**Vat**	**Final Selling Price**
5	Hat	$ 20.00			
6	Shirt	$ 75.00			
7	Pants	$ 235.00			
8	Jersey	$ 145.00			
9	Shoes	$ 225.00			

Figure 10.34 Worksheet for Activity 7

You are required to do the following:

1 Create the spreadsheet shown in Figure 10.34.

2 Calculate the 'Marked-up' price.

3 Calculate the 'VAT' on the 'Marked-up' price.

4 Calculate the 'Final selling price'.

Activity 7 continued

Here is how it is done.

The values for Mark–Up and VAT are placed at the top of the worksheet, so that they can be easily changed.

1   Enter the data as shown in Figure 10.34.

2   Move to cell C5. Type the formula =B5+ (B5* B1).

3   Copy the formula to cells C6, C7, C8 and C10.

4   Move to cell D5. Type the formula =C5 * B2.

5   Copy the formula to cells D6, D7, D8 and D10.

6   Move to cell E5. Type the formula =C5 + D5.

7   Copy the formula to cells E6, E7, E8 and E10.

Figure 10.35 shows the various formulae used to calculate the 'Final selling price'. Figure 10.36 shows the completed worksheet for the activity.

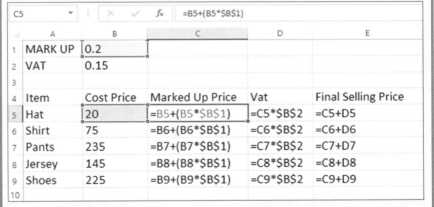

C5			fx	=B5+(B5*B1)	
	A	B	C	D	E
1	MARK UP	0.2			
2	VAT	0.15			
3					
4	Item	Cost Price	Marked Up Price	Vat	Final Selling Price
5	Hat	20	=B5+(B5*B1)	=C5*B2	=C5+D5
6	Shirt	75	=B6+(B6*B1)	=C6*B2	=C6+D6
7	Pants	235	=B7+(B7*B1)	=C7*B2	=C7+D7
8	Jersey	145	=B8+(B8*B1)	=C8*B2	=C8+D8
9	Shoes	225	=B9+(B9*B1)	=C9*B2	=C9+D9
10					

Figure 10.35 Various formulae for calculating a final selling price

C5			fx	=B5+(B5*B1)	
	A	B	C	D	E
1	MARK UP	20%			
2	VAT	15%			
3					
4	Item	Cost price	Marked-up price	VAT	Final selling price
5	Hat	$ 20.00	$ 24.00	$ 3.60	$ 27.60
6	Shirt	$ 75.00	$ 90.00	$ 13.50	$ 103.50
7	Pants	$ 235.00	$ 282.00	$ 42.30	$ 324.30
8	Jersey	$ 145.00	$ 174.00	$ 26.10	$ 200.10
9	Shoes	$ 225.00	$ 270.00	$ 40.50	$ 310.50
10					

Figure 10.36 Completed worksheet for Activity 7

Sorting

To 'sort' means to arrange cells in order. A typical spreadsheet package enables you to sort data (text or numbers) into ascending or descending order. If you do not specify an order, the rows and columns are sorted in ascending order (lowest to highest). This means the lowest is at the top of the sheet and the highest is at the bottom. The opposite applies for descending order.

Data can be sorted in a number of ways. For example, a teacher who enters the names of students and end-of-term marks for five subjects can sort the column of names into alphabetical order, with the students' marks being moved accordingly, as well. The teacher could also create a worksheet to rank the students according to a particular subject, again with a corresponding movement of all the other rows.

When sorting a list of data, most spreadsheet packages use the following guidelines:

* Rows with blank cells are placed at the bottom of the sorted list.
* Hidden rows are not moved.
* Numbers used as text are sorted before text alone.

Sorting data

Follow these steps to sort data:

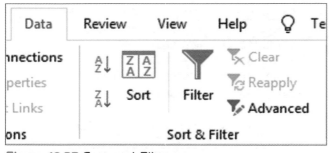

Figure 10.37 Sort and Filter group

1 Select the cells you would like to sort.

2 Click on the **Data tab**.

3 Click on the desired **AZ** or **ZA Sort icon** (ascending or descending) in the Sort & Filter group (Figure 10.37). The table will be sorted.

4 For more complex sorting options, click the **Sort icon**. The Sort dialog box appears as in Figure 10.38.

Sorting using multiple criteria

You may need to sort the data in a worksheet by more than one field. For example, a bookstore may want to sort all their books by author's name. The owner may then want to sort each author's books alphabetically by title. The sorting procedure for a multiple sort is exactly the same as that for a single criterion, except that after the first criterion is selected, you then move down to a second sort field and add additional sort criteria.

Sorting using multiple criteria

Follow these steps to sort using multiple criteria:

1   Select the cells you would like to sort.

2   Click on the **Data tab**.

3   Click the **Sort icon**. The Sort dialog box appears as in Figure 10.38.

4   In the 'Sort by' box, select the primary column (first field) by which you want your data sorted.

5   Click in the **Order box** and select **A-Z** or **Z-A**

6   If you wish to sort a second column click the 'Add Level' button at the top of the Sort dialog box.

7   Click in the **Order box** and select **A-Z** or **Z-A**.

8   If you wish to sort a third column, repeat steps 5 and 6.

9   Click **OK**.

Figure 10.38 Sort dialog box

Creating graphs and charts

An important feature of any spreadsheet package is the ability to convert worksheet data into one of many graphical forms. Graphs and charts are very useful because they:

* simplify numerical data that may otherwise be confusing
* make the data easier to interpret
* grab your attention almost instantly
* allow information to be assimilated quickly.

Therefore charts can be important tools for data analysis and the presentation of data.

Chart types and their uses

Each of the following chart types has a different use:

* **Column charts:** These charts compare numerical values for several categories. A column chart is used when the order of the categories is not important.
* **Bar charts:** These charts also compare numerical values for several categories. However, a bar chart is used when the category text is long or the category being shown is 'Duration'. A chart to compare the time taken for different journeys is a good example of this type of use.
* **Line graphs:** These charts show trends – how one category changes compared to another. They plot the data as a series of points, and then link those points with a line so that you can estimate values between the ones recorded. For example, line graphs are used to show how a population has changed over time, or the amount of liquid that was in a bucket as it was poured in over time.
* **Pie charts:** These charts show categories as the proportions of a whole. The quantities in the particular category of interest are added up and then each one is turned into a percentage.

How to create a chart

The first step in creating a chart is to select the data values you want to place in it. A spreadsheet package enables you to plot any row or column of data against any other row or column of data. For example, if you want to represent the first-quarter sales for the months of January to March for the five branches of the Home Maker's Furniture Store for the values shown in Figure 10.33, you need to select the cells A4:D9.

After selecting the data values, you need to select a type of chart that is relevant to the situation. The type of chart you choose depends on the type of data you have and how you would like to represent it. Some charts are best for representing certain types of data. For example:

* the data that represents sales of different branches of a company over a specified period may be displayed using a column graph
* data that represents portions of a whole might best be represented using a pie chart.

If any values in the data selected are changed after the chart has been created, the changes are immediately reflected in the chart. Also, more data can be inserted between the first and last rows or columns. These changes will also be automatically included in the chart. Before creating a chart, make yourself familiar with the elements of a chart. Figure 10.39 shows a completed chart for the first-quarter sales of the Home Maker's Furniture Store.

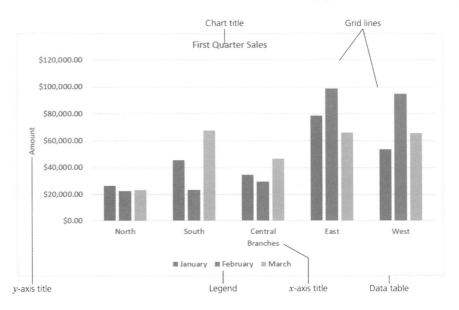

Figure 10.39 Sales chart with its elements named

Chart elements

A chart can include the following elements:

* **Axes:** These are the vertical and horizontal lines against which data is plotted. The *x*-axis is referred to as the **category axis** and the *y*-axis is known as the **value axis**.
* **Data range:** This is the data selected to create the chart.
* **Series:** These are the row or column headings that make up the cells of values from the worksheet that is used to create the graph.
* **Titles:** There are three titles: for the chart, category axis and value axis. They are lines of text used to describe the chart elements.
* **Gridlines:** These are incremental lines that may appear along each axis; they help you to read values from the graph more easily.
* **Legend:** This is a cross-reference to show each series is represented in the chart, that is, a key.
* **Data labels:** These are the actual values, percentages or names given to a bar or segment in a chart.
* **Data table:** These are the cells of values that are included at the bottom of the chart used to chart the graph.

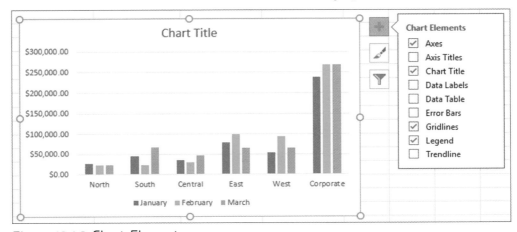

Figure 10.40 Chart Elements

Creating a chart in Excel

Creating a chart using Excel's Chart options is a very simple process.

1   Select the data in the worksheet to be used to create the chart. Select **Insert tab / Charts group** (see Figure 10.41) and choose the type of chart from those is displayed. Click the **Arrow button** to launch the Insert Chart dialog box (see Figure 10.42) for more options. Clicking the **All Charts tab** displays other chart options (see Figure 10.43).

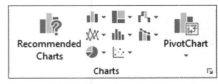

Figure 10.41 Insert tab, showing options on the Charts group

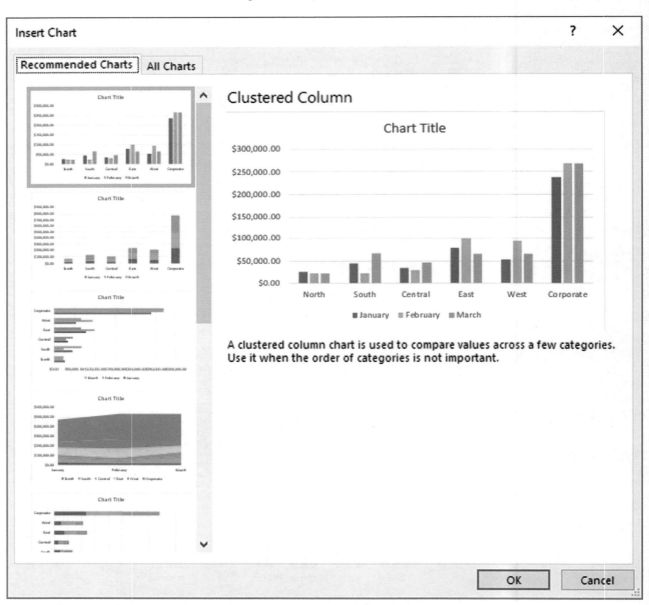

Figure 10.42 Recommended charts tab in the Insert Chart dialog box

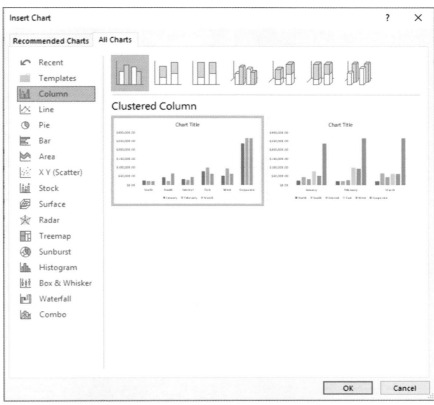

Figure 10.43 All charts tab in the Insert Chart dialog box

2 Select the type of chart you require from the options provided.

3 **Chart Design:** The Design tab shown in Figure 10.44 provides a number of options to change the features of the chart, such as titles, labels, legends, data tables, axes, gridlines, and many more. The following groups are provided: Chart Layouts, Chart Styles, Data, Type and Location.

Figure 10.44 Chart Styles group from the Design tab

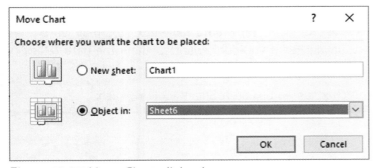

Figure 10.45 Move Chart dialog box

4 **Chart Location:** You can choose where the chart is placed. Click the **Move Chart** icon located in the Location group at the end of the Chart Tools Design tab (see Figure 10.44). The Move Chart dialog box appears (see Figure 10.45). Make the appropriate selections.

Activity 8

Use the worksheet in Figure 10.46 to create a column graph to show the first-quarter sales for the Home Maker's Furniture Store.

◢	A	B	C	D	E
1			Home Maker's Furniture Store		
2		January	February	March	Total
3	North	$ 26,500.00	$ 22,442.00	$ 23,456.00	$ 72,398.00
4	South	$ 45,600.00	$ 23,246.00	$ 67,543.00	$ 136,389.00
5	Central	$ 34,568.00	$ 29,687.00	$ 46,578.00	$ 110,833.00
6	East	$ 78,540.00	$ 98,755.00	$ 65,981.00	$ 243,276.00
7	West	$ 53,546.00	$ 94,786.00	$ 65,847.00	$ 214,179.00
8	Corporate	$ 238,754.00	$ 268,916.00	$ 269,405.00	$ 777,075.00

Figure 10.46 Worksheet to form the basis of a graph

Here is how it is done.

1 Select the cells **A2** to **D7**.

2 Click on the **Insert tab**.

3 From the **Chart group**, select the type of chart you require by clicking on the **Down** arrow and selecting from the options.

4 Click the **Add Chart** elements option from the Chart Layout group. Click the **plus +** sign, and the Chart Elements dialog box appears.

5 For each tab, do the following:

- **Titles:** In the 'Chart title' field, type 'FIRST QUARTER SALES'. In the 'Category (X) axis' field, type 'Branches'. In the 'Value (Y) axis' field, type 'Amount'.
- **Axes:** Ensure the 'Category (X) axis' and the 'Value (Y) axis' boxes are checked, and check the **Automatic radio button**.
- **Gridlines:** Check **Value (Y) axis: Major gridlines**.
- **Legend:** Check the **Placement: Right radio button**.
- **Data Labels:** Check the **None radio button**.
- **Data Table:** Check the **Show data table box**. (You may leave the box unchecked if you don't want to show the data table.) Click **Next**.

6 Leave the chart as an object in Sheet 1. Click **Finish**.

Activity 8 continued

The chart created by this process is shown in Figure 10.47.

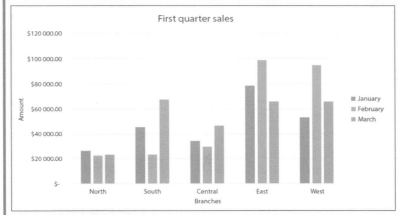

Figure 10.47 A graph showing the first quarter sales

Activity 9

Create a pie chart to represent the total sales for the five branches.

Here is how it is done.

1 Select columns **A3** to **A7** and **E3** to **E7**. (Select the cells **A3** to **A7**. Then hold down the **Ctrl** key and select the cells **E3** to **E7**.)

2 Click on the **Chart Wizard icon**.

3 With the Standard Types tab displayed, select **Pie** from the 'Chart type' box. Then select the first chart from the 'Chart sub-type' box. Click **Next**.

4 Select the **Series tab**. Type 'Total Sales' in the 'Name' field. Click **Next**.

5 On the **Titles tab**:

- In the 'Chart title' field, type 'First Quarter Total Sales'. (There are no other options available in this tab.)
- On the Data Labels tab, check the **Percentage button**.

6 Click **Next**. Click **Finish**.

The pie chart produced should look like Figure 10.48.

Figure 10.48 A pie chart of total sales

Figure 10.49 Print pane

Printing a worksheet

Printing allows you to get a hard copy of your worksheet. However, before you print an Excel workbook, it is important to decide exactly what information you want to print. For example, if you have multiple worksheets in your workbook, you need to decide if you want to print the **entire workbook** or only the **active worksheets**. There may also be times when you want to print only a **selection** of content from your workbook.

You need to access the Print pane from the File menu to print an entire workbook, an active worksheet or a selection from a worksheet.

Accessing the Print pane

Follow these steps to access the Print pane:

1   Select **File tab/Print**.

2   The Print pane will appear (see Figure 10.49).

Printing active worksheets

Worksheets are considered active when selected. Follow these steps to print active worksheets:

1   Select the worksheet you want to print. To print multiple worksheets, click the first worksheet, hold down the **Ctrl key** on your keyboard, and then click any other worksheets that you want to select.

2   Navigate to the Print pane.

3   Select **Print Active Sheets** from the Print Cells drop-down menu (see Figure 10.50).

4   Click the **Print button**.

Printing an entire workbook

Follow these steps to print an entire workbook:

1   Navigate to the Print pane (see Figure 10.50).

2   Select **Print Entire Workbook** from the Print Cells drop-down menu.

3   Click the **Print** button.

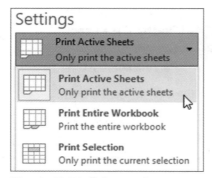

Figure 10.50 Print options

Printing a selection

Follow these steps to print a selection from a worksheet:

1   Select the cells you want to print.

2   Navigate to the Print pane.

3   Select **Print Selection** from the Print Cells drop-down menu.

4   A preview of your selection will appear in the Preview pane.

5   Click the **Print** button to print the selection.

6   If you prefer, you can also set the print area in advance so that you are able to visualise which cells will be printed as you work in Excel. Simply select the cells you want to print, click the **Page Layout tab**, select the **Print Area command**, and then choose **Set Print Area**.

The importance of importing and exporting data between and among software applications

Excel is part of the Microsoft Office, which is an integrated software package. One of the key advantages of an integrated package is the ability to share information between and among its applications.

For example, Excel lets you easily import textual data into an Excel workbook. This capacity means that anything you can get as a text file – such as a financial report generated by an accounting system – can be imported into Excel and then examined.

Excel can also be used to bring information from various files and documents together, so that it exists in a single location. It is possible to import text, images and tables into Excel.

You can also retrieve data from an Access table to an Excel spreadsheet, which means that you can use the business graphing capabilities of Excel to create a pie chart, a bar chart, or whatever kind of chart is suitable for your data. Alternatively Excel data can also be exported to a Word document, so that you can easily add charts and graphs to a report.

Summary 10

1 A spreadsheet package is an application package that can be used for any job that involves repetitive numerical calculations. It is a large grid divided into rows and columns. The intersection of a row and a column is called a cell. Each cell is identified by its cell reference (column and row position). A cell can hold one of three kinds of information: label (text), value (number) or formula.

2 Formulae are used to perform operations on numbers. A formula must start with an equals (=) sign, which is followed by numbers, different operators or cell references that are part of the calculation. Excel also contains built-in functions for performing calculations, including:

* =SUM(First cell:Last cell). Finds the sum of a row or column of numbers.
* =MAX(First cell:Last cell). Finds the maximum value in a row or column of numbers.
* =MIN(First cell:Last cell). Finds the minimum value in a row or column of numbers.
* =AVERAGE(First cell:Last cell). Finds the mean of a row or column of numbers.

3 Formulae usually contain cell addresses and not the values in the cell, so that if a value is changed in a cell, all the values in the dependent cells will be automatically updated. This is referred to as 'automatic re-calculation'.

4 A formula can be copied or moved from one cell to another cell or to a range of cells. When the formula is moved, all cell references in the formula change with respect to the formula's new cell location. This is called 'relative cell addressing'. However, it may be necessary to move or copy a formula but keep the cell reference in the formula fixed. This is done using absolute cell referencing.

5 Most of the editing features available in a word processor are also available in Excel – for example, 'Delete', 'Cut', 'Copy', 'Paste', 'Find' and 'Replace'.

6 Formatting enables you to control the appearance of cells and the worksheet in general. Commands that control the formatting can be triggered from the toolbar or from the Format pull-down menu. Formatting includes:

* Alignment of cells (left-, centre- or right-justified)
* Representation of numbers (general, number, currency, accounting)
* Changing the column width, row height, font size and style and including borders and patterns.

7 A group of continuous cells that form a square or a rectangle is called a range of cells and is identified by the addresses of the first and last cells. You can use a single command to affect a range of cells. For example, a range of cells can be formatted for currency, or the contents of the cells can all be centre-justified, by selecting the cells and using one command.

8 A spreadsheet enables data to be sorted in ascending or descending order according to the content of one or more fields.

9 Excel enables users to convert worksheet data easily into a wide range of graphs. Simply select the data cells that you want to use to create the graph and then follow the steps using the Chart Wizard.

10 Worksheets can be printed using the printer icon in the Standard menu or using Print in the File menu.

Questions 10

Copy and fill in the blanks questions

1 A spreadsheet uses _____ to carry out operations on the numerical data.

2 The _____ bar displays the contents of the active cell.

3 The _____ box identifies the active cell.

4 The intersection of a row and a column is called a _____.

5 A _____ is a piece of data that can be used in a calculation.

6 A _____ can be used as a title or heading to describe an aspect of the worksheet.

7 The _____ key moves to the first cell in a row in Excel.

8 A formula in Excel includes _____ (such as cell references, text or numbers) and _____.

9 A _____ is a predefined formula in Excel that can automatically calculate results.

10 The _____ function is used to find the mean of a set of values.

11 The _____ function is used to find the largest value in a set of values in a row or column.

12 The _____ function returns the number of entries in its argument list that represent numbers.

13 A _____ error occurs when the cell reference containing the formula is also part of the formula.

14 An _____ is the information passed to a function, on which it operates.

15 The first step in creating a chart is to select the data _____ to place in it.

True or false questions

1 A spreadsheet package is an application package.

2 When you save an Excel file, it is given the file extension '.doc'.

3 A workbook initially contains four worksheets.

4 The Title bar displays the name of the program, as well as the name of the current workbook if it has been saved.

5 The rows in a spreadsheet run up and down and are numbered, while the columns run left to right and are lettered.

6 Each cell in the spreadsheet can be identified by its cell reference.

7 All formulae in Excel start with a plus sign (+).

8 An Excel formula is an instruction to perform operations on values.

9 Clicking the Tab key in Excel will move from the current active cell to the first cell in a row.

10 Numbers are automatically left aligned in Excel.

11 To autofit a column, double-click the right boundary of the column heading.

12 Formatting relates to the way in which numbers are represented in Excel.

13 An expression in a formula in a spreadsheet package follows the same order of precedence as for normal arithmetic.

14 A worksheet may be sorted using multiple criteria.

15 Incremental lines that may appear along each axis of a graph to help you to read values from the graph more easily are known as gridlines.

Multiple-choice questions

1 Which one of the following applications may require the use of a spreadsheet?

a Creating a flyer

b Editing a picture

c Preparing end-of-term school reports

d Editing a video

2 Which one of the following is a formatting feature in Excel?

   a Editing and deleting contents of cells

   b Inserting and deleting rows and columns

   c Copying and moving data within a worksheet

   d Changing the alignment of cells

3 Which of the following default justifications is applied when textual data is entered in a spreadsheet?

   a Right

   b Left

   c Centre

   d Justified

4 Which of the following represents a cell that is used in absolute cell referencing?

   a A5

   b !A5

   c A5

   d A!5

5 Which of the following number formats would you use for lining up currency symbols and decimal points?

   a General

   b Currency

   c Number

   d Accounting

6 Which of the following is true about an Excel formula?

   a Begins with an @ sign

   b Includes arguments

   c Cannot contain brackets

   d Does not follow the same order of precedence as for normal arithmetic

7 Four numbers are stored in cells A1, B1, C1 and D1 of an Excel spreadsheet. Which of the following formula would **not** calculate the average of the numbers?

   a =(A1+B1+C1+D1)/4

   b =AVERAGE(A1:D1)

   c =A1+B1+C1+D1/4

   d =SUM(A1:D1)/4

8 Which of the following means that the column is not wide enough to display the value?

   a #####

   b #NAME?

   c #NUM!

   d #VALUE!

9 Which of the following is **not** true about sorting data in Excel?

   a Data can be sorted in ascending and descending order.

   b Rows with blank cells are placed at the bottom of the sorted list.

   c Hidden rows are not moved.

   d Numbers used as text are sorted after text alone.

10 The actual value, percentage or name of a bar or segment of a chart created in Excel is referred to as a:

   a gridline.

   b data label.

   c data table.

   d legend.

Short-answer questions

1 Explain how a spreadsheet can be used in the following places:

   a The home

   b At school

   c The club

2 Describe what is meant by the following and give examples to illustrate your answer.

   a Cell

   b Cell reference

   c Label

   d Value

   e Formula

   f Worksheet

   g Workbook

3 Write down the formula you would put in a cell to do the following:

   a Add cells A3, D3 and E3 together.

   b Subtract B5 from D6.

   c Multiply cell F1 by C5.

   d Divide cell G4 by H8.

   e Find 8% of cell E10.

   f Add the cells B2 to B10 inclusive.

   g Find the average of the cells from C3 to C10.

   h Find the maximum value from the cells D3 to D40.

   i Find the minimum value from the cells D3 to D40.

   j Add the cells B3, C4 and D4, and then divide the total by A1.

4 You need to find the total of the cells A1 to A8 inclusive and store the value in A10. Explain three ways in which to do this.

5 Explain the difference between relative cell referencing and absolute cell referencing.

6 List the guidelines that Excel uses when sorting text in terms of blank cells, numbers used with text and hidden rows.

7 Explain the meaning of these error messages:

   a #####

   b #NAME?

   c #REF!

   d CIRCULAR

Worksheet questions

1 Create the spreadsheet shown in Figure 10.51.

   a Insert a formula in cell D4 to calculate the area of the square.

   b Insert a formula in cell D7 to calculate the area of the rectangle.

   c Insert a formula in cell D10 to calculate the area of the circle.

   d Insert a formula in cell D9 to calculate the area of the triangle.

	A	B	C	D	E	F
1				Area Generator		
2						
3	Square	Length of side		Area		
4		15				
5						
6	Rectangle	Length	Breadth	Area		
7		22	13			
8						
9	Circle	Radius		Area		
10		8				
11						
12	Triangle	Base	Altitude	Area		
13		14	19			

Figure 10.51

2 The worksheet shown in Figure 10.52 shows the names and starting balance of some customers of the People's Bank. Each customer is paid 3% interest on their starting balance. Create the worksheet shown in Figure 10.52 and complete the following:

a Calculate the interest that each customer earns.

b Calculate the 'Year End Balance' of each customer.

c Format the cells with currency and two decimal places.

d Change the starting balance for Larry Adams to 54600.

e Insert the details for the new customer Jerry Ben who deposited $15 674 between customers Birbal and Balfour.

	A	B	C	D	E	F
1				The People's Bank		
2						
3	Surname	First Name	Starting Balance	Interest Rate	Interest Earned	Year End Balance
4	Adams	Larry	45600	3%		
5	Balfour	Marie	76259			
6	Birbal	Varun	58648			
7	Chin-Fat	Gary	125648			
8	Douglas	Sheena	54782			
9	Henry	Ria	35489			
10	Jackson	Penny	75146			
11	Mason	Joseph	12467			

Figure 10.52

3 The spreadsheet in Figure 10.53 shows the prices of various items at different supermarkets located in different parts of Trinidad. You are required to do the following:

a Create the spreadsheet shown in Figure 10.53.

b Display the highest, lowest and average price of each item.

c Create a bar chart to compare the prices of baked beans from each supermarket. Label the chart appropriately.

J6				fx				
	A	B	C	D	E	F	G	H
1				Price Survey				
2								
3	Item	Brand	Weight	Supermarket North	Supermarket South	Supermarket East	Supermarket West	Supermarket Central
4	Toothpaste	Coolgate	200g	25.65	23.65	25.75	24.75	23.95
5	Toothpaste	Coolgate	400g	19.95	19.75	19.85	18.65	18.45
6	Soap	Luxury	200g	13.5	13.25	13.45	13.25	13.75
7	Sardines	Oceans	250g	13.95	13.74	13.65	13.25	13.09
8	Baked Beans	Salad	400g	19.95	19.75	19.35	19.05	18.95
9								
10								
11	Item	Brand	Weight	Maximum Price	Minimum Price	Average Price		
12	Toothpaste	Coolgate	200g					
13	Toothpaste	Coolgate	400g					
14	Soap	Luxury	200g					
15	Sardines	Oceans	250g					
16	Baked Beans	Salad	400g					

Figure 10.53

4 The spreadsheet in Figure 10.54 shows the income and expenses for the first six months of the year in 2018 for Ms Jennifer Grant.

a Create the spreadsheet shown in Figure 10.54.

b Insert a row between rows 1 and 2.

c Bold all the headings.

d Insert a column between columns A and B.

e Change the font size of the entire worksheet to 12.

f Centre justify all the headings.

g Enter the label 'Total Income' in cell A7.

h Insert a formula in cell C7 to calculate the total income for the month of January.

i Copy the formula to calculate the total income for the other months.

j Enter the label 'Monthly Expenditure' in cell A17.

k Enter a formula in cell C17 to find the total expenses for the month of January.

l Copy the formula to cell H17 to find the total expenses for the other months.

m Enter the label 'Item Total' in cell I10.

n Enter a formula in cell I10 to find the total amount spent on Phone for the first six months of 2018.

o Copy the formula down to cell I17.

p Enter the label 'Balance after expenses' in cell A20.

q Enter formulae to calculate the balance after expenses for each month.

r Format the numbers as currency.

s Create a bar chart to show the total amount of money spent on clothes over the six months period.

t Create a pie chart to show the total amount of money spent on each item for the entire period.

u Save the worksheet as 'Half-year expenses 2018'.

	A	B	C	D	E	F	G
1					Income 2018		
2		January	February	March	April	May	June
3	Salary	20115	20115	20115	20115	20115	20115
4	Investment returns	5467	5467	5467	5467	5467	5467
5	Part-time salary	6345	6345	6345	6345	6345	6345
6							
7					Expenses 2018		
8	Expenses	January	February	March	April	May	June
9	Phone	865	823	950	810	874	915
10	Electricity	600	620	600	650	610	720
11	Gas	1500	1550	1525	1400	1495	1530
12	Groceries	5000	5000	5000	5000	5000	5000
13	Rent	3000	3000	3000	3000	3000	3000
14	Car expenses	1300	300	500	650	1500	300
15	Clothes	2300	1500	1400	1200	800	1324
16	Miscellaneous	1500	1000	1800	1600	1400	1200

Figure 10.54

Research questions

1 Do research to find out how a spreadsheet can be used to help with teaching these subjects:

a Mathematics

b Agricultural Science

c Business Studies

You are required to give examples to show how the spreadsheet package will be used.

2 Do research on the internet to explore low-fat menus and various exercise programmes.

a Compare calories from a healthy home-cooked meal to a fast-food meal.

b Create a spreadsheet to calculate the total calories consumed and the total exercise with calories burned.

Crossword

Down

1 An option that allows labels consisting of more than one word and that exceed the width of a cell to move to another line in the same cell

2 A type of line that makes it easier to read the values from a chart

4 When formatting numbers, you can use this if you do not want a specific number format

Across

3 A function that allows you to find the mean of a row or column of cells

5 The location data is held when you Copy, and then use the Paste command in Excel

6 A function that can be used to find the largest value in a row or column

STEM project

You conducted an agricultural science experiment in which you have measured the height in centimetres of six seedlings on a weekly basis over an eight-week period. The measurements you made are as follow:

Seedling A: 2, 3, 4, 4.5, 5, 6, 7, 8

Seedling B: 1, 2, 2.5, 3, 3.7, 4.2, 4.5, 5, 7

Seedling C: 1.5, 2.5, 3.5, 4.5, 5, 5.5, 6.5, 7.5

Seedling D: 2, 3, 4, 5, 6, 7, 8, 10

Seedling E: 0.5, 1, 1.5, 2, 2.5, 3, 3.5, 4

Seedling F: 2, 3.5, 4.5, 5.5, 6.5, 7.7, 8.9, 11.

Use an Excel spreadsheet to record your data. You have been asked to calculate the growth rates of each of the six seedlings and compare them. You need to present your findings to the class and discuss the possible reasons for the differences in the growth rates. You may use a bar chart as part of your presentation.

1 What is the most appropriate title for your spreadsheet?

2 In a step-by-step approach, explain how you plan to create your spreadsheet (and bar chart).

3 Produce your spreadsheet and bar chart. Write a list of possible reasons for the different growth rates.

4 Compare your spreadsheet (and bar chart) with that of a classmate. Discuss your reasons for the different growth rates of the seedlings. What do you both discover?

Hints

1 What are the factors affecting the growth of seedlings?

2 Revise the steps in producing an Excel spreadsheet before doing this question.

3 How can your spreadsheet be useful to students doing a similar project in the future?

Digital citizenship

As citizens of a country, we try to be safe, healthy, law-abiding, and ethical in all our actions. Today, the internet has created a global platform in which billions of people all over the world interact using various technologies. This platform has created a digital society that provides its citizens with opportunities for education, employment, entertainment and social interaction.

Figure 11.1 A digital society provides its citizens with both opportunities and responsibilities.

As in any society, digital citizens are expected to act in a certain way according to accepted norms, rules and laws. Digital citizenship means learning how to use technology in ways that are appropriate, responsible and intelligent. It includes digital literacy, ethics, etiquette, online safety, norms, rights, culture, commerce, among others.

In this chapter, we will look at some of the issues related to being part of a digital society. These include the following:

- ✳ Netiquette
- ✳ Laws relating to computer crimes and cybercrimes
- ✳ Copyright organisations
- ✳ APA and MLA referencing styles.

Figure 11.2 Good netiquette involves asking these questions before posting online.

Did you know?

Flaming is writing content online to intentionally cause responses such as rage, sadness, humiliation and self-doubt.

Figure 11.3 Many countries have laws to protect their citizens and organisations from computer crimes and cybercrimes.

Netiquette

All digital citizens should follow good netiquette in the cyberworld. Here are some tips for practising good netiquette.

* Do not send or post a flame.
* Do not post rude and insulting messages. You may disagree strongly with someone, but do not call them names or threaten them.
* Stay on topic. Do not post about cricket in a football forum.
* Do not post copyrighted material if you do not own the rights.
* Only forward jokes and chain letters if the recipient wants them.
* Do not type in ALL CAPS. This is referred to as 'shouting'. Some people see it as offensive and it is also hard to read.
* Do not share offensive photographs or videos.
* Respect peoples' privacy. Do not post peoples' names, email addresses, photos or personal videos without their permission.
* Forgive other people's mistakes.
* Follow the same standards of behaviour online that you would practise in real life.
* Respect other people's time and bandwidth. Do not send too many large files that take a long time to download.

Laws relating to computer crimes and cybercrimes

The exponential growth in computer and internet usage and mobile devices in the Caribbean, along with the emergence of e-commerce, e-government and other e-services, has resulted in computer crimes and cybercrimes. A **computer crime** is any illegal act that involves the use of a computer or related devices. An illegal act committed online or via the internet is referred to as a **cybercrime**.

An assessment of five Commonwealth Caribbean countries revealed an increase in cybercrime.

In Trinidad and Tobago, the most common forms of cybercrime are:

* automatic teller machine (ATM) 'skimming', where criminals install hidden devices on the ATM to steal people's personal information
* business email compromise, where criminals hack into a company's email account and, by pretending to be the owner, trick company employees or customers into making payments into the attackers' account
* financial phishing scams, which involves criminals obtaining personal financial information such bank account details and pin numbers from people in order to steal money from their bank accounts or credit cards
* ransomware attacks, where criminals trick people into downloading software that then locks or encrypts the files on their computers and the victims have to pay a ransom to have the files unlocked or decrypted
* online character assassinations, where attackers post lies or twisted facts about their victims to damage those people's reputations.

Figure 11.4 Never open or download attachments in unusual emails or emails from people you do not know, as they may contain ransomware.

Reports have also found that people do not report these cybercrimes because they are worried about damaging their reputations and they do not think the authorities can solve the crime. To protect organisations and individuals from computer crimes and cybercrimes, many Caribbean governments are passing laws to deal with these crimes. For example, the Jamaican Cybercrimes Act (2015) regards these actions as illegal and punishable by fines and/or jail sentences:

* **Unauthorised access to computer programs or data:** The law states that anyone who knowingly obtains, for themselves or another person, any unauthorised access to any program or data held in a computer commits an offence.
* **Access with intent to commit or facilitate commission of an offence:** A person who knowingly accesses any program or data held in a computer with the intent to commit or facilitate (make possible) any crime commits an offence.
* **Unauthorised changes to computer programs or data:** Changing programs or data without authorisation is illegal.
* **Unauthorised access or take-over of computer functions or services:** Anyone who knowingly obtains unauthorised access to any computer in order to, directly or indirectly, take-over any computer service or function without permission commits a crime.
* **Unauthorised obstruction of computer operations:** A person who, without permission or any lawful reason, directly or indirectly deliberately causes damage to a computer, affects the operation of a computer or prevents access to any files, data or programs stored on a computer commits a crime.
* **Computer-related fraud or forgery:** A person who, in order to commit a crime or allow a crime to be committed, unlawfully: possesses, receives or manufactures devices or data for sale; or imports, distributes, reveals or makes available a computer, and access code or passwords; or any data or device designed or adapted mainly to commit an offence, commits a crime.
* **Intention to cause loss of property or data:** It is illegal to cause another person to lose property by interfering with data or any function of a computer, or to intend that this altered data be thought of and used as the original data.
* **Use of computer for malicious communication:** A person commits an offence if they use a computer to send data to another person that is offensive or threatening, or that causes annoyance, inconvenience, distress, or anxiety to that person or any other person.
* **Make devices or data available for the commission of an offence:** A person commits an offence if they possess, receive, manufacture, sell, import, distribute, disclose or otherwise make available a computer, a key or any other data or device designed or adapted to commit an offence.

Figure 11.5 A hacker who accesses another person's computer without permission is committing a crime.

In addition to the Cybercrimes Act (2015), the Obscene Publications (Suppression) Act of 1927 makes it illegal for anyone in Jamaica to possess, distribute and publish obscene writings, drawings, photographs and other material.

Copyright organisations

In *Interact with IT* Book 1, you learned about copyright. In this book, you will learn about some organisations in the Caribbean that are responsible for protecting the rights of content creators. The Broadcasting Commission of Jamaica is the statutory body established to monitor and regulate the electronic media in Jamaica. This organisation assesses the media laws and makes recommendations to update these laws based on a changing media framework. The Commission works with the following Jamaican organisations to fulfill its mandate:

* Jamaican Copyright Licensing Agency (JAMCOPY)
* Jamaica Music Society Ltd (JAMMS)
* The Jamaica Association of Authors Composers & Publishers (JACAP)
* Jamaica Reggae Industry Association (JaRIA)
* Jamaica Intellectual Property Office (JIPO).

Under Jamaica's Copyright Act of 1993, copyright applies to original literary, dramatic, musical or artistic works, sound recordings, films, broadcasts or cable programme and typographical arrangements of published editions.

The Jamaican Copyright Licensing Agency (JAMCOPY) is Jamaica's national Reproduction Rights organisation (RRO) and Collective Management Organisation (CMO) for copyright in text and image-based published works. JAMCOPY provides licensing and education solutions that make it easy for businesses, government and educational institutions to manage their copyright compliance efficiently. These solutions include making access easy, and allowing users in these organisations to reuse and share content within the organisation and across national borders.

As a collective management organisation, JAMCOPY is authorised by the creators and publishers of material published in printed and digital format to collectively manage their exclusive rights to publish and reproduce their works in any form. JAMCOPY's main functions are to:

* negotiate licences with users to photocopy or digitise specified portions of text or image-based copyrighted works
* collect royalties from these users
* distribute the royalties to authors and publishers
* educate the public and promote respect for copyright
* take legal action against infringers of members' photocopying rights
* keep members informed about new developments in copyright legislation and administration
* lobby for changes to current legislation to improve protection of members' rights.

In addition, the Jamaica Reggae Industry Association (JaRIA) represents the interests of the reggae industry. The Jamaica Intellectual Property Office (JIPO) is an agency of the Ministry of Industry, Commerce, Agriculture and Fisheries, which registers trademarks, and patents of creative work and protects intellectual property of content and media creators.

Figure 11.6 TTCO protects the copyright of carnival performers under Works of Mas.

Similar to Jamaica, the islands of Trinidad and Tobago also have several copyright organisations. Three of these organisations are:

* Awesome Copyright
* Copyright Music Organisation of Trinidad and Tobago (COTT)
* Trinidad and Tobago Copyright and Collection Organisation (TTCO).

TTCO covers authors and composers under traditional copyright, carnival and other elements under Works of Mas. It also covers performers, producers and broadcasters under neighbouring rights. These organisations perform similar functions to that of the JAMCOPY.

Evaluating web resources

In Book 1, we examined these criteria to evaluate Web resources:

* **Source or publishing body:** Does the source come from a national or international organisation? Does it come from an educational institution?
* **Author:** Can you identify the author of the website? An author can be an individual, company, educational institution, government agency or non-profit organisation. What are the qualifications or credentials of the author? Is the author affiliated with a reputable institution?
* **Objectivity:** Are there biases in the web page? Is this the site of a company selling products or an individual or organisation with a specific agenda?
* **Date (currency):** Is there a date to show when the website was last updated? Are the links from the site up-to-date?
* **Complete (accurate):** Is the website well-researched with all information properly cited? Can the information be verified using other sources?

Applying APA and MLA style of references

In Book 1, you learned how to reference online and offline text material using APA and MLA styles of referencing. In this chapter, we will look at how to use the APA and MLA styles of referencing for materials such as CD-ROM, graphics, sound and video.

Did you know?

The term 'Works cited' is sometimes referred to as 'References'. These terms mean the same thing. Use 'Works cited' when citing sources using the MLA (Modern Language Association) style. Use the title 'References' when citing sources using the APA (American Psychological Association) style.

How to use the APA referencing style

Material	APA reference	APA in-text
CD-ROM (offline)	General format: Author, Initial. (year). Title [CD-ROM]. Place of publication: Publisher. Birbal, R. & Taylor, M. (2008). ICT for Senior High Schools [CD ROM]. Essex: Pearson Education.	Birbal and Taylor (When used as part of a sentence) (Birbal & Taylor, 2008) (Used at the end of a sentence)
Online graphics	Image with author: General format: Figure number. Artist Surname, First Initial. Second Initial. (Year). *Title of the artwork* [Format]. Retrieved from URL. Figure 1. Lynch, P. J. (2006). *Oblique view of Human Heart* [Image]. Retrieved from http://www.interactive-biology.com/75/show-me-a-diagram-of-the-human-heart-here-are-a-bunch/	Lynch (2006)
Online graphics	Image without author: General format: Title of work [Type of work]. (Year image was created). Retrieved from URL The Human Heart [Image]. 2019. Retrieved from https://www.teachpe.com/anatomy-physiology/the-circulatory-system/the-heart	(The Human Heart, 2019)
Online sound	General format: Author Surname, First Initial. Second Initial. OR Author screen name. (Producer). (Year, Month Day {of podcast}). *Title of podcast* [Audio podcast]. Retrieved from URL Smith, C. (Producer). (2017, April 17). *Authenticity* [Audio podcast]. Retrieved from https://www.bbc.co.uk/programmes/b01n7094/episodes/downloads	(Smith, 2017). Smith (2017). Subject to availability and terms of use at https://www.bbc.co.uk/usingthebbc/terms/terms-of-use bbc.co.uk - © copyright [2019] BBC
Online video	General format: Author, A. A. [Screen name]. (year, month day). Title of video [Video file]. Retrieved from http://xxxxx [MrInclusivevacation]. (2016, December13). *Jamaica Tourism* [Video file]. Retrieved from https://www.youtube.com/watch?v=AryUc4Lhnmc	(MrInclusivevacation, 2016)

How to use the MLA style of referencing

Material	MLA reference	MLA in-text
CD-ROM (offline)	General format: Name of Author (if given). "Title of Part of Work." Title of Product. Edition or release, if relevant. Publication medium CD-ROM. City of Publication: Publisher, Year of publication. Birbal, Roland and Taylor, Michele. "Activities" ICT for Senior High Schools. CD-ROM. Essex: Pearson Education, 2008.	(Birbal and Taylor, 2008)
Online graphics	General format: Artist if Available. "Description or Title of Image." Online image. Date of image. <u>Title of Larger Site</u>. Name of Providing Library, Consortium or Library System (if appropriate). Name of organization (if appropriate). Date of download. <http://address.website.org>. Lynch, P, J. "Oblique view of Human Heart." Online image. 2006. <u>Interactive Biology</u>. 2/1/2019. http://www.interactive-biology.com/75/show-me-a-diagram-of-the-human-heart-here-are-a-bunch/	(Lynch, 2006)
Online sound	General format: Creator if Available. "Description or Title of Sound." Date of Sound. Online sound. <u>Title of Larger Site</u>. Date of download.<http://address.website.org>. Smith, C. "Authenticity". (2017, April 17). Online sound. <u>BBC The Digital Human</u>. 2/1/2019. https://www.bbc.co.uk/programmes/b01n7094/episodes/downloads	(Smith, 2017) Smith (2017)
Online video	General format: Last name, First name of the individual who posted the content OR the name of the company who posted it OR the username. "Title of the Video." *Title of the Website*, Name of the Publisher (only include if it is different than the author or title), Date it was posted, URL. MrInclusivevacation. "Jamaica Tourism". YouTube, 13 Dec. 2016, https://www.youtube.com/watch?v=AryUc4Lhnmc	(MrInclusivevacation, 2016)

Summary 11

1 Digital citizenship means learning how to use technology in ways that are appropriate, responsible and intelligent. It encompasses digital literacy, ethics, etiquette, online safety, norms, rights, culture, commerce and many more.

2 Netiquette means respecting other users' views and being polite when posting your views online.

3 A computer crime is any illegal act that involves the use of a computer or related devices.

4 A cybercrime is an illegal act committed online or via the internet.

5 Many countries have passed laws to protect citizens and organisations from computer crimes and cybercrimes.

6 Copyright organisations protect the rights of content creators.

7 Copyright organisations in Jamaica include: The Jamaican Copyright Licensing Agency (JAMCOPY), Jamaica Music Society Limited (JAMMS) and The Jamaican Association of Authors Composers & Publishers (JACAP).

8 CD-ROM, graphics, sound and video can be referenced using APA and MLA styles of referencing.

Questions 11

Copy and fill in the blanks questions

1 _____ citizenship means learning how to use technology in ways that are appropriate, responsible and intelligent.

2 _____ means respecting other users' views and being polite when posting your views online.

3 _____ is writing content online that intentionally invokes responses such as rage, sadness, humiliation and self-doubt.

4 An illegal act committed online or via the internet is referred to as a _____.

5 A _____ crime is any illegal act that involves the use of a computer or related devices.

True or false questions

1 The internet has created a global platform in which billions of people all over the world interact using various technologies.

2 Digital citizens must act in a certain way according to accepted norms, rules and laws.

3 Digital citizenship encompasses digital literacy.

4 Every digital citizen should be aware of good netiquette in the cyberworld.

5 'Netiquette' means respecting other users' views and being polite when posting your views online.

6 It is okay to post about cricket in a football forum.

7 You must not disagree with what someone says online.

8 Many countries throughout the world have passed laws to protect citizens and organisations from computer crimes and cybercrimes.

9 There is an increase in cybercrimes in the Caribbean.

10 Jamaica has a Cybercrime Act that makes it illegal to commit computer crimes and cybercrimes.

11 People found guilty of some computer crimes and cybercrimes in Jamaica can be imprisoned.

Multiple-choice questions

1 Digital citizenship means learning how to use technology in ways that are:

   a appropriate, responsible and intelligent.

   b appropriate, efficient and entrepreneurial.

   c investigative, entrepreneurial and friendly.

   d none of the above.

2 Which option is an example of good netiquette?

   a Typing your comments in ALL CAPS

   b Posting any videos you receive to all your friends without their permission

   c Forwarding chain letters to your friends

   d Staying on-topic in a forum

3 Which option shows the correct format to reference a CD-ROM using the APA format?

   a Author, Initial. (year). *Title* [CD-ROM]. Place of publication: Publisher.

   b Author, Initial. (year). "Title of Part of Work." *Title* [CD-ROM]. Publisher: Place of publication.

   c Author, Initial. (year). Title [CD-ROM]. Place of publication: Publisher.

   d Author, Initial. (year). "Title of Part of Work." *Title* [CD-ROM]. Publisher: Place of publication.

4 Which option shows the correct format to reference a CD-ROM using the MLA format?

   a Author, Initial. (year). Title [CD-ROM]. Place of publication: Publisher.

   b Author, Initial. (year). *Title* [CD-ROM]. Publisher: Place of publication.

   c Name of Author (if given). "Title of Part of Work." Title of Product. Edition or release, if relevant. Publication medium CD-ROM. City of Publication: Publisher, Year of publication.

   d Name of Author (if given). Title of Product. "Title of Part of Work." Edition or release, if relevant. Publication medium CD-ROM. Place of Publication: Publisher, Year of publication.

Short-answer questions

1 **a** Explain the term 'digital citizenship'.

   b List three aspects of 'digital citizenship'.

2 **a** What does the term 'netiquette' mean?

   b Describe five tips for good netiquette.

3 **a** What is the function of a copyright organisation?

   b Name three copyright organisations in Jamaica.

4 For each of the following, state the law that may have been broken according to the Jamaican Cybercrimes Act (2015).

   a James copied the file containing the end-of-term examination from his teacher's laptop and shared it with his friends.

   b Mary was upset with her friend Kim, so she uploaded a lot of false statements on Facebook to damage her reputation.

   c Billy used his computer to hack into the school database to change his examination grades.

   d Shelly used her computer programming skills to download copyright software to distribute to her friends.

   e Mr Data installed a virus in his company's network because the company did not give him a pay raise.

Research questions

1 Copy the table into your notebook. Do research on the internet to find information about three major cybercrimes committed in the last five years, and then complete the table.

Type of cybercrime	Year committed	Description of crime	Loss incurred

2 Copy the table below into your notebook. Do research on the internet to find out which Caribbean islands listed in the table have laws to protect citizens from computer crimes and cybercrimes. Then complete the table by filling in the names of the relevant Acts or Laws alongside each island (where applicable).

Name of island	Name of Law or Act
Jamaica	
Trinidad and Tobago	
Barbados	
St Lucia	

Crossword

Down

1 Acronym for Jamaican Copyright Licensing Agency

2 Respecting other users' views and being polite when posting your views online

4 Acronym for Jamaica Music Society Limited

Across

3 Writing content online that intentionally invokes responses such as rage, sadness, humiliation and self-doubt

5 A type of citizenship that means learning how to use technology in ways that are appropriate, responsible and intelligent

6 An illegal act committed online or via the internet

STEM project

Students at your school are planning to do a netiquette video campaign to help prevent cyberbullying and other inappropriate use of the internet. Your class has been asked to produce a video presentation highlighting the most important issues and showing the proper netiquette for each issue. This presentation will be shown in your school cafeteria on a television screen during lunchtime every day.

1 What is an interesting and attention-catching, but accurate title for this presentation?

2 Outline five major steps that your class will take to produce this presentation. Which step(s) are related to the content of this chapter? Explain these steps in detail.

3 Due to the positive results that this presentation has had in your school, the school has decided to produce a DVD with the PowerPoint presentation to share with other schools. What must you do to ensure that this DVD is copyright-protected and properly referenced in the Jamaica National Library DVD Collection?

Hints

1 Which types of research did you carry out to help you decide on the content of the video presentation, for example, look at other presentations that students enjoy watching, trial ideas with other students, and so on?

2 Speak to your school or community librarian about copyright protection and referencing.

12 Problem solving and algorithm development (1)

Objectives

At the end of the chapter, you will be able to:

❑ define an algorithm

❑ explain the properties of writing an algorithm

❑ define the term 'flowchart'

❑ explain the purpose of some flowchart symbols

❑ draw a flowchart for simple algorithms

❑ develop algorithms for simple everyday problems

❑ develop algorithms for simple linear mathematical problems

❑ develop algorithms using the 'if ... then' statement

❑ dry run simple algorithms.

In *Interact with IT* Book 1, you were introduced to the steps involved in problem solving, one of which is the use of **algorithms**. In this chapter, you will learn how to write algorithms, which are essential to writing computer programs.

What are algorithms?

An algorithm is a formula or set of unambiguous steps that, if followed exactly, will solve a particular problem. We use algorithms every day: a recipe for baking a cake or the steps to find the average of a set of numbers are both examples of algorithms. However, some problems, such as 'how to be happy', cannot be solved by an algorithm, as it is a problem with no clear rules. In order to create algorithms, the rules required to solve the problem must be clear and complete.

Can you think of any problems that do not have clear rules for solving them and therefore cannot be solved by an algorithm?

Algorithms can be expressed in any language, from natural languages such as English or French to computer programming languages such as BASIC or Pascal. Developing elegant algorithms – algorithms that are simple and require the fewest steps possible – is one of the principal challenges in computer programming.

Before we start writing algorithms for some common everyday and computing problems, we will look at the instructions for writing algorithms.

Figure 12.1 Algorithms can be written in any language.

Instructions for writing algorithms

When you write algorithms, you need to:

* always be aware of the assumptions that you are making
* remember that there is no single correct answer, as the same algorithm can often be expressed in more than one way
* keep in mind that, with more than one way to solve a problem, different algorithms may be equally valid solutions for the same problem
* as you write and after you are finished, check your algorithm to make sure it satisfies all of the properties of writing an algorithm.

We have summarised the properties of writing an algorithm here in the form of questions you can ask as you check your algorithm:

1 **Inputs specified:** Did you describe all of the data (or materials) needed for the algorithm?

2 **Processing specified:** Did you describe the processing involved and the order in which it must be done?

3 **Outputs specified:** Did you precisely describe the results of your algorithm?

4 **Precision:** Is your algorithm precise? An algorithm must be expressed very precisely. An ambiguous algorithm, if misinterpreted, might be ineffective at solving the problem it was designed for. In everyday life, when we think of instructions, we usually mean instructions for other people to follow, rather than for a machine to follow, and we can conveniently make many unstated assumptions and get away with being ambiguous. For example, if a member of your family asks you to go out and buy bread, they may be assuming you know where to find a shop that sells bread. They can make certain assumptions about your prior knowledge. However, unlike instructions for people, instructions for computers can leave no room for misinterpretation, so algorithms require an extreme level of precision that will take some getting used to.

5 **Finiteness:** Are you sure that the algorithm actually finishes?

We can represent an algorithm in the following three ways:

* As a **narrative**, using English statements to describe the solution to the problem, similar to the problem in Example 1
* As a **flowchart**, which is a visual representation of the solution using specific symbols and arrows
* As **pseudocode**, which (as the name implies: pseudo – fake code) is not the actual program code, but closely resembles it.

Now, let us review a simple example from Book 1.

Figure 12.2 Remember to constantly check your algorithm to make sure it contains all of the properties for writing an algorithm.

Figure 12.3 Making tea is quite a complicated process

Example 1

Karen wants to make a cup of hot green tea with milk and no sugar for her mother.

> **Ingredients/Items:** Cup, hot water, green tea and milk are all available.

Possible algorithm

First: Boil the water.

Next: Pour hot water into the cup.

Next: Place the tea bag in the cup of hot water.

Next: Leave the tea bag to infuse for one to two minutes.

Next: Remove the tea bag.

Next: Add two teaspoons of milk.

Last: Serve the tea to mother.

The tea is now ready, because a person knows what to do at each stage, without too much difficulty or specific instructions. Yet, each of these actions is actually quite involved. Boiling the water involves:

1   fetching a pot from the cupboard

2   turning on the tap

3   filling the pot with water

4   placing the pot on the stove

5   lighting the stove

6   determining when the water is boiled.

Just think what a complex task it is to boil the water! It involves:

*   checking to see where the pot is in the cupboard
*   holding it in a special way to remove it and place it under the tap
*   opening the tap and deciding how much water is needed
*   turning on and lighting the stove.

All of these tasks are just for boiling the water. Then, after boiling the water, we still have to find and arrange the teacup and tea bag, (for example, place the tea bag into the water). Then we need to determine when two minutes is up, remove the tea bag and fetch the milk. As the algorithm nears its end, we need to measure and add two teaspoons of milk, and finally serve the drink to mother.

We can also further refine (improve) all of the tasks just mentioned to make the instructions even more precise so that there is absolutely no room for error in making the tea.

Let us look at another example of an algorithm for a simple everyday problem.

Example 2

John wants his younger brother to make a cheese sandwich with tomato and lettuce for him. His younger brother does not know how to prepare the sandwich but is eager to try. John has outlined the steps for him.

> **Ingredients/Items:** Knife, bread, cheese, tomato and lettuce are all available.

1 Fetch the bread from the refrigerator.

2 Take out two slices.

3 Fetch a tomato from the refrigerator.

4 Wash the tomato under the kitchen tap.

5 Slice the tomato using a knife.

6 Wash away the seeds.

7 Place two slices of tomato on top of one of the slices of bread.

8 Fetch the cheese from the refrigerator.

9 Using a knife, cut one slice of cheese.

10 Place the slice of cheese on top of the two slices of tomato.

11 Fetch the lettuce from the refrigerator.

12 Break off one leaf from the lettuce.

13 Wash the leaf under the kitchen tap.

14 Place the leaf on top of the cheese slice.

15 Place the other slice of bread on top of the tomato, cheese and lettuce.

Your cheese sandwich with tomato and lettuce is now complete. As with the previous example, many of the tasks can be broken down even further to make a more exact algorithm. For example, one assumption in this algorithm is that John's younger brother knows how to use a knife.

Figure 12.4 By following the step-by-step process, John's brother completed all the tasks to make a cheese sandwich with tomato and lettuce.

Exercise 1

Algorithms for simple tasks
Write algorithms to solve each of the problems below. State all your assumptions clearly.

1 Prepare a bowl of cold cereal.

2 Change a tyre on a car.

3 Prepare a cup of hot cocoa tea.

4 Make scrambled eggs.

5 Brush your teeth.

Writing algorithms for computer programs

Writing an algorithm as a step towards developing a computer program is likely to need even more detail than was needed to do the simple everyday human tasks we have looked at so far.

Computer programs involve three types of instructions: input, processing and output. When writing an algorithm, we have to determine the input, processing and output instructions. We start by describing an algorithm in a way that a human can readily understand. Then we continuously refine it until eventually we can describe the sequence in a way that a computer can understand. The solution is then written in a particular programming language.

Example problems

Let us start by looking at how to write algorithms for two example problems.

Problem 1

Write an algorithm that requests a user to enter and calculate the sum of three numbers, and then display the sum of the three numbers.

Possible algorithm

You can begin writing the algorithm by asking the following questions and supplying the answers:

Questions	Responses
What is the input instruction?	Ask the user to enter the three numbers.
What is the processing instruction?	Calculate the sum of the three numbers.
What is the output instruction?	Display the sum of the three numbers.

Problem 2

Write an algorithm that requests a user to enter a temperature in degrees Celsius, and then convert it to degrees Fahrenheit and display both values.

Possible algorithm

Question	Algorithm
What is the input instruction?	Enter the temperature in degrees Celsius that you would like to convert.
What is the processing instruction?	Convert the temperature to degrees Fahrenheit.
What is the output instruction?	Display the temperature in degrees Celsius and the converted value in degrees Fahrenheit.

Another way to identify these three main instructions, that is, input instructions, processing instructions and output instructions, is to look at the problem statement.

Input instructions

Input instructions allow information or data to be accepted by the computer and stored. The input is the information the computer needs to solve the problem. Words such as 'Enter', 'Input' and 'Read' in problem statements usually indicate what data the computer requires.

Example 3

What are the input instructions here?

1   Read the price of an item and calculate the discount of 25%.
2   Enter the name and birth year of a parent and calculate their age.
3   Input the radius of a circular table top and find the area.

Let us analyse these instructions to determine the inputs and what we need to store.

1   Read the price of an item.
2   Enter the name and year of birth of a parent.
3   Input the radius of a circular table top.

Processing instructions

Processing instructions manipulate the input data. They involve calculations, (mathematical operations: addition, subtraction, multiplication, division) and may form part of three types of control structures. In programming, control structures include:

* sequencing instructions, where the instructions are executed line by line
* repeating or looping instructions, which involves the repeating of a piece of code
* selecting and comparison instructions, where the instructions are executed based on a particular choice.

Did you know?

A **control structure** is a simple decision-making construct. It is a block of code that checks the variables and makes a decision on the direction to go based on given factors. A control structure indicates the direction or flow of the program, which is called the **flow control** of the program.

We make decisions everyday that are based on particular parameters (factors or requirements). These parameters help us decide on a particular direction or the best solution. An example of a control structure in real life is: 'Is it sunny outdoors? If so, go out and play. Is it raining outdoors? If so, stay indoors.'

These processing instructions include commands and constructs.

* A **command** is a word that instructs the computer what must be done to accomplish a specific task. Commands are specific to a particular programming language: for example, WRITE, PRINT, READ, INPUT, and so on.

* A **construct** is a group of instructions that work together with commands to accomplish a specific task. An example is the 'IF–THEN' construct:

IF a < 10 THEN

READ Num

Problem statements that contain the words 'calculate', 'compute', 'convert', 'add', 'sum', 'subtract', 'minus', 'multiply', 'divide', 'percentage' and 'average' indicate what needs to be done. Problem statements can also imply what needs to be processed by looking at what results are required for output; for example: 'Print the area of the room'.

Example 4

What are the processing instructions here?

1   Read the price of an item and calculate the new price after a 25% discount.

2   Enter the mass in pounds and convert it to kilograms.

3   Input the name and year of birth and compute and print the age of a person.

Let us analyse these instructions to determine what we need to process.

1   Calculate the new price after a 25% discount.

2   Convert it to kilograms.

3   Compute the age of a person.

Repeat statements and comparison statements

These are the repeating instructions and comparison instructions mentioned above.

* Comparison/Selection/Decision statements involve determining whether a condition is true or false in order to perform a set of instructions. For example:

> Read the weekly hours worked by an employee. If the hours worked are greater than 40, then calculate overtime salary at 1.5 times the standard hourly rate of $8.50, for those hours over 40.

The condition that is checked is the number of hours worked to find out if it is more than 40.

∗ Repeat statements/loopings/iterations are used when a problem has to be done a number of times. For example:

> Read the marks for three subjects, English, Maths and Spanish, for each student. Then find the average mark of each student in a class of 15, over the three subjects.

The process of finding the average for the three subjects has to be repeated 15 times.

Output instructions

Output instructions allow information to be displayed on the screen. Problem statements that include key words such as 'print', 'output', 'display', 'return' and 'write' indicate what data should be output to the screen.

Example 5

What are the output statements here?

1   Enter the name and year of birth of a person and compute and display the age of the person.

2   Write an algorithm to print a conversion table of degrees Celsius to degrees Fahrenheit, 10 °C to 20 °C inclusive.

Let us analyse these instructions to determine what we need to output.

1   Display the age of the person.

2   Print a conversion table.

Now we will analyse a few problems.

Exercise 2

Algorithms for computational problems

1 Write an algorithm to find and display the total and average of three numbers.

2 Write an algorithm to find and display the area of a rectangle.

3 Write an algorithm to find and display the square of a number.

4 Write an algorithm to input the name of an item and price. Calculate the discount on this price at 15% and the discounted price. Display the price, the discount and the discounted price of the item.

Another way to represent the three main instructions, that is, input (I) instructions, processing (P) instructions and output (O) instructions, also called IPO, is to represent them in the form of an IPO chart, as shown in Examples 6 to 10 below.

Example 6
Write a program to enter the length and width of a rectangle and find and print the area.

Input	Processing	Output
Length Width	Calculate Area Area = length * width	Area

Example 7
Write a program to read the mass on an item in pounds and convert it to kilograms. Kg = lb * 2.2, where kg is kilograms and lb is pounds. Output the weight in pounds and kilograms.

Input	Processing	Output
Pounds – lb	Calculate kilograms kg = lb * 2.2	lb, kg

Example 8
Write a program to **read** the answer to the problem: John has 60 oranges. He sold 15 to Jack and 25 to Martha. How many oranges does John still have? (The answer is 20.) Return the comment "Correct" if the answer is right and "Incorrect" if the answer is wrong.

Input	Processing	Output
Answer	If Answer = 20 then print "Correct" otherwise print "Incorrect"	"Correct" or "Incorrect"

Example 9
Write a program that reads the result of 10 cricket matches played by a team and find the percentage of matches won by the team. Output the percentage matches won.

Input	Processing	Output
MatchResult	• Repeat 10 times Read MatchResult add 1 to TotalWins if MatchResult is a "Win" • PercentageWins = (TotalWins/10)*100	PercentageWins

Example 10

A school has a club system implemented. Points are awarded to each club based on the performance of its members. 1st place – 4 points, 2nd place – 3 points, 3rd place – 2 points, 4th place – 1 point, and last place – no points awarded. Read the names of 10 members of the Blue club and the place they came in the events; calculate and print the total points awarded to the house.

Input	Processing	Output
Name	• Repeat 10 times • Check Place If Place = 1 then add 4 to Total If Place = 2 then add 3 to Total If Place = 3 then add 2 to Total If Place = 4 then add 1 to Total	Total

Exercise 3

Analyse the following problems by dividing them into input and storage, processing and output:

1 Write a program to enter an individual's year of birth and the current year, and to calculate and return the individual's age.

2 Write a program to enter a number, triple the number, and output the result.

3 A box can hold two and a half dozen cans of peas. Read the number of boxes and the price of a can of peas. Calculate and print the total cost of all the cans of peas.

4 Write a program to read a month in the year and print 'This is the month of #myfreedomday' if the month entered is 'March'.

5 Persons shorter than four feet in height are not allowed to ride the rollercoaster. Write a program to read a person's height and if their height is less than four feet, output 'Sorry you are not allowed to ride the rollercoaster'.

6 Persons are awarded reward points depending on how much money they spend on their purchase; if they spend $5.00, they are awarded one reward point. Read the person's amount spent and calculate the points rewarded for that purchase. Add the points to the person's total reward points. Print the person's total reward points.

7 Write a program to input a number N. If the number is greater than 50, subtract 10 from the number; otherwise multiply the number by 2 and add 5. Print the number and the result.

8 Write a program to determine the average age of students in a class of 20. Read the age of each student and print the average.

Flowcharts

Flowcharts are diagrams used to help us visualise the sequences of algorithms. They use a set of symbols with a little text in each. Simple tasks have simple flowcharts and complex tasks can have flowcharts with thousand of components. They are especially useful for novice programmers if they can fit on one page; however, if they take up several pages they become difficult to follow and may be ineffective. Programmers use many different symbols to draw flowcharts but we will start with four basic symbols that are connected by arrows.

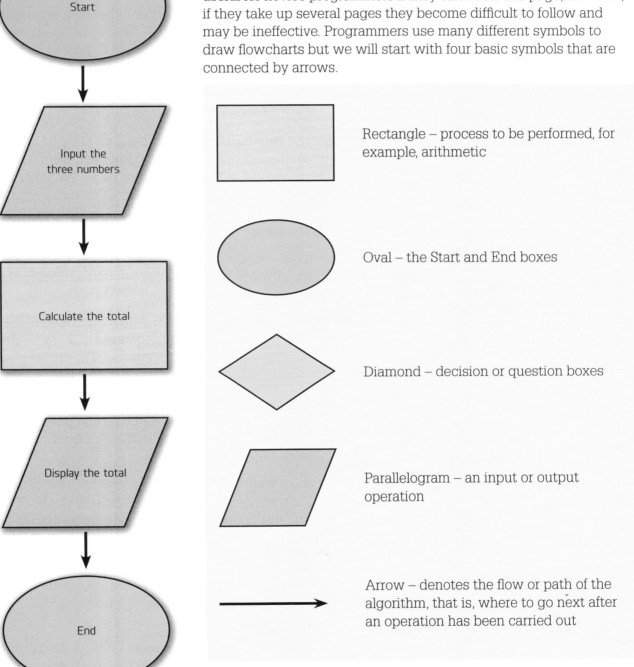

Rectangle – process to be performed, for example, arithmetic

Oval – the Start and End boxes

Diamond – decision or question boxes

Parallelogram – an input or output operation

Arrow – denotes the flow or path of the algorithm, that is, where to go next after an operation has been carried out

Figure 12.5 Flowchart: Finding the sum of three numbers

So, if we take our example of finding the sum of three numbers and displaying the sum of the three numbers, we can make a flowchart as shown in Figure 12.5.

Refining an algorithm

Refining an algorithm makes it easier to convert it to programming code. However, before we go through the steps to refine an algorithm we need to consider a few things.

Constants

Constants are data that do not change, but remain the same during the execution of a program or algorithm. For example: Given the formula 'Degrees Fahrenheit = (32 + 9 * degrees Celsius / 5)', the values **32**, **9** and **5** are constants; they are values that do not change during the execution of the formula.

Variables

Again, consider the formula 'Degrees Fahrenheit = (32 + 9 * degrees Centigrade / 5)'. Depending on the value of degrees Celsius, the degrees Fahrenheit value would change accordingly. **Variables** represent the values that change during the execution of a program or algorithm. 'Degrees Fahrenheit' and 'degrees Celsius' are variables in this equation.

Different programming languages use different types of variables to represent the different types of data. In this Student's Book, we will only consider two types of data:

* **Literal or string data:** Literal or string data represent all the data that is not purely numeric. Some examples of literal or string data are names of persons, address, colours, and so on.
* **Numeric data:** Numeric data represents only number values such as the age of a person, marks made in a subject, and so on.

The rules for developing variable names differ in each programming language. In a programming language called BASIC, the rules are as follows:

* Numeric variables must begin with a letter and may be followed by letters and/or numbers, for example A, A1, SUM, Count, XYZ.
* Literal variables must begin with a letter and may be followed by letters and/or numbers and must end with a dollar sign ($), for example A$, A1$, Name$, Address$.

How do variables get their values? How do we input the data? Where will it be stored? These are some of the questions you may be asking yourself.

The data that you input will be stored in main memory. Each item of data will be stored in a memory location. We can think of a memory location as a container to hold the data until it is required for processing. We can label each container so that it becomes easier to know which ones will hold the input, processing and output values. The label we give to each container is called a variable.

For example, to input three numbers into the computer, we have to specify three locations:

* The location to hold the first number can be identified by the letter A
* The location to hold the second number can be identified by the letter B
* The location to hold the third number can be identified by the letter C.

The letters A, B and C are variable names, because the values that they represent can change each time the program or algorithm is executed.

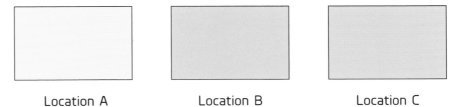

Location A   Location B   Location C

Let us go through the steps to refine one of the previous example algorithms by including variables in the algorithm.

Problem 3

Write an algorithm to find the sum of three numbers and display the sum of the three numbers.

Possible algorithm

1 Prompt and enter the three numbers. (The word 'prompt' means a message must be displayed to indicate to the user what they have to enter.)

2 Calculate the sum of the three numbers.

3 Display the sum of the three numbers.

The first line of the algorithm can now be written as:

Enter three numbers A, B, C

This means that whatever three values you enter will be stored in the locations with variable names A, B and C.

The total of the three numbers will also be stored in a memory location. We can call this location 'Total'.

The second line of the algorithm can now be stated as:

Calculate the total using the formula TOTAL = A + B + C

To display the Total we will use the word 'Output'. Therefore the output statement of the algorithm will be:

Output TOTAL

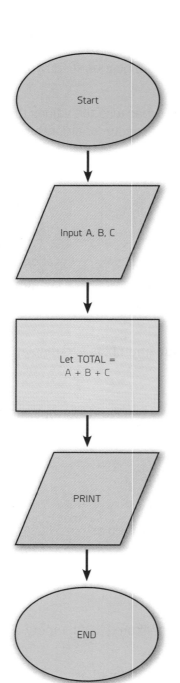

The new algorithm, which is a little more refined, can be stated as:

Prompt and enter three numbers A, B, C

Calculate the total using the formula TOTAL = A + B + C

Output TOTAL

The algorithm can be further refined. For example 'Enter three numbers' can be replaced by the word 'Input' as this is really what you want to do. The words 'Calculate the total using the formula' can be replaced by the word 'Let', and the word 'Output' can be replaced by 'Print'. Our new algorithm will now be:

Prompt and INPUT A, B, C

LET TOTAL = A + B + C

PRINT TOTAL

The steps for refining an algorithm are summarised in Table 12.1.

Table 12. 1 Stages of refining an algorithm

Questions	Algorithm (rough) – narrative	Algorithm refined	Algorithm refined further – pseudocode
What is the input instruction?	Prompt and enter the three numbers	Prompt and enter three numbers A, B, C	Prompt and INPUT A, B, C
What is the processing instruction?	Calculate the sum of the three numbers	Calculate the total using the formula: TOTAL = A + B + C	LET TOTAL = A + B + C
What is the output instruction?	Display the sum of the three numbers	Output TOTAL	PRINT TOTAL

The flowchart for the example in Figure 12.6 will have the same symbols as the one we have seen before, but the content of the boxes will be changed to reflect the more refined algorithm.

Figure 12.6 Flowchart: The sum of three numbers

Let us look at another example.

Problem 4

Convert a temperature in degrees Celsius to degrees Fahrenheit.

Possible algorithm

The summary for the steps to writing the possible algorithm is shown in Table 12.2.

Table 12.2 Converting temperature

Question	Algorithm – narrative	Algorithm refined	Algorithm refined further – pseudocode
What is the input instruction?	Enter the temperature in degrees Celsius that you would like to convert.	Prompt and enter the temperature in degrees Celsius C (The letter C is the variable used to hold the value of degrees Celsius.)	Prompt and INPUT C
What is the processing instruction?	Convert to degrees Fahrenheit by using the formula: Degrees Fahrenheit = (32 + 9 * degrees Celsius / 5)	Convert to degrees Fahrenheit by using the formula: F = (32 + 9 * C / 5) (The letter F is the variable used to hold the value of degrees Fahrenheit.)	LET F = (32 + 9 * C / 5)
What is the output instruction?	Display the temperature in degrees Celsius and the converted value in degrees Fahrenheit.	Output C and F	PRINT C and F

In a flowchart, the algorithm would look like this one in Figure 12.7.

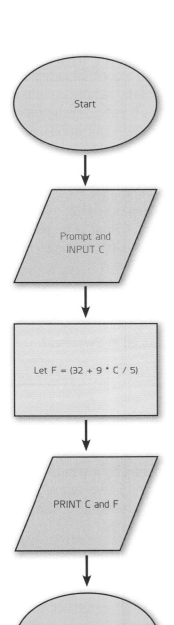

Figure 12.7 Flowchart: Convert temperature

Dry running your algorithm

How do you know that your algorithm works? Quite simply, you will have to test it. This is an important part of the algorithm design process. It involves carrying out a **dry run**. This means inputting values and working through the steps in the algorithm logically and carefully, one by one, while keeping track of the results. At a higher level the process is a little more involved as it entails using different sets of data. At this level we would dry run our algorithms by using simple data.

Let us look at a dry run of the following algorithm. We will use the values 5, 7 and 9 for the variables A, B and C. Adding these values we get 21, which will be stored in the location Total. Print Total will result in the value 21 being printed. Dry run the algorithm using different values to see if it works.

Algorithm	Dry run
INPUT A, B, C	A = 5, B =7, C = 9
LET TOTAL = A + B + C	TOTAL = 5 + 7 + 9 TOTAL = 21
PRINT TOTAL	Value printed 21

Exercise 4

1 Refine all the algorithms that you developed in Exercise 2.

2 Dry run all the algorithms in question 1.

Conditional algorithms

So far we have only dealt with linear problems. However, instances may occur in problems that require decisions about whether to proceed in one particular direction or another. These types of algorithm require a **condition statement**. A condition, also known as a branch, determines which step to proceed to.

* The IF statement is used to state a condition that, if true, specifies a statement or group of statements in the procedure to be carried out.
* The ELSE statement can be used with the IF statement to specify a statement or group of statements to be carried out if the condition expressed by the IF statement is false.
* The ENDIF statement marks the end of the IF structure. We might write a general conditional algorithm like this:

IF (condition) THEN   (statements)

ELSE   (statements)

ENDIF

The following are some conditions that can be tested using the IF structure:

Symbol	Meaning	Example
=	equals	IF A=B THEN
>	is greater than	IF A > B THEN
<	is less than	IF A < B THEN
>=	is greater than or equal to	IF A >= B THEN
<=	is less than or equal to	IF A <= B THEN
<>	is not equal to	IF A <> B THEN

Problem 5

Write an algorithm that requests a user to enter two numbers and complete the following task:

If the first number is larger than the second, then divide the first number by the second and output the result; else, multiply the two numbers and output the result.

Possible algorithm

The summary for the steps to writing the possible algorithm is shown in Table 12.3.

Table 12.3 Multiply or divide two numbers

Algorithm	Algorithm refined	Algorithm refined further
Enter two numbers	Prompt and enter two numbers X and Y	Prompt and INPUT X,Y
If the first number is larger than the second number, then divide the first number by the second number; else multiply the first number by the second number.	If X is greater than Y then Divide X by Y else Multiply X by Y	IF X > Y THEN LET ANSWER = X/Y ELSE LET ANSWER = X * Y ENDIF
Output the answer	Output answer	PRINT ANSWER

In a flowchart, the algorithm would look like the one in Figure 12.8.

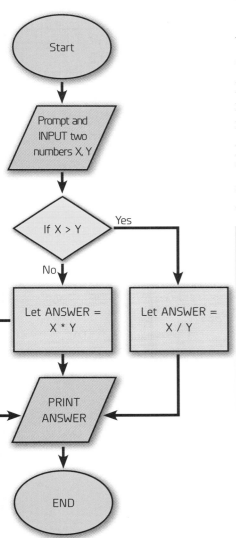

Figure 12.8 Flowchart: Multiply or divide two numbers

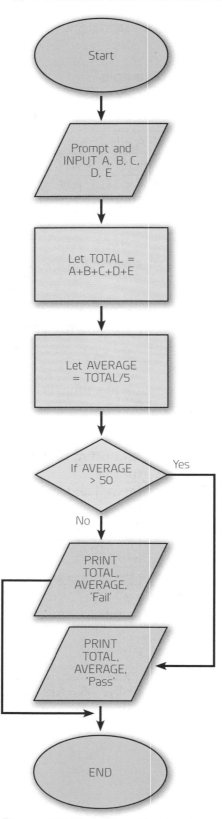

Problem 6

Calculate the total and average mark made by a student in five subjects. If the student made an average of 50 or more, output the total mark, average mark and the message 'Pass'; else print the total mark, average mark and the message 'Fail'.

Possible algorithm

The summary for the steps to writing the possible algorithm is shown in Table 12.4.

Table 12.4 Total and average student marks

Algorithm	Algorithm refined	Algorithm refined further
Enter the marks made in the five subjects	Prompt and enter five marks A, B, C, D, E	Prompt and INPUT A,B,C,D,E
Find the total	Calculate the total marks using the formula Total = A + B + C + D + E	LET TOTAL = A + B + C + D + E
Find the average	Calculate the average mark using the formula Average = Total/5	LET AVERAGE = TOTAL/5
If average is greater than fifty, then output the total mark, average mark and 'Pass'; else output the total mark, average mark and 'Fail'.	If Average is greater than 50 then output Total mark, Average mark and the message 'Pass' Else Output Total mark, Average mark and the message 'Fail' Endif	IF AVERAGE > 50 THEN PRINT TOTAL, AVERAGE, 'Pass' ELSE PRINT TOTAL, AVERAGE, 'Fail' ENDIF END

In a flowchart, the algorithm would look like the one in Figure 12.9.

Figure 12.9 Flowchart: Total and average student marks (from IF statement only)

Summary 12

1 An algorithm is a formula or set of unambiguous steps that, if faithfully followed, will solve a particular problem.

2 Some problems cannot be reduced to an algorithm as they are problems with no clear limiting rules.

3 Algorithms can be expressed in any language, from natural languages such as English or French to programming languages such as BASIC or Pascal.

4 Inventing elegant algorithms that are simple and require the fewest steps possible is one of the principal challenges in programming.

5 Many different algorithms might be acceptable for each problem.

6 An algorithm must specify the input, processing and output tasks. It must also be precise and finite.

7 Flowcharts are diagrams used to help us visualise the sequences of algorithms. They use a set of symbols with a little text in each.

8 Refining an algorithm makes it easier to convert it to programming code.

9 A dry run involves inputting values in an algorithm and working it through by hand to see if it works.

Questions 12

Copy and fill in the blanks questions

1 An _____ is a formula or set of unambiguous steps that, if followed exactly, will solve a particular problem.

2 _____ are diagrams used to help us visualise the sequences of algorithms.

3 _____ an algorithm makes it easier to convert it to programming code.

4 Each item of data is stored in a _____.

5 _____ means inputting values and working through the algorithm by hand to see if it works.

6 We can use _____ to represent values that change during the execution of a program or algorithm.

7 A _____ is a data item that does not change during the execution of a program or algorithm.

True or false questions

1 Algorithms can only be written using the English language.

2 For every problem we can develop an algorithm that will solve it.

3 An algorithm must be expressed very precisely.

4 Computer programs involve three types of instructions: input, processing and output.

5 Flowcharts are diagrams used to help us visualise the sequences of algorithms.

6 Flowcharts are especially useful for professional programmers.

7 Refining an algorithm makes it easier to convert it to programming code.

8 Constants are data that change during the execution of a program or algorithm.

9 All programming languages use the same variables to represent the different types of data.

10 Dry running means inputting values and working through the steps in an algorithm logically and carefully, one by one, while keeping track of the results.

Multiple-choice questions

1. Which three types of instructions do computer programs need?

   a Input, processing, preciseness

   b Input, output, finiteness

   c Input, processing, output

   d Input, preciseness, finiteness

2. The formula given is: Area of a circle = Pi multiplied by the square of the radius ($A = \pi r^2$). Which of the following is the constant in the equation?

   a A

   b r

   c π

   d None of the above.

3. Which of the following is a numeric variable?

   a 2A

   b X1$

   c $AB

   d XYZ

4. Which of the following is a literal variable?

   a $XY

   b XY$

   c 2A$

   d N

5. Prompt and INPUT A,B,C

   LET Z = A x B

   LET X = Z/C

   PRINT X

   END

   What value will be printed if A = 6, B = 8 and C = 2?

   a 16

   b 7

   c 24

   d 48

6. Prompt and INPUT P1, P2, P3, P4, P5

   LET TOTAL = P1+ P2 + P3+ P4 + P5

   LET D = TOTAL * .15

   PRINT TOTAL, D

   END

   What will be printed if P1 = 20, P2 = 15, P3 = 35, P4 = 16, P5 = 14?

   a 70, 14

   b 100, 15

   c 100, 115

   d None of the above.

7. Prompt and INPUT LENGTH, WIDTH

   AREA = LENGTH * WIDTH

   P = (LENGTH+WIDTH) * 2

   PRINT AREA, P

   END

   What will be printed if LENGTH = 15 and WIDTH = 10?

   a 15, 10

   b 150, 50

   c 50, 150

   d 300, 150

8. What are the values of K, B and Z after you dry run the following algorithm?

   K = 3

   LET K = K + 3

   LET B = K + 2

   LET Z = B + K

   PRINT K, B, Z

   END

   a 6, 8, 14

   b 9, 11, 20

   c 5, 8, 13

   d None of the above.

9. What are the values of Z and P after you dry run the following algorithm?

   LET X = 16

   LET Y = 2

   LET Z = X/Y

   LET P = Z * Y

   PRINT Z, P

   END

   a 2, 16

   b 4, 6

   c 6, 8

   d 8, 16

Short-answer questions

1. Write an algorithm to bake a batch of chocolate brownies.

2. Write an algorithm to find a word in the dictionary.

3. Jug A has orange juice and Jug B has apple juice. Write an algorithm to place the contents of Jug A into Jug B and the contents of Jug B into Jug A.

4 Write an algorithm to find and print the area of a circle.

5 Write an algorithm to convert a mass in kilograms (kg) to pounds (lb). Display the amount in kilograms and pounds. 1 kg = 2.2 lb Draw a flowchart of the algorithm. Dry run the algorithm using two different values.

6 Flour is sold at $40.00 a bag. Write an algorithm to input an order number and the quantity ordered. Calculate the cost of the order. Print the order number, quantity and cost.

7 Write an algorithm to calculate simple interest on savings in a bank. The algorithm should allow the user to input the principal, rate and time, and output the principal and the interest earned. Simple Interest = (Principal x Rate x Time)/100

8 Draw a flowchart of the following algorithm.

INPUT A, B

IF B = 0 THEN

PRINT "Cannot go further"

ELSE

LET C = A/B

PRINT C

ENDIF

What will be printed if:

a A= 48 and B = 2?

b A= 48 and B = 0?

9 Draw a flowchart of the following algorithm.

INPUT C

IF C <= 100 THEN

PRINT C

ELSE

LET C = (C + .20 * C)

PRINT C

ENDIF

What will be printed if:

a C = 120?   **b** C = 100?

STEM project

The daily operations of Roads R Us, a road toll company in a large Caribbean country, include the collecting of toll fees for vehicles of four possible classes, providing customers with change, updating the tag on customers' accounts and keeping track of the number of times government vehicles cross the toll point. Employees at the toll booths process thousands of dollars daily.

There are three lanes going into the capital city and three lanes leaving the capital city, with moderate traffic all day and peak traffic in the early morning and late afternoon. There are six employees and two supervisors on each shift at the toll booths.

1 Identify three possible problems that may occur in the above scenario. Explain how you will identify these problems.

2 Use an algorithm to work out a solution for each problem you identify.

3 Choose the most probable problem and refine it as much as possible to present to Roads R Us. Use a flow chart to support your presentation.

Hints
1 How does a road toll system work?
2 Explain what an algorithm is in your own words. What are its components?
3 List any assumptions that you have made.

13  Applications of IT (2)

Objectives

At the end of the chapter, you will be able to:

❑ state some of the uses of computers in the fields of:
  ❑ law enforcement and the military
  ❑ medicine
  ❑ entertainment
  ❑ weather forecasting
  ❑ mass media.

Many of us go through our daily routine without noticing how many times we come into contact with computers. Computer technology has become such a part of our daily lives that, if it were taken away, we would be completely lost without it.

Computers in law enforcement

Computers play an important role in law enforcement.

* National crime databases have been set up to hold information such as:
  – criminal records
  – profiles of wanted persons
  – data on stolen cars
  – fingerprints of convicted individuals
  – details of drivers with suspended or cancelled licenses.
* Computers are also used to:
  – maintain criminal databases
  – examine forensic evidence
  – communicate with other law enforcement departments and agencies
  – provide electronic surveillance
  – control traffic systems and CCTV (closed circuit television) camera systems
  – provide assistance to officers through easy access to information
  – computerise many of the traditional office tasks.

Security cameras (CCTV camera systems)

Cameras act as a visible warning to a criminal. They can also capture video footage of a crime in progress and the images can be used to identify the criminals. Most cameras these days are linked to computer systems that can store and process the raw data. Some of these cameras are found on traffic lights.

Biometric identification systems

Biometrics refers to the science of identifying an individual through their body characteristics, such as face geometry, hand geometry (for example, fingerprints), iris or retinal scans, veins and voice patterns. In law enforcement, these methods have become some of the main ways by which individuals are identified. Figure 13.2 shows examples of different biometric identification systems.

Figure 13.1 Computers affect all aspects of our lives.

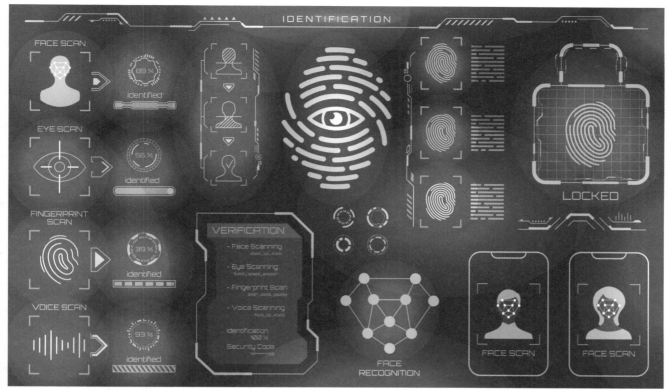

Figure 13.2 Different biometric identification systems used in law enforcement

Fingerprinting

Fingerprints obtained from a crime scene can be matched against a database of known criminals' fingerprints to identify a suspect. Computers are used to store and analyse the complex patterns of people's fingerprints.

Figure 13.3 Computers can identify a person from a surveillance camera image.

Computer-assisted facial image identification systems

Computer-assisted facial image identification systems can mean using computers to:

* identify a person from an image captured through a surveillance camera or photograph
* do a three-dimensional facial reconstruction from the skull of a person, to show what the person might look like if they were alive.

Profiling (computer composites)

Police officers can use appropriate software to compose a picture of an alleged criminal based on the description of a witness. Computers can then compare this picture to those stored in the national databases.

Traffic control

Computerised traffic light systems are able to adjust the traffic lights throughout the day depending on the flow of traffic. These systems use a sensor in the road to detect the flow of traffic, and the traffic lights are adjusted accordingly.

Electronic surveillance

Electronic surveillance can help the police track criminals' movements and activities. Different forms of electronic surveillance include:

* wiretapping (listening to criminals' telephone, cell phone and internet conversations)
* obtaining copies of email and online communication
* determining location information (finding out where you are from calls going to your cell phone)
* analysing communication, (for example, monitoring when and where credit cards are used).

Computers in medicine

Computers and computer technology have become essential tools in medicine. They are used to:

* monitor patients' vital signs
* maintain databases of patients, diseases and drugs
* aid in detecting and diagnosing diseases
* assist in generating case-specific advice through the use of expert systems
* help doctors collaborate and administer treatment over the internet
* perform research.

Patient monitoring system

A patient monitoring system is a computerised unit that monitors a person's vital signs, such as blood pressure, temperature and heart rate, using sensors attached to the patient. The unit records the information at specific intervals and may sound an alert if any of the readings show irregular or dangerous abnormalities.

Patients' records databases

Most doctors' offices in the Caribbean still use manual databases to store information about their patients' diagnoses, symptoms and treatment. Doctors could easily access records of their patients' health history, as well as their personal information, if this information were computerised. Computerised records can also reduce the time spent looking for patient records in the case of an emergency. They can also make it easy to identify trends in diseases.

Figure 13.4 Computerised medical records provide easy access to a patient's medical history in emergencies.

Computer-aided detection and diagnosis

Computer technology, such as the following two systems, helps doctors to detect or diagnose abnormalities in the tissues of their patients:

* **Magnetic resonance imaging (MRI) machine:** This machine uses magnets to create two-dimensional and three-dimensional images of tissues, such as the brain, to detect strokes, tumours, infections and even haemorrhages.
* **Computer axial tomography (CAT) scan machine:** This machine is an X-ray tube that takes as many as 30 pictures per second as it rotates around the patient. The computer system reconstructs a three-dimensional view of the image from the pictures taken. This helps in the diagnosis of diseases.

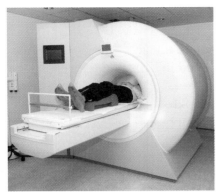

Figure 13.5 A CAT scanner in action

Expert medical system

An expert medical system analyses data and provides answers to questions in the field of medicine. This system has the following advantages:

* Doctors can use this system if they need help with a medical decision because of lack of knowledge or experience.
* Experts can use this system to reach faster and more accurate conclusions or decisions.
* Doctors and experts can access the theory on which the given conclusion or decision is based.

This system has the following disadvantages:

* Doctors often rely on instinct and common sense as part of their decision-making process, which this system does not have.
* Unlike real doctors, this system cannot learn from its mistakes.

Figure 13.6 The internet allows doctors to consult with patients in different or remote locations.

Practicing medicine over the internet

Doctors can use the internet to send information to patients, send X-rays to other medical institutions, and even work together with other doctors or surgeons on 'live' surgery in different parts of the world. Some doctors are now diagnosing patients' illnesses and prescribing medication online.

The explosion of information on the internet has led to an increase in people self-diagnosing themselves. Self-diagnosis is the process of identifying a medical condition oneself by doing research in books and on the internet. However, this can potentially be very dangerous, as an untrained person can misinterpret the medical information or not realise if the information on the internet is factually incorrect.

Entertainment

Computers play a key role in modern entertainment, such as:

* the way in which we play and listen to music
* the special effects and animation used in films and television programmes
* the different types of video and computer games available.

Music and sound

The natural sounds of most musical instruments have been digitised into electronic versions. This means that these sounds can now be played from a single instrument, such as a keyboard. When the keyboard is connected to your computer, you can record, playback, edit and improve music.

Computers also play a role in the way in which music is distributed and consumed. People today can download popular music to cell phones and MP3 players from the internet. They can do this legally for a small fee through various websites.

Figure 13.7 Computer animation

Films and animation

Computers play an important role in the making of many films, such as 'Black Panther' and 'Avengers'. Computer-generated images (CGI) and animations are now becoming part of many popular films today. Computer animations are also used in many television programmes, especially those for children.

Games

Computers are used in games purely for entertainment, and in education for both learning and entertainment (known as 'edutainment'). In both cases, computer games have become a big industry. The Nintendo Wii U, 2DS and Nintendo Switch, PlayStation 4 Pro and Slim, Microsoft X-Box One S and 360 and Game Boy (special computer game-playing consoles), as well as computer games for personal computers, have become very popular, earning millions of dollars every year.

Figure 13.8 Computer games are a popular form of entertainment.

Computers in weather forecasting

Weather forecasting is the practice of trying to predict what the weather conditions will be like by measuring and observing the current weather conditions around the world.

In weather forecasting, computers are used to:

* gather and store data
* analyse the data
* display the data in interesting and easy-to-understand ways.

Data obtained from a variety of sensors and instruments is sent to a supercomputer to be logged and analysed. Supercomputers, along with other complex instruments, use this information to predict weather conditions.

* Doppler radar gives the locations of storms. It also gives an indication of wind speeds, wind direction and rainfall.
* Weather balloons with radiosondes measure the pressure, temperature and humidity in the air at many locations around the world. Radiosondes are packages of lightweight measuring instruments that produce electrical signals that can be sent back to the Earth by radio.
* Satellites such as the GOES-8, orbiting high above the Earth, take pictures to help create surface weather maps showing types of clouds and rainfall. These satellites allow meteorologists to observe clouds across the entire globe.

Figure 13.9 Doppler radar gives scientists information about weather conditions such as storms and rainfall.

The supercomputer uses the information gathered using these instruments, together with mathematical models, to make predictions about the weather. The mathematical models are programs that contain complex mathematical equations. These models try to predict weather conditions based on historical data. However, even with the fastest computers, meteorologists cannot forecast day-to-day weather for more than one week ahead, because elements of the weather may change completely.

Figure 13.10 A supercomputer showing a predicted weather pattern

Many new models are currently being developed. Some of these models will help to forecast tropical features, such as hurricanes. Other models of the future will help to forecast weather features on a smaller scale, such as thunderstorms and severe weather events in fairly specific locations. Forecasters will be able to issue better and more timely warnings and advice. In the United States of America (USA), the National Weather Service's National Centers for Environmental Prediction (NCEP) run the computer models. All weather forecasters in the USA rely on these models.

Computers in mass media

Mass media is the use of media specifically designed to reach large sections of the public or very wide audiences. They include media such as print (newspapers, books, magazines, and so on), television, radio, cinema, recordings (pre-recorded DVDs, video tapes, CDs, and so on), the internet and, most recently, cell phones.

Some of the main hardware and software used in mass media are:

* print media
* cinema and television
* recordings
* radio
* internet and social media
* cell phones.

Print media

Computers are used to produce books, newspapers and magazines with the use of word-processing software and other desktop applications. Popular novels are written and sold, and posters, banners and billboards are produced using wide-format printers and plotters, allowing their messages to be viewed by thousands or even millions of people.

Figure 13.11 Computers and editing software are used to produce all material viewed on television.

Cinema and television

Cinema and television enable advertisements, documentaries and films to be viewed by large audiences. In today's society, cinemas have become popular in many countries and most homes have television sets. The production of these media utilises computers and computer-related devices, as well as audio and video editing software.

Recordings

Video and audio programmes also reach large audiences through the use of pre-recorded video tapes, DVDs, CDs, Blu-ray Discs and others. Many homes have computers, CD, DVD and Blu-ray Disc players, which can be used to view or listen to these recordings.

Figure 13.12 Disc players allow people to watch recorded films on CD at home.

Radio

Numerous radio stations around the world broadcast audio programmes. Although many programmes are broadcast live, some are pre-programmed. When personnel cannot be present to run a programme, they use sophisticated software programmed to run on autopilot. Many, if not all radio stations, have switched their entire operations over to digital production. Today, most radio stations use digital turntables, instead of the old-fashioned vinyl record turntables, which are seldom used anymore.

Figure 13.13 Inside a radio station

A fairly recent development is the introduction of satellite radio. This type of radio broadcast covers a much wider geographical area than the traditional radio stations. A listener can listen to the same radio programme or radio station wherever they are in the country. Radio stations such as XM Satellite Radio and SIRIUS Satellite Radio are two of the leading satellite radio stations in America.

Internet and social media

With the arrival of the internet and digital technology, many printed texts are being changed to digital format. This has led to the production of the electronic book or ebook, which is a portable reading device that can wirelessly download books, blogs, magazines and newspapers. Examples such as the Kindle and Kindle 2 allow the user to pay for and download books off the internet to read at their convenience.

Websites, blog sites and emails are used to broadcast information to a wide geographical area. Twitter is a free online social network that allows a user to send and read other users' updates (also called 'microblogging'). As of 1 March 2019, the top three most-followed persons on Twitter were Katy Perry, Justin Bieber and Barack Obama with over 100 million followers.

Figure 13.14 The ebook allows users to download and read books, blogs, magazines and newspapers.

Many viewers and listeners now use podcasts quite extensively. A podcast is an audio or video programme that is uploaded to the internet. This programme can be listened to live or downloaded to computers, MP3 and MP4 players, CDs and DVDs, for later viewing or listening.

Figure 13.15 Recording a podcast

Cell phones

Cell phones are one of the most popular devices of the twenty-first century. Everyone carries their phones almost everywhere, from restrooms to bedrooms. Some people even take their cell phones to bed with them. Therefore, we can safely say that this device is one of the most revolutionary mediums to reach large audiences.

The arrival of mobile internet, mobile radio and mobile TV means that programmes can now reach a person wherever they are every day. This form of media has the characteristics of being personal, always carried and always on. Many companies use these characteristics to communicate by broadcasting information to individuals via text messaging, mobile internet, mobile radio and mobile TV.

Summary 13

1   In law enforcement, computers are used in communication, security cameras, biometric identification systems, profiling, traffic control, electronic surveillance and traditional law enforcement office tasks.

2   In medicine, computers are used to maintain databases of patients' records, patient monitoring systems, computer-aided detection and diagnosis, expert medical systems and in practicing medicine using the internet.

3   In entertainment, computers are used to create, edit, record and enhance music and sound, and create films, animation and games.

4   In weather forecasting, computers are used to gather, store, analyse and display data.

5   In mass media, computers are used to broadcast information to large audiences via print media, cinema and television, recordings, radio, the internet and social media, and cell phones.

Questions 13

True or false questions

1   Supercomputers, together with sensors and instruments, can predict the weather.

2   An expert medical system can learn from its mistakes.

3   Monitoring when and where credit cards are used is also part of electronic surveillance.

4   Hand geometry is not a part of biometric identification.

Multiple-choice questions

Choose the best answer to each question.

1   Which system allows you to record video footage of a crime in progress?

   a CCTV   b CAT scans

   c MRI   d Profiling

2   Electronic surveillance involves all of the following except:

   a MRIs.   b wiretaps.

   c email interception. d location tracking.

3   This machine uses magnets to create a two- and three-dimensional image of tissues.

   a CBA   b CAI

   c MIR   d MRI

4   Many films now use this in their production process.

   a CIG   b CAT

   c CBA   d CGI

5   This device gives the location of storms.

   a Weather balloons

   b Doppler radar

   c Radiosondes

   d Electrical signals

Short-answer questions

1   Explain what an expert medical system is.

2   Discuss the advantages and disadvantages of practicing medicine on the internet.

3   Your friends insist you go with them to watch a new CGI film. In your own words, explain what CGI means and give examples.

4   Differentiate between a CAT scan and an MRI scan.

5   List at least three biometric forms of identification used in law enforcement.

Crossword

Down

1 The process of identifying a medical condition oneself by researching on the internet (2 words)

2 Gives the locations of storms (2 words)

4 Can capture footage of a crime in progress

Across

3 A way to identify an individual through their body characteristics

5 This can be matched against a database of known criminals to identify a suspect

6 The process by which police use specialised software to compose a picture of a suspect

7 An X-ray tube that takes pictures of a patient as it rotates around the patient

8 A type of media that can be created with word-processing software

STEM project

Fifty years ago, typewriters were used for typing and preparing documents in offices. However, as computers are now widely available and continue to evolve, what do you think computers will be more used for fifty years from now?

1 List two areas that use ICT in their daily operations that did not use it initially in the preparation of document.

2 Explain how ICT is used in the areas highlighted in question 1.

3 List the steps for using a typewriter to produce a named office document and compare this to the steps for producing this document using a computer.

4 How has natural language processing improved the ways in which information is processed, recorded and researched in the twenty-first century?

Hints

1 Do research on how typewriters were used since they were invented and until today.
2 Use a typewriter and compare its use to the use of a computer.
3 Do research on new and evolving uses of ICT in the twenty-first century.

Computing careers in an ICT department

In Chapter 13 of *Interact with IT* Book 1, we looked at some careers in both traditional and non-traditional ICT departments of large organisations such as banks, insurance companies, government agencies and educational establishments, as well as smaller companies. In this chapter, we will look at some of those careers in more detail, as well as explore a few other ICT careers in non-traditional ICT departments.

Figure 14.1 The computer industry offers a wide choice of careers.

Careers in a traditional ICT department

The organogram in Figure 14.2 shows the structure of a traditional ICT department.

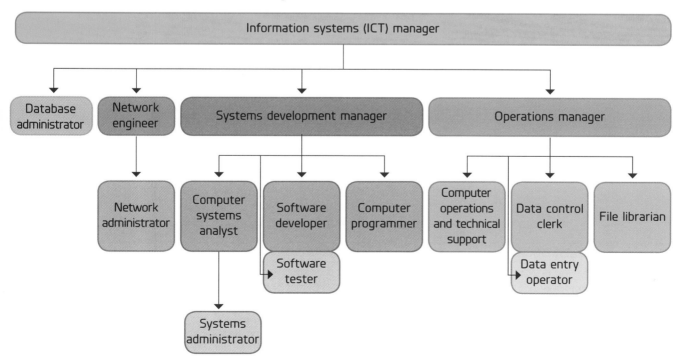

Figure 14.2 The structure of a traditional ICT department

Did you know?

New or emerging careers are being established in IT where the focus is on green technology.

Information systems (ICT) manager

ICT managers plan, coordinate, manage and staff the ICT departments of large organisations. They play an important role in defining the technological direction of the organisation. As such, they must clearly understand the organisation's purpose and goals, and its unique data-processing needs. An ICT manager must be aware of the latest developments in the ICT field and be able to chart the long-term vision, plans and policies for the way in which ICT can be used in the organisation.

Educational qualifications	Duties
• Degree courses in computer studies, along with extra studies such as business administration and human resource management. • Master of Business Administration (MBA) degree with a strong emphasis on information technology and other business courses.	• Communicate with, motivate and lead a number of highly-skilled people. • Be aware of the latest developments in the ICT field. • Read reports the system's performance. • Discuss system problems and new computerisation projects with other departments. • Prepare budget projections, including equipment and training.

Database administrator

Database administrators (DBAs) are responsible for the administration and management of a company's database. This involves the effective and efficient storage, retrieval, customisation and archiving of data.

Educational qualifications	Duties
• Degree in computer studies or information systems, and many other courses attended. • Master's degree in computer science with an emphasis on database design, or an MBA may be required for large organisations.	• Interact with managers and users to ensure database effectiveness. • Ensure that the database performs at its optimum. • Develop policies and procedures to ensure system security and integrity. • Select and maintain database management software. • Coordinate database design. • Establish a back-up and recovery procedure in case of failure or loss of data.

Network engineer

Network engineers plan, design, install and maintain the equipment in a network. Their work covers all types and sizes of networks – LAN, MAN, WAN – as well as different types of data including video and audio, as many computer networks now also handle broadcasting and telephony. They work closely with network administrators, particularly once the network is built, to make sure it is reliable and can grow to meet the customer's needs. In smaller companies, the network engineer and network administrator jobs may be combined.

Educational qualifications	Duties
• Degree in computer science or in electronic engineering. • Professional qualifications such as those from the CISCO Networking Academy.	• Plan and design the network. • Oversee the installation of hardware and software in the network. • Test the network to ensure it is functioning properly. • Monitor the network's performance. • Troubleshoot and solve problems on the network.

Network administrator

Network administrators are responsible for the creation, administration and security of computer networks. The creation of a network starts with planning and designing, after which the hardware and software are installed. This is followed by a short period of testing to ensure that the network is functioning properly.

Educational qualifications	Duties
Degree in computer studies along with some professional qualification in networking, for example, Microsoft Certified Systems Engineer (MCSE) certification.	• Plan and design the network, and manage the installation of hardware and software. • Test the network to ensure that it is functioning properly. • Set up user accounts and arrangements for access. • Ensure that staff are trained to use the network hardware and software. • Monitor the network's performance to ensure it is working at its optimum. • Troubleshoot and solve network problems and create security policies. • Set up systems to ensure compliance by users of the network.

Systems development manager

A systems development manager develops, implements and maintains a company's computerised system.

Educational background	Duties
• Degree or a Master's degree in computer science, engineering or a related field. • Experience in network design and software engineering, and managing teams of people.	• Manage teams to design, develop, implement, operate and administer computer software. • Oversee development and training of personnel.

Computer systems analyst

Systems analysts look at the operations of a manual or computerised system in an organisation and find solutions to specific end-user problems by implementing a new computerised system or upgrading an existing one. They are directly in charge of the development of the system from start to finish. Before starting a project, systems analysts must understand the existing system thoroughly. They do this by planning and conducting studies to determine if the existing system must be upgraded, or if a new system is needed.

Educational qualifications	Duties
• Degree in computer science or the equivalent is usually required. • Good problem-solving skills, as analysis and problem solving is a major part of the job. • Good communication skills as they need to express their thoughts clearly in speech and in writing. • Strong business background, in order to create better systems for the overall success of the company.	• Discuss their exact needs with system users. • Design new systems and integrate existing procedures into new system specifications. • Recommend the purchase of hardware and software. • Test and debug the new system. • Create documentation for the system. • Assist in training employees to use the system. • Evaluate the performance of the system.

System administrator

System administrators run the computer system. Typically, this will be a key server or servers on a network. They work closely with the network administrator, network engineer, help desk and data security staff. They are often specialists in the system software that runs on servers, such as Linux.

Educational qualifications	Duties
• Degree in computer studies. • Professional qualification in networking, for example Microsoft Certified Systems Engineer (MCSE) certification, or CISCO certification.	• Maintain and update the software on the server. • Manage and run backups and recovery. • Monitor and manage traffic on the server so it does not get overloaded. • Maintain and repair the hardware.

Software engineer

Software engineers are specialists who design or create software. They may or may not write actual programming code, but they must be competent in programming. They work together with both the business functions and the programmers, explaining the business functions to the programmers and the technology to the non-technical personnel.

Educational qualifications	Duties
• Degree in computer science. • Relevant qualifications or knowledge in the related programming languages such as Java, C++, C#.Net, and so on. • Good communication and teamwork skills. • Certification in business functions. • Master's and PhD degrees in computer science are required for promotion to senior management.	• Develop and implement software services. • Evaluate software and software designs. • Perform design trade-off depending on budget.

Software testers

Software testers, also known as software test engineers, are hired by companies to perform quality control tests on the software that they produce. Their responsibility is to find any bugs in the program.

Educational qualifications	Duties
• Computer degree not required. • Must be knowledgeable on computer operations.	• Set up and run simple to complex tests. • Document the results of the tests.

Computer programmer

Computer programmers write programs according to specifications determined mainly by computer engineers, software developers or systems analysts. A programmer's job is usually very demanding. Programmers may regularly work long hours and weekends to meet deadlines.

Educational qualifications	Duties
The qualifications for this job vary between a diploma from a technical college and a degree from a university.	• Discuss program specifications with the systems analyst. • Write, test and debug programs. • Update, repair, modify and expand existing programs.

Operations manager

Operations managers are responsible for the overall operations of a computer department on a daily basis. In companies with small information system departments, the operations manager and information systems manager jobs are often combined.

Educational qualifications	Duties
Degree in computer science or information technology.	• Supervise the use and maintenance of equipment. • Supervise data reception and preparation. • Schedule processing activities, allocate staff duties and consult with IT manager.

Computer operator

Computer operators monitor and control computer hardware systems (especially mainframes) through the central console, which is the main terminal that gives instructions to the operating system).

Educational qualifications	Duties
• Acquire the skills needed for the work through on-the-job training. • Additionally, ordinary-level examination passes and a diploma from a technical institute may be required.	• Start up and shut down the system. • Respond to messages from system software and carry out the actions required. • Observe equipment operations and report faults to the supervisor. • Perform routine equipment maintenance, such as cleaning drive-heads. • Load input and output units with materials such as tapes for tape drives and paper for printers. • Keep a log of of all tasks carried out on the system.

Data control clerk

Data control clerks screen, edit and validate the input and output for a data processing unit. They also run scheduled or requested jobs to provide clients with the necessary data.

Educational qualifications	Duties
• High-school diploma. • Two or three years of experience. • Office management and computer courses are advantageous, as are skills such communication and attention to detail.	• Regulate workflow according to operating schedules. • Be responsible for the receipt, safekeeping and retrieval of data, software, hardware, and security items. • Distribute materials on request and follow up on overdue items. • Help with the destruction of information-system materials.

Data-entry operator

Data-entry operators enter data into a system in a form that is suitable for processing.

Educational qualifications	Duties
• General knowledge of data-entry machines and their operations. • An ability to enter data at a rapid rate with very few errors.	• Transcribe data from a variety of source documents into the computer. • Keep records on the data transcribed. • Verify the data entered.

File librarian

A file librarian is responsible for keeping a company's data files and software organised and up-to-date.

Educational qualifications	Duties
• On-the-job training skills. • Ordinary-level examination passes and a diploma from a technical institute may also be required.	• Maintain and protect programs and data. • Catalogue and store magnetic tapes and disks. • Clean and inspect storage media. • Keep records of the disks and magnetic tapes stored.

Figure 14.3 A data security analyst protects a company's computer network from threats and damage.

Other careers in a non-traditional ICT department

Data security analyst (data security specialist)

Security problems have become more common with the growth of networks, as skilled hackers from outside an organisation may find it easy to gain access to a company's network. Data security analysts look after the protection of a company's computer-based information banks, and constantly analyse and assess the potential threats to a computer system.

Educational qualifications	Duties
• The educational background that someone in this field needs will depend on the sensitivity of the data and the complexity of the network. • Degree in computer studies, along with extra certificates in networking such as the Microsoft Certified Systems Engineer (MCSE) and CISCO courses, is a distinct advantage.	• Keep information safe from floods, fire, power outages, fraud, theft, invasion of privacy and viruses. • Set up procedures to protect vulnerable information. • Develop, document and implement data security policies and guidelines. • Identify and fix security vulnerabilities, and remove any security loopholes. • Work with different types of security software. • Keep up-to-date with cryptographic tools and techniques, and with all the different types of security hardware and software. • Have in-depth knowledge of operating systems and network technology.

Computer consultant

Computer consultants give an independent and objective opinion on how to use ICT to meet the needs of an organisation. A consultant is usually contracted for a short period of time to provide technical assistance to an organisation in areas such as systems analysis, design and programming, and the formation or upgrading of a data-processing department.

Educational qualifications	Duties
• Constantly upgrade skills and keep up-to-date with the latest technology in the field. • Extensive working experience. • First degree in information systems and management, along with a master's degree in computer science or business administration.	• Hold discussions with users to identify and clarify their information needs. • Identify and evaluate potential hardware and software. • Assist in the design, development and implementation of a company's computer system. • Assist in the development of programs, applications and documentation. • Develop training programmes for users.

Electronic data processing (EDP) auditor

Electronic data processing (EDP) auditors ensure that all aspects of a company's information systems operate as designed. EDP auditors provide ICT managers with expert opinions about the reliability of results and operations of computer systems.

Educational qualifications	Duties
• Degree in computing or information systems and management. • Extensive experience in the computer field. • Ability to pay close attention to detail. • Logical and analytical approach to investigation.	• Inspect programs, systems, operational procedures, documentation, control techniques, disaster plans and insurance and fire protection. • Use sample data to test the accuracy of computer programs and the control procedures built into them. • Check and report on the use of computing facilities. • Examine the input and output of programs for accuracy and report discrepancies to management. • Recommend changes to ensure system integrity and accuracy and implement if required.

Computer engineer

Computer engineers are found in all levels of the computer industry. They design, develop, test and supervise the manufacture of components (such as new computer chips or circuit boards) and peripheral devices. If their employer is a large company, then different engineers take care of the assembly and testing of new designs for overall effectiveness, cost, reliability and safety. Some computer engineers working for hardware dealers or manufacturers also maintain and repair computer hardware sold to clients.

Educational qualifications	Duties
• Degree in computer engineering or electrical engineering. • Additional qualifications in computer science, computer programming and any other similar computer-related field are also desirable.	• Design, develop, test and supervise the manufacture of components and peripheral devices. • Assemble and test new designs for effectiveness, cost, reliability and safety. • Maintain and repair computer hardware sold to clients.

Computer technician

Computer technicians, sometimes called computer repair technicians, are called in when a computer system is not working as it should. They maintain, repair and install hardware and software. They may be employed by an organisation or can be outsourced, which means they may have their own business and be called to perform a service (independent service providers).

Educational qualifications	Duties
• Qualifications vary and can range from computer repair courses to courses with various levels of certification, for example: A+ certification, NET+, MCSE (Microsoft Certified Systems Engineer) and MCP (Microsoft Certified Professional), to computer technician degree programmes and higher-level degree programmes.	• Troubleshoot and diagnose computer problems. • Repair, replace and test computer parts. • Receive and set up hardware. • Communicate and return failed hardware to vendor. • Maintain and set up servers and networks. • Set up and back up desktop computers and servers.

Software trainer (IT trainer)

Software trainers (IT trainers, design) develop and deliver training courses to individuals and organisations on a variety of software applications.

Educational qualifications	Duties
• Formal certification is not a requirement to become a trainer. • Technical qualifications may necessary for more complex technical trainer jobs. Technical trainer courses are available for those wanting to become skilled trainers. • Excellent presentation and communication skills.	• Assess client's needs. • Prepare learning materials and aids. • Set up the learning environment and resources. • Deliver and evaluate the course.

Multimedia artist and animators

Multimedia artists and animators use computers to develop moving pictures for use in game development, on the internet, and in films and television. They may work with a web developer, designer or programmer to develop their design.

Educational qualifications	Duties
• Qualifications obtained from a variety of courses offered at the level of associate, bachelor's or master's degrees. • Formal training in art, drawing, illustration or a related area.	• Create animated images and special effects. • Create storyboards for films and video games. • Create drawing or illustrations by hand or computer.

Computer sales representative

Sales representatives are important as they are responsible for bringing in the company's profits. Computer sales representatives must understand the products they are selling, (hardware, software or services), as may often have to do demonstrations for customers.

Educational qualifications	Duties
• Ordinary-level passes and a good knowledge of computers, or specialised training in computer repairs and computer applications, or a degree in computers (depending on the company and the position requirements). • Good communication skills, a pleasant personality and patience. • Good business sense, since part of their earnings usually comes from commission on sales.	• Explain specifications, functions and capabilities of hardware and/or software products. • Help customers to install new equipment. • Attend trade shows and seminars to keep up-to-date. • Demonstrate equipment to clients.

Mobile app developer

People are increasingly using smartphones and tablets for communication, entertainment and work. For these reasons, the mobile app developer has become one of the fastest-growing information technology careers in the world.

Educational qualifications	Duties
• Software programming skills and knowledge. • Attending coding boot camps. • Pursuing an associate or a bachelor's degree in computer science or related computer qualifications.	• Discuss specifications with systems analyst or client. • Write programs. • Test programs for correct operation and results. • Debug and document programs. • Update, repair, modify and expand existing programs.

Summary 14

1 The ICT manager plans, coordinates, manages and staffs the information systems department of a large organisation.

2 A database administrator (DBA) manages a company's database.

3 A systems analyst looks at the operations of a manual or computerised system.

4 A software developer or engineer designs, develops, maintains, tests and evaluates software.

5 Programmers write programs and update, repair, modify and expand existing programs.

6 Network engineers plan, design, install and maintain network equipment.

7 Network administrators create, administer and manage the security of computer networks.

8 A system administrator is responsible for running a computer system.

9 A operations manager is responsible for the overall operations of a computer department.

10 A computer operator monitors and controls computer hardware systems.

11 A data control clerk screens, edits and validates the input and output for a data-processing unit.

12 A data-entry operator enters data into a system in a form that is suitable for processing.

13 A file librarian keeps a company's data files and software organised and up-to-date.

14 A data security analyst (specialist) looks after the protection of a company's computer-based information banks.

15 A computer consultant provides technical assistance to an organisation in areas such as systems analysis, design and programming.

16 Electronic data processing (EDP) auditors ensure that all aspects of a company's information systems perform as stated in the design.

17 Computer engineers develop, test and supervise the manufacture of components and peripheral devices.

18 Software engineers design or create software.

19 Computer technicians maintain, repair and install hardware and software.

20 Software testers perform quality control tests on the software to find any bugs in the program.

21 Software trainers, design, develop and deliver training courses to individuals and organisations.

22 Multimedia artists and animators use computers to develop moving pictures for use in game development, on the internet, and in films and television.

23 Computer sales representatives market computer products and services.

24 Mobile app developers create application software for mobile devices.

Questions 14

Copy and fill in the blanks questions

1 The _____ monitors and controls a computer system from the central console.

2 A _____ updates, repairs, modifies and expands existing programs.

3 A _____ administers and manages a company's database.

4 A _____ enters data into a system in a form that is suitable for processing.

5 A _____ creates application software for cell phones.

6 A _____ explains the specifications of the different hardware and software products sold by their company to customers.

True or false questions

1 A systems analyst selects and maintains database management software.

2 A data security analyst analyses and assesses the potential threats to a computer system.

3 Electronic data processing auditors make recommendations for changes to ensure system integrity and accuracy.

4 Multimedia artists do not need formal art training and qualifications.

5 Computer engineers are not responsible for maintaining and repairing computer hardware sold to clients.

Short-answer questions

1 Describe two functions for each job:

   a Operations manager

   b Network administrator

   c Database administrator

2 List three duties of a computer technician.

3 Explain the difference between a computer engineer and a software engineer.

4 State three duties of a mobile app developer.

Project

1 You are asked to advertise a post that has become available in your company. Create a flyer, leaflet or brochure to advertise one of the computing careers. Include descriptions of the job functions of the post and the qualifications required to fill that post.

2 You own a small business and want to hire a computer technician and a software trainer as part of your staff. Create an advertisement to hire these new employees.

3 You applied for a job as a data security analyst and you are asked to present a resume at the interview. Design a resume using the security analyst qualifications and any additional information you think you will need to create a winning résumé. (Hint: Ask your English teacher for assistance.)

STEM project

Your friend Kayli is a Grade 9 or Form 3 student at your school. She is unsure about her choice of subjects for Grade 10 or Form 4. She likes Mathematics and Science, and is very good at IT. However, she also likes to do practical things and does not see herself sitting at a computer all day, although she is very interested in finding hackers, stopping the theft of data and the reducing the occurrence of viruses on computers. She has come to you to discuss her possible career options, so that she can make the best subject choices as she plans to start working after Grade 11 or Form 5. You can ask one of your classmates to play the role of Kayli.

1 How can you best help Kayli with the IT knowledge you now have? Write down your thoughts.

2 Collect and collate useful information to help Kayli. What information do you think will be most useful? How do you plan to access this information?

3 Inform her of three ICT jobs that you think would best suit her, using her interests to guide your suggestions. For each job you have suggested, explain its key tasks and day to day responsibilities.

4 What feedback did you get from Kayli? How can you further help her with her job choice?

Hints

1 Revise this chapter and Chapter 13 in *Interact with IT* Book 1 of this series.

2 Research jobs in your country by internet searches, interviewing IT persons in businesses, and so on.

Glossary

3D printer a device that creates a physical object from a digital model by layering materials

absolute cell references symbols inserted into a spreadsheet formula that prevent the cell references from changing when a formula is copied from one location to another

access point a device attached to a LAN network that translates computer signals into wireless signals, which it broadcasts to wireless NICs on the network

active cell the cell in an Excel spreadsheet in which any information entered from the keyboard will be stored

additive processes laying down of successive layers of material until an object is created

arguments cell references, text or numbers in a formula

algorithms a formula or set of unambiguous steps which, if faithfully followed, will solve a particular problem

application software programs developed to perform specific tasks or to solve a particular problem

authoring tools (authorware) programs that programmers use to write code to create these multimedia presentations or applications

automatic recalculation if a value is changed in a cell, all the values in the dependent cells will be automatically updated

bandwidth the capacity of a channel to transmit a volume (amount) of data in a given time

barcode a set of vertical lines of differing thickness with a string of numbers printed at the bottom, which contains information that can be accessed by a scanner

bluetooth a standard that allows any sort of electronic equipment to automatically make their own wirelss connections

bit smallest unit of storage in a computer, can be a 0 or a 1

Blu-ray disk (BD) optical disk technology developed to enable recording, rewriting and playback of high-definition (HD) video

boot process of loading operating system software into a computer's main memory from the hard disk

byte eight adjacent bits

cell the intersection of a row and a column in a spreadsheet, which can hold a label, value or formula

character a byte representing a letter, number, symbol, punctuation mark or blank space

cell pointer the border that identifies the active cell in a spreadsheet; that is, the cell in which any information entered from the keyboard will be stored

cell reference (cell address) the cell in a spreadsheet that is formed by combining the column position and the row position (cell address)

cold booting hold in the power button to shut down the computer

command a word that instructs the computer what must be done to accomplish a specific task

computer crime any illegal act that involves the use of a computer or related devices

condition statement determines which step to proceed to

constants values that do not change during the execution of a program or algorithm

construct a group of instructions that work together with commands to accomplish a specific task

cut delete or remove a piece of text such as a character, word, phrase, line or block of text

cybercrime an illegal act committed online or via the internet

data communication the transmission of data from one location to another for direct use or for further processing

desktop a visual background on a computer screen that contains icons representing, for example, files, folders and programs

digitising tablet a board that can detect the position of a pointing device, such as a stylus or a puck, on its surface, which is used for drawing

direct access data that can be accessed without having to access any other data either before or after the data you want

dot matrix printer contains a print head with pins (18 or 24), arranged in a rectangular matrix of rows and columns, which move forward and strike an inked ribbon, which then strikes the paper

dry run inputting values and working through the steps in an algorithm logically and carefully, one by one, while keeping track of the results

e-commerce buying and selling of merchandise over the World Wide Web

erasable programmable ROM (EPROM) PROM that can be erased and then reprogrammed, after which it acts as a ROM

File Transfer Protocol (FTP) a set of rules for communicating over the internet

flash memory memory device that can hold data even if there is no power (non-volatile)

formatting changing the appearance of text in a document

formulae instructions that tell the computer to work out the answer for the values entered, such as a mathematical equation

gutter margin the space allotted at the side of a page for binding

hacker person who tries to gain access to a computer system without authorisation

hardcopy   permanent output and refers to output printed onto paper

header row   the first row in a table that contains the merge fields

human-readable   output that can be read by people

icons   small pictorial figures that represent programs, folders, files, tasks, procedures, and so on

immediate access store (IMAS)   primary storage (also known as main memory)

impact printers   produce their output when the printing mechanism presses against a ribbon which then hits (impact) the paper

inkjet printer   produce their output by spraying small, electrically charged droplets of ink from the printer head

in-line port   blue port is used to playback and record sounds from devices such as an MP3 player, electric guitar, turntables and DVD players

integrated software   set of related programs combined in a unified package

IP address   32-bit address consisting of four sets of up to three digits each, separated by full stops, for example 196.361.232.4.

joystick   a device that lets you control the movement of an object on the screen by operating a small lever, used mainly in computer games

keyboard, alphanumeric   containing letters and numbers

keyboard, Braille   keys marked with raised dots to help users who are blind

keyboard, special functions   designed to help someone type or enter data more easily

label   a text entry in a spreadsheet

LAN   a collection of microcomputers, such as in an office building, department or school that can share peripherals, files and programs, as well as communicate with each other on the network

laser printer   use laser beams, magnetically charged toner and heat to transfer an image to paper

line printer   impact printer that appears to print a line at a time; the two main types are chain printers and band printers

log   record of events or progress (for example, users logged in)

machine readable   output that cannot be read by people, but only by machines

main memory   primary storage (also known as immediate access memory)

merge field   the name of a data item that will be stored in the data source and later be merged into the main document

mouse, optical   mouse, using light emitting diode (LED) to detect its position on the surface of your desk or table

mouse, traditional or mechanical   mouse, cable-connected to computer, ball in base

multi-access system   a system that allows a number of users with online terminals or PCs to interact with the same computer at the same time

multimedia authoring   the process of creating, enhancing or editing a multimedia presentation or application

multiprocessing   computer system's ability to support more than one process (program) at the same time using multiple processors

multiprogramming   computer's ability to run two or more programs at the same time using a single processor

multitasking   ability of a computer to run more than one program at the same time

non-impact printers   output formed without making any direct physical contact with the paper

network   a group of two or more computers linked together so that they can share resources (hardware, software and data) and communicate with one another

network interface card (NIC)   a device that enables wireless or wired capabilities on a device that did not previously support it

online system   a system where the terminals or PCs and the computer are linked interactively

operators   mathematical symbols that are used in formulae (+, [n-dash], *, /, ^)

packet   small numbered pieces of data that can travel quickly and easily across data lines

pixel   smallest unit on the screen that can be turned on and off or coloured in different shades

plotter   wide-format printer producing high-quality graphics; three basic types are pen, inkjet and electrostatic plotter

program   set of instructions for the computer to follow to accomplish a given task

programmable ROM (PROM)   you can program (write to) a PROM once, after which it becomes ROM

protocol   set of rules that defines how computers interact or communicate with each other

puck   mouse-like device that is moved over the surface of the tablet, which has cross-hairs to position it accurately and a number of buttons for different actions

random-access memory (RAM)   volatile read/write memory in which data can be accessed in any order

read-only memory (ROM)   holds data and instructions necessary for starting up the computer when it is switched on

relative cell referencing (addressing)   a spreadsheet formula that changes relative to the position of a cell; when a formula is copied, the structure of the formula is copied but the cell addresses change accordingly

resolution clarity or sharpness of an image when displayed on the screen

router device that acts as an interface between two networks by taking information provided by the modem and routing it to the various connected devices

scanner, flatbed flat, glass surface holding paper with scan head moving underneath

search engine a website that allows users to find information quickly and easily; also sometimes called a web portal

slide each page of information in a PowerPoint presentation

slide show a number of related slides in a PowerPoint presentation that can be viewed in sequence

smartphone cell phone with information access, giving a variety of functions similar to a computer

softcopy temporary output and it refers to information displayed on a screen or in audio or voice form through speakers

software all the different types of programs that can be run on a computer

software house company that specialises in writing software

source documents documents on which data is first recorded before it is entered into the computer

speech-generating device (SGD) an electronic output device that is used to help individuals with severe speech impairments or other issues who have difficulty in communicating

spreadsheet application package that can be used in any job that involves repetitive numerical calculations; a large grid divided by rows and columns

stylus a pen-like pointing device for a graphics/digitising tablet

switch device that connects multiple devices on the same network to facilitate communication among the devices

system software software that enables the running of application software and the management of the system resources

TCP/IP Transmission Control Protocol/Internet Protocol – a set of rules that define how computers communicate with each other to transfer data over the internet

thermal printer has a print head made up of pins arranged in a matrix. 'Direct thermal printers' have a print head where the pins are heated electrically and burn the characters onto heat-sensitive paper which is coated with a head reactive dye. In 'thermal wax transfer printers' the print head melts a wax-based ink from a transfer ribbon onto the paper

thumbnail a miniature image of a graphic, document or slide

user interface user-controllable part of the operating system that allows you to communicate, or interact, with the operating system

value a piece of data that can be used in a calculation

variables values that can change during the execution of a program or algorithm

voice recognition systems process the spoken word and match it to a word stored in the computer's memory

volatile memory that does not hold its data without power

window rectangular boxed area on a computer screen

WiFi means of communicating data wirelessly, within a fixed location

word the number of bits a computer's CPU can process in one operation

workbook a window in Excel that occupies the majority of the screen and initially contains three worksheets

worksheet sub-part of a workbook

Index

Acknowledgements

The Publishers would like to thank the following for permission to reproduce copyright material. Every effort has been made to trace or contact all copyright holders, but if any have been inadvertently overlooked the Publishers will be pleased to make the necessary arrangements at the first opportunity.

Photo acknowledgements

p. 2 *br* © Aberenyi/Adobe Stock; **p. 3** *tl*, **p. 11** *cc* © Bogdan/Adobe Stock; **p. 3** *br* © Popova Olga//Adobe Stock; **p. 4** *tl* © Audrey Design/Adobe Stock; © USB 2.0 Promoter, © USB 2.0 Promoter Group - under Text acknowledgements; **p. 4** *cl* © Mehmet/Adobe Stock; **p. 4** *bl* © Patrik Slezak/Adobe Stock; **p. 4** *cc* © Jipen/Alamy Stock Photo; **p. 4** *cr* © Anatoly Fedotov/123rf; **p. 4** *bc* © Fototocam//Adobe Stock; **p. 5** *tl* © Nnudoo/Adobe Stock, ©Thunderbolt®; **p. 5** *tc* © Happy Vector 071/Adobe Stock, ©Thunderbolt®; **p. 5** *cl* © Belkin, ©Thunderbolt®; **p. 5** *cc* © Amin , ©Thunderbolt®; **p. 6** *tl* © Studio KIVI/Adobe Stock; **p. 6** *cl*, **p. 11** *bl* © Mseisenhut/Adobe Stock; **p. 6** *cl* © Alexey/Adobe Stock; **p. 6** *cl* © Dervish 77/Adobe Stock; **p. 6** *cl* © Primo Chill; **p. 6** *br* © C0nan Payne; **p. 7** *tl*, **p. 11** *br* © Gudella Photo/Adobe Stock; **p. 7** *tr* © Nikky Tok/Adobe Stock; **p. 7** *bl* © Firewings/Adobe Stock; **p. 7** *bc* © Tootles/Adobe Stock; **p. 7** *br* © Clifford Farrugia/Adobe Stock; **p. 8** *tl* © Citadelle/123rf; **p. 8** *cl* © AVD/Adobe Stock; **p. 8** *cl* © Citadelle/123rf; **p. 8** *bl* © P Billam/Adobe Stock; **p. 9** *cl* © Ronstik/123rf; **p. 9** *cl* © Teerawut Masawat/123rf; **p. 9** *bl* © Design 56/Adobe Stock; **p. 10** *bl* © Arthur Mustafa/Adobe Stock; **p. 11** *cl* © Anatoly Fedotov/123rf; **p. 11** *cc* © Bogdan/Adobe Stock; **p. 11** *bl* © Mseisenhut/Adobe Stock; **p. 11** *br* © Gudella Photo/Adobe Stock; **p. 13** *tr* © Daniel Krason/Adobe Stock; **p. 15** *tl* © Creativa Images/Adobe Stock; **p. 15** *bl* © Zlikovec/Adobe Stock; **p. 16** *tl* © Gerald Bernard/Adobe Stock; **p. 16** *bl* © Andrew Buckin/Adobe Stock; **p. 17** *tl* © KY Tan/Shutterstock; **p. 17** *cl* © Ever/Adobe Stock; **p. 17** *br* © LD Prod/Adobe Stock; **p. 19** *br* © Anya Berkut/123rf; **p. 20** *tl* © Denis Yankin//Shutterstock; **p. 20** *br* © Adam Gregor//Shutterstock; **p. 21** *tl* © Peter Devlin/Alamy Stock Photo; **p. 21** *bc* © The Simplify/Adobe Stock; **p. 21** *br* © Tyler Olson/Adobe Stock; **p. 22** *tl* © Juksy/Shutterstock; **p. 22** *bl* © George JMC Little/Adobe Stock; **p. 23** *tl* © Yulai Studio/Shutterstock; **p. 23** *cr* © PTN Photof/Adobe Stock; **p. 24** *cr* © Murat Baysan/Adobe Stock; **p. 25** *cr* © Sergey Yakovlev/123rf; **p. 25** *bl* © Rachel Torres/Alamy Stock Photo; **p. 31** *cr* © Nikita Kuzmenkov/Adobe Stock; **p. 32** *cr* © Sondem/Adobe Stock; **p. 33** *tl* © K Sena 32/Adobe Stock; **p. 33** *cl* © Nikky Tok/Shutterstock; **p. 33** *bl* © Fosupaksorn/Adobe Stock; **p. 35** *tl* © Mr Aphirak Arkasamnuai//Shutterstock; **p. 35** *bl* © Dja 65/Adobe Stock; **p. 36** *tl* © Jack F/Adobe Stock; **p. 36** *cl* © Vetkit/Adobe Stock; **p. 36** *bl* © Mik CZ/Adobe Stock; **p. 37** *tl* © Kirill 4 Mula/Adobe Stock; **p. 38** *tl* © JMS Photography/Adobe Stock; **p. 38** *cl* © YM German/Shutterstock; **p. 38** *tl* © Ryan King 999/Adobe Stock; **p. 44** *cl*, **p. 48** *tl* © Shutter Stock Studio/Shutterstock; **p. 44** *cr*, **p. 51** *tl* © Nicolas Portais/123rf; **p. 44** *bl*, **p. 50** *br* © Brian Jackson/Adobe Stock; **p. 44** *br*, **p. 47** *tc* © Charnsitr/Adobe Stock; **p. 46** *tl* © DND Project/Shutterstock; **p. 46** *tc* © De Serg/Shutterstock; **p. 47** *tl* © Konovalov Pavel/Adobe Stock; **p. 47** *br* © Jacky Kids/Adobe Stock; **p. 50** *tl* © Miro Jurin/Shutterstock; **p. 50** *bl* © Relax Photography/Adobe Stock; **p. 52** © Hodder Education is not affiliated with or otherwise sponsored by Dropbox, Inc., © 2018 Google LLC All rights reserved. Google Drive is a trademark of Google LLC, © Livedrive® is a trademark of Livedrive Internet Ltd.; **p. 57** *bl* © Photobank /Adobe Stock; **p. 58** *bl* © Juan-Carlos García/Adobe Stock; **p. 68** *bl* © George JMC Little/Adobe Stock; **p. 68** *br* © George JMC Little/Adobe Stock; **p. 69** *bl* © Syda Productions/Adobe Stock; **p. 72** *tl* © Sergej Toporkov/Adobe Stock; **p. 72** *bl* © Sergey Peterman/123rf; **p. 75** *bl* © Pedro Luz Cunha/Alamy Stock Photo; **p. 78** *tl* © Vivitta/Shutterstock; **p. 85** *tl* © Jacob Lund/Adobe Stock; **p. 85** *cl* © Zakhar Marunov/Adobe Stock; **p. 85** *cl* © Ra3rn/Adobe Stock; **p. 85** *bl* © Destina/Adobe Stock; **p. 86** *tl* © Gudella Photo/Adobe Stock; **p. 86** *tl* © Scan Rail/Adobe Stock; **p. 87** *tl* © Flair Images/Adobe Stock; **p. 88** *bl* © Design Elements/Adobe Stock; **p. 89** *cr* © Vtls/Adobe Stock; **p. 89** *bl* ©Oleksandr Delyk/Adobe Stock; **p. 97** *bl* © Jakub Jirsák/Adobe Stock; **p. 101** *br* © N Media/Adobe Stock; **p. 113** *tr* © Subbotina Anna/Shutterstock; **p. 144** *cl* © Rocket Clips/Adobe Stock; **p. 150** *tr* © Raw Pixel.com/Adobe Stock; **p. 197** *cc* © Raw Pixel.com/Adobe Stock; **p. 198** *tl* © Michael J Berlin/Adobe Stock; **p. 198** *bl* © Koya 979/Adobe Stock; **p. 199** *tl* © Rawf8/Adobe Stock; **p. 199** *bl* © Sergey Nivens/Adobe Stock; **p. 200** *tl* © Christelle Delforge/Adobe Stock; **p. 202** *bl*, **p. 203** *bl* © Sveta/Adobe Stock; **p. 207** *br* © Maciek 905/Adobe Stock; **p. 208** *bl* ©Dragon Images/Adobe Stock; **p. 210** *bl* © Photo Everywhere/Adobe Stock; **p. 228** *bl* © Phonlamai Photo/Adobe Stock; **p. 229** *t* © Mad Dog/Adobe Stock; **p. 229** *bl* © Andrey Popov/Adobe Stock; **p. 230** *bl* © P and P Stock 001/123rf; **p. 231** *tl* © Andrey Ushakov/Adobe Stock; **p. 231** *bl* © P and P Stock 001/Adobe Stock; **p. 232** *cl* © Gorodenkoff/Adobe Stock; **p. 232** *bl* © Amirraizat/Adobe Stock; **p. 233** *tl* ©Matyas Rehak/Adobe Stock; **p. 233** *bl* © Jarrett Cohen/NASA/Goddard; **p. 234** *cl* © Raw Pixel.com/Adobe Stock; **p. 234** *br* © Vastram/Adobe Stock; **p. 235** *tl* © Shapik Media/Adobe Stock; **p. 235** *bl* © George JMC Little/Adobe Stock; **p. 236** *tr* © Monkey Business/Adobe Stock; **p. 239** *tr* © Scan Rail/Adobe Stock; **p. 244** *tl* © Kasto/Adobe Stock.

t = top, *b* = bottom, *l* = left, *r* = right, *c* = centre

Screenshot acknowledgements

pp. 5, 76–77, 91, 104–119, 122–143, 151–195 © Used with permission from Microsoft. **p. 93–96** ©2018 Google LLC, used with permission. Google and the Google logo are registered trademarks of Google LLC.

Text acknowledgements

pp. 1, 10, 16, 50, 69, 72, 73, 75–81, 91, 101–149, 150–196, 200, 206, 249, 251–254 © Used with permission from Microsoft. **pp. 12, 69, 90** © Apple® Macintosh® is a trademark of Apple Inc. **pp. 51, 71, 93–95, 111, 253** © 2018 Google LLC All rights reserved. Google and the Google logo are registered trademarks of Google LLC. **pp. 52, 91, 232** © Mac® is a trademark of Apple Inc. **pp. 69, 102** © Apple® iWork® Pages® is a trademark of Apple Inc. **pp. 69, 101, 102** © Copyright © 2019 Adobe. All rights reserved. **p. 72** © OS X® is a trademark of Apple Inc. **p. 75** © macOS® is a trademark of Apple Inc. **p. 81** © Apple® iMac® is a trademark of Apple Inc. **p. 81** © iPhone® is a trademark of Apple Inc. **pp. 102, 232** © Apple® is a trademark of Apple Inc. **p. 205** © Facebook © 2019. **p. 235** © 2019 Twitter, Inc.